Fearon's

English
Composition

Fearon's

English Composition

Joanne Suter

Fearon Education
Belmont, California

Pacemaker Curriculum Advisor: Stephen C. Larsen
Stephen C. Larsen holds a B.S. and an M.S. in Speech Pathology from the University of Nebraska at Omaha, and an Ed.D. in Learning Disabilities from the University of Kansas. In the course of his career, Dr. Larsen has worked in the Teacher Corps on a Nebraska Indian Reservation, as a Fulbright senior lecturer in Portugal and Spain, and as a speech pathologist in the public schools. A full professor at the University of Texas at Austin, he has nearly twenty years' experience as a teacher trainer on the university level. He is the author of sixty journal articles, three textbooks and six widely used standardized tests including the Test of Written Learning (TOWL) and the Test of Adolescent Language (TOAL).

Subject Area Consultants: M.B. Clarke and A.G. Clarke
Both M.B. Clarke and A.G. Clarke earned Ph.D.s in English at the University of California, Berkeley. Together they have developed composition and reading materials for a wide range of educational publishers. Both also score national writing tests for the Educational Testing Service. M.B. Clarke teaches composition at the University of California, Davis, and A.G. Clarke teaches writing at American River College near Sacramento.

Editor: Emily Hutchinson
Text Designer: Dianne Platner
Cover Design: Dianne Platner
Production Manager: Teresa A. Holden
Production Editor: Mary A. Dickinson
Graphics Coordinator: Joe C. Shines
Cover: holographic manuscript of Charles Dickens, compliments of the
        San Francisco Public Library

Other photos: UPI/BETTMANN Newsphotos 2, 28, 60, 90, 104, 146, 176, 192, 332, 352, 368; The BETTMANN Archive 132, 296; Reuters/BETTMANN Newsphotos 282; Schomburg Center, New York Public Library 14, 44, 260.

Other photos courtesy of: Peter Radsliff 12; Linda Brown/Sterling Lord Literistic, Inc. 76; Los Angeles Times 120; Robert Foothorap/G.P. Putnam's Sons 162; Quintana Roo Dunne/Simon & Schuster 208; Harcourt, Brace & World 228; Michael Weinstein/Pantheon Books 246; Bantam Doubleday Dell Publishers 310.

ISBN 0–8224–0802–3

Printed in the United States of America
1. 9 8 7 6 5 4 3 2

Table of Contents

A Note from the Publisher to the Student

"If you can walk, you can dance.
If you can talk, you can sing."

This charming folk saying comes from the African nation of Zimbabwe. It reminds us that basic skills can be used for enjoyment as well as survival. Writing sentences, paragraphs, and papers to get a good grade is useful. But writing to express yourself, make somebody laugh, or present your own ideas, is even better than useful. It's interesting and fun.

Anyone who can talk and read can also learn to write. The thought processes are the same. *English Composition* will show you, step by step, how to write a good sentence and a complete paragraph. And anyone who can write one good paragraph can write four more. That's all a simple essay is—a chain of five good paragraphs. By the time you finish Chapter 14, you will have written your own essay. And you will have discovered that putting words on paper is really not so different from saying words out loud.

The purpose of this book is to make it easier for you to succeed at school, at work, and in the outside world. Chapter by chapter, you will strengthen your composition skills. You will learn how to build interesting paragraphs that give information or tell how to do something. You will learn how to write clear descriptions and opinions. By the time you finish this book, you will know how to write notes, letters, book reports, and test answers. And you will know something about writing stories and poems.

All through the book you'll find notes in the margins of the pages. These friendly notes are there to make you stop and think. Sometimes they comment on the material you're learning. Sometimes they give examples, and sometimes they remind you of something you already know.

Watch for the study aids throughout the book. At the beginning of every chapter, you'll find **learning objectives**. These will help you focus on the important points covered in the chapter. And you'll find **Words to Know**, a look ahead at the vocabulary you may find difficult. At the end of each chapter, a **summary** will give you a quick review of what you've just learned.

Everyone who put this book together worked hard to make it useful, interesting, and enjoyable. The rest is up to you. We wish you well in your studies. Our success is in your accomplishment.

Carol Hegarty
Publisher

Unit One

Writing Sentences

Chapter 1

What Is a Sentence?

Chapter 2

Avoiding Sentence Fragments and Run-on Sentences

Chapter 3

Writing Different Kinds of Sentences

Chapter 4

Writing Better Sentences

Chapter 5

Choosing the Correct Words

What Is a Sentence?

Willa Cather lived in Nebraska when it was still frontier land. She built her characters on the immigrant settlers she knew there. O Pioneers! and My Antonia are two of her best-known novels about life on the prairie.

Colorful characters make fiction come alive.

Writers at Work: Willa Cather (1876–1947)

Chapter Learning Objectives

- ☐ Explain what makes a group of words a complete sentence.
- ☐ Identify the subject and predicate as the two main parts of a sentence.
- ☐ Write and punctuate a complete sentence.

Words to Know

noun   a word that names a person, a place, or a thing

example: The furry **monkey** ate a large, yellow **banana**.

verb   a word that expresses action or being

example: The shark **swam** toward the tiny boat.

example: The passengers **were** white with fear.

subject   the part of the sentence that tells who or what the sentence is about

example: The **cook** wore a clean, white apron.

predicate   the part of the sentence that tells something about the subject

example: The girl **wore a yellow raincoat**.

sentence   a group of words that expresses a complete thought; a sentence has a subject and a predicate. It begins with a capital letter and ends with a punctuation mark.

simple subject   the most important noun or pronoun in the sentence; what the sentence is about

example: The tall, thin **man** ran down the dark alley.

simple predicate   the verb or verb phrase in the sentence

example: A robber **escaped** with $5,000 in gold.

command   a sentence that gives an order

example: Leave me alone.

Identifying Sentences

You use sentences every day when you speak and when you write. **Sentences** are one way we communicate with each other. We use them easily and automatically.

"The bus stops at Main Street," you might say. If so, you have used a sentence. Or you may write a note in class and pass it to a friend. You use sentences in the note. You might write, "Will you meet me after school?" That's a sentence. Your teacher might say, "Bring me the note." That's a sentence too.

How is talking on the telephone different from communicating in person?

How is talking on the telephone different from communicating in writing?

What makes these groups of words sentences?

1. Each expresses a complete thought and makes sense on its own.

2. Each contains a **subject** and a **predicate**.

Let's look at the first reason. What do we mean when we say a sentence expresses a complete thought and makes sense on its own?

Read this group of words:

The gray car raced around the corner.

It's a complete sentence. It has a subject (gray car). It has a predicate (raced around the corner). It begins with a capital letter and ends with a period. It also makes sense. We understand it. But what if a sentence said, "Jack is the moon." Why isn't this a sentence?

Now read this group of words:

> the gray car

Do these words make sense on their own? Do they express a complete thought? Or are you wondering what the writer wants to say about the gray car? The gray car is just a phrase. It isn't a sentence.

A sentence makes sense by itself. It expresses a complete thought.

Activity 1

On your own paper, make each group of words below into a complete sentence.

The big, yellow cat _____ . (What did it do?)

> *The big, yellow cat watched the tiny mouse.*

1. The army of red ants _____ . (What did it do?)

2. Big Joe Green _____ . (What did he do?)

3. _____ turned on the radio. (Who did it?)

4. A terrible thunderstorm _____ . (What did it do?)

5. _____ eats everything in sight. (Who or what does it?)

6. The girl in the swimming pool _____ . (What did she do?)

7. _____ tore open the letter. (Who did it?)

8. _____ fell to the hard ground. (Who or what did it?)

9. _____ wore an ugly mask. (Who or what did it?)

10. The last dinosaur on earth _____ . (What did it do?)

Make sure your sentences begin with capital letters and end with periods.

A sentence must have a subject and a predicate.

Read this sentence again:

> The gray car raced around the corner.

Read an article in your local newspaper. Underline the simple subject and the simple predicate in three of the sentences.

The **simple subject** in this sentence is *car*. The simple subject of a sentence is almost always a **noun** or pronoun. It tells who or what did something. *Car* is the *what* in the example above.

> simple subject: car

The **simple predicate** in the sentence above is *raced*. The simple predicate of a sentence is always a **verb** or verb phrase. The simple predicate tells what the subject did.

Raced tells what the *car* did.

> simple predicate: raced

Activity 2

Copy each of the following sentences. Notice that each one begins with a capital letter and ends with a period. Underline the simple subject of each sentence with one line. Underline the simple predicate with two lines.

> example: <u>Maggie</u> <u>broke</u> the red balloon.

1. Linda screamed.

2. An elephant broke the bars of the cage.

3. Her umbrella had red and yellow stripes.

4. Richard won $2 million.

5. The accident happened at midnight.

Every sentence has two parts, a subject and a predicate. The simple subject is a noun or pronoun. The simple predicate is a verb or verb phrase.

Punctuating Sentences

Every sentence begins with a capital letter.

When a sentence just states facts, it ends with a period.

> example: The dog barked at Harry.

But some sentences ask questions. They end with question marks.

> example: Who took Harry's dog?

And a sentence that expresses very strong feelings, like fear or excitement, ends with an exclamation point.

> example: I won tickets to the Michael Jackson concert!

Activity 3

Copy each of the following sentences on your paper. Capitalize the first word in each sentence. End each sentence with a period, a question mark, or an exclamation point. (Remember, most sentences end with periods.)

1. the movie begins at seven o'clock

2. will your brother go with us

3. there is a spider on your neck

4. the basketball team won again

5. did you finish your work

Why is it important to know what a sentence is? Remember that when you write, you're trying to communicate with someone else. You want your ideas to make sense. You want to be understood. And it's very hard to understand writing that is not broken up into sentences.

> The dark clouds meant rain last night we decided to stay home it was lucky a storm flooded the roads.

In your own words, explain why it's important to write in sentences.

The ideas in the writing above are unclear. They run together and are hard to read. Punctuation clears up these ideas. It separates them, so we understand what the writer is saying. Look at the same words written in sentences.

> The dark clouds meant rain. Last night we decided to stay home. It was lucky. A storm flooded the roads.

Communicate clearly. Let your readers know where your ideas begin and end. Write in complete sentences. Try it!

Activity 4

On your paper write five sentences of your own. A topic is suggested for each of your sentences.

1. _____ (summer)
2. _____ (jet planes)
3. _____ (a special friend)
4. _____ (a television star)
5. _____ (your next-door neighbor)

A Special Kind of Sentence

The **command** is a special kind of sentence. Sometimes commands are used in this book when you're asked to do an activity or to think about something. When you tell someone to do something (give a command), you can call that person by name:

example: Paul, take out the garbage.

In this case, Paul is the subject of the sentence.

Another way is to just give the command.

example: Take out the garbage.

Take is the simple predicate in this sentence. But it seems this sentence has no subject. And there must be a subject in a complete sentence. In a command, the subject is an understood "you." It's as if the sentence reads this way:

You take out the garbage.

A command can end with a period or, if it shows strong feeling, with an exclamation point. The following command shows strong feeling:

Stop that right now!

Challenge

1. Write and punctuate a sentence that is a command.

2. Write and punctuate a sentence that is a question.

3. Write and punctuate a sentence that expresses strong feeling.

Writing With Style

There are many ways to make the same point. Part of a writer's job is finding the best way to say something. A writer wants each sentence to be clear, to the point, and pleasant to the ear. Think of how your favorite song states its ideas. Imagine how you would say the same things, how you would want to sound. The following sentences are all grammatically correct. They all make the same point. Which sentence do you like best? Why?

a. The frightened young girl tumbled off the cliff.

b. Off the cliff tumbled the young girl who was very frightened and she fell and fell and fell.

c. The girl fell off the cliff.

d. The young girl tumbled in a fright off the edge of the cliff.

Many of you may have chosen sentence *a* as the best sentence. It's clear and simple, but it still has enough description to give the reader a picture of the event.

Vocabulary Builder

Context Gives Clues to Meaning

When you read a word you don't know, you may be able to guess its meaning from the context. Context means the other words that surround the word you're trying to define. The way a word is used in a sentence very often gives you clues to its meaning.

The car speeding north collided with the car heading south.

You might be able to guess the meaning of the word *collided* from the rest of the sentence, in other words, from its context.

The word *collided* means *crashed together.*

In each sentence below, one word is underlined. Decide the meaning of the underlined word from its context. Write down your definition of the word. Then check the dictionary to see if you have written a correct definition. Put a star next to your definition if it comes close to the dictionary definition.

1. The cans of fruit and vegetables were stored in the kitchen <u>pantry</u>.
2. The oil leak might <u>contaminate</u> the lake.
3. The new computer worked fine except for one small <u>defect</u>.
4. He seemed <u>depressed</u> after his dog died and he lost all his money.
5. The <u>marlin</u> struggled on the end of the line, but Susan reeled it in.
6. She was having trouble seeing the blackboard, so she went to an <u>optometrist</u>.
7. The seven-foot tall basketball star seemed <u>gigantic</u> to the little boy.
8. Martha was <u>astonished</u> when a purple elephant appeared in her bedroom.

Chapter Review

Chapter Summary

- ☐ Complete sentences make your writing clearer.

- ☐ A sentence expresses a complete thought and makes sense on its own.

- ☐ A sentence contains a subject (sometimes understood, not stated) and a predicate.

- ☐ A sentence begins with a capital letter. It ends with a period, a question mark, or an exclamation point.

Writing Practice

Look at this picture:

What does it make you think about? What ideas does it give you? How does it make you feel? How would you describe the picture?

Write three sentences about the picture. Make sure each sentence is complete and is properly punctuated.

Chapter Quiz

A. Decide if each of the following items is a complete sentence. If it isn't a complete sentence, write **No** on your paper after the number. If it is a complete sentence, copy it on your paper. Then underline the subject with one line and the predicate with two lines.

1. The queen wore a golden crown.

2. The waitress dropped the soup bowl.

3. Hit the ground with a crash.

4. The chubby baby waved the rattle.

5. The huge, yellow lion.

6. The crowd in the park.

7. The committee talked about the party decorations.

8. Lisa snores.

9. Fell from the tree.

10. Heavy winds broke the frozen trees.

B. Use each pair of nouns and verbs below to write a complete sentence. Remember: the noun will be the subject of your sentence and the verb will be the predicate.

1. dog   chased

2. man   watched

3. book   dropped

4. car   crashed

5. boat   sailed

Chapter 2

Avoiding Sentence Fragments and Run-on Sentences

Zora Neale Hurston supported herself as a maid, secretary, and chauffeur as she taught herself to write. Just as she did, the characters in her novels struggle courageously to overcome poverty and hardship. Orphaned at age 9, she put herself through Barnard College, graduating in 1928. Her best known books are Jonah's Gourd Vine *and* Their Eyes Were Watching God.

Learning to write, like any other skill, takes patience and practice.

Writers at Work: Zora Neale Hurston (1901–1960)

Chapter Learning Objectives

- ☐ Identify sentence fragments.
- ☐ Correct sentence fragments.
- ☐ Identify run-on sentences.
- ☐ Correct run-on sentences.
- ☐ Write complete sentences that begin with capital letters, end with punctuation marks, and express complete thoughts.

Words to Know

fragment   a group of words that is not a complete sentence but is punctuated as if it were

example: Wearing a silly clown costume.

run-on sentence   two or more sentences that have not been properly separated or properly joined

example: The singer sang a song the rude crowd kept talking.

conjunction   words used to join or link words, phrases, ideas, and sentences; common conjunctions are *and, but,* and *or*

example: Dogs **and** cats **and** birds **and** lizards filled the pet shop, **but** we could not take them home.

Sentence Fragments

People have to learn different skills to use any form of communication.

What skills does a writer have to learn?

A fragment is a part broken off of something. A piece broken off of a dinner plate is a fragment. A splinter of wood broken off of a larger piece is a fragment. In writing, a sentence **fragment** is a part of a sentence broken off from the whole sentence. Sometimes people mistakenly treat sentence fragments as if they were whole sentences.

The coach left the football. *Under the bench.*

The words in *italics* are a sentence fragment. They have been treated like a sentence, but they aren't. The group of words has no verb. You learned in Chapter 1 that a sentence always has a predicate, part of which must be a verb. Therefore, *Under the bench* cannot be a sentence.

Be sure that if you begin a group of words with a capital letter and end it with a period, it's really a sentence. Does your sentence express a complete thought? Does it contain a subject and a predicate?

fragment: The truck in the left lane.

It has no predicate.

sentence: The truck in the left lane lost its load.

simple subject: truck

simple predicate: lost

In a sentence fragment, the first word is capitalized. End punctuation is used. However, a fragment doesn't express a complete thought. As a developing writer, you will learn to recognize fragments and to avoid using them. You want your sentences to express whole ideas and feelings, not just fragments of them.

Activity 1

Three of the five items below are complete sentences and two are sentence fragments. On your own paper, write the numbers of the fragments. After each number that you write, explain why it's a fragment. (Is it missing the subject or the predicate?)

1. The beautiful dolls stood in the front window.

2. A tall, dark man in a white coat.

3. The suitcase was stuffed with clothes.

4. Screamed and ran from the room.

5. They invited Susan.

Activity 2

Rewrite the items you identified as fragments in Activity 1. Make them into complete sentences. Use your imagination to finish the sentences.

Sometimes sentence fragments can be corrected by joining them to other sentences. At other times the fragment can be corrected by adding words to it to make a complete sentence.

> wrong: On the train. The twins saw a movie star.

> right: On the train the twins saw a movie star.

> wrong: The restaurant was too crowded. And noisy as well.

> right: The restaurant was too crowded and noisy as well.

or

> right: The restaurant was too crowded. It was noisy as well.

Activity 3

Correct any sentence fragments you find on the next page. Either turn them into separate, complete sentences or join them to another sentence.

> example: The bank robbers in masks. They went into the crowded bank.

> right: The bank robbers in masks went into the crowded bank.

or

> right: The bank robbers wore masks. They went into the crowded bank.

1. On her lucky day. She found a ten dollar bill.
2. The audience clapped loudly. For her great magic show.
3. In great pain. The injured skier limped down the mountain.
4. Ken thought he saw a ghost. Was only a dream.
5. The ball was hit. To far left field.
6. The sign showed. The way to Cleveland.
7. Homework after school. She hated to do it.
8. Just in time. The bell rang to end the boxing match.
9. Alexander the Great. He won many battles.
10. Dinner was ready. Sat down to eat.

Always Be Clear!
Sometimes in conversation we answer questions with fragments. Read the following examples:

question: Where did you go?

answer: to the movies

question: What did you see?

answer: *Return of the Sea Slime*

But in writing, it's always better to answer questions in complete sentences.

Why did you like the book?

wrong: Because it was exciting.

right: I liked the book because it was exciting.

This method is especially important when you answer test questions. Writing in complete sentences makes your answers clearer.

Activity 4

Write five sentences about the last time you quarreled (or went to a movie or had fun) with a friend or a relative. Describe what happened, how people acted, and so on. Make sure each of your sentences is a complete thought with a subject and a predicate.

Run-on Sentences

Sometimes writers forget to separate their sentences. They forget to mark the end of one sentence with a period and the beginning of the next with a capital letter. Sentences that aren't properly separated from each other are called **run-on sentences**. Read the following sentences from a job application. The person has been asked why he feels he would make a good worker in a day-care center.

> I am from a large family, I was the oldest and helped with the younger ones, and, well, I am patient but firm with children.

The item above has been punctuated as if it were one sentence. Really, it is three sentences.

> I am from a large family. I was the oldest and helped with the younger ones. I am patient but firm with children.

Run-on sentences easily confuse your reader. Avoid run-ons. When you keep your reader in mind, you're helping yourself as well. Your ideas and feelings will come through clearly. You'll make a good impression when you write in a way the reader can follow.

Warning!

A comma cannot separate two sentences. Only an end mark (a period, an exclamation point, or a question mark) and a capital letter can separate sentences.

> wrong: The witch laughed, her evil spell had worked.

> right: The witch laughed. Her evil spell had worked.

Activity 5

Some of the items below are correctly written. Others contain run-on sentences. Number your paper from 1 to 10. Write C next to the number if the sentences are written correctly. Write RO next to the number if the sentence is a run-on.

1. The alarm clock buzzed. It was time to start another day.
2. The last boy in line got no lunch the food had all been eaten.
3. The movie ended with a kiss it was a silly ending.
4. The bugs escaped from the box. Her collection was ruined.
5. The garbage truck banged and clattered and woke up all the people.
6. The pig grunted loudly, the chickens clucked in the chicken coop.

7. Do you think *The Blob* was a scary movie my cousin almost fainted when he saw it.

8. Ann fell off her bike and hurt her knee.

9. Ann fell off her bike she hurt her knee.

10. The television suddenly went off. The power was out.

How can you correct run-on sentences?

There are two easy ways to correct them.

1. Write two separate sentences.

> run-on: *Popcorn once was free now they charge a dollar for a box.*

> corrected: *Popcorn once was free. Now they charge a dollar for a box.*

*Conjunctions are joining words. **And**, **but**, and **or** are conjunctions often used to join two sentences.*

2. Join the sentences with a comma and a **conjunction**.

> run-on: *Popcorn once was free now they charge a dollar for a box.*

> corrected: *Popcorn once was free, but now they charge a dollar for a box.*

Activity 6

*Notice that there is a complete sentence with a subject and predicate on **each side** of the comma and conjunction.*

Underline the comma and the conjunction in each of the following sentences.

> example: I wanted to wear jeans, but it was a costume party.

1. The Smith family brought salad, and the Browns brought dessert.

2. The guitar string broke, and the singer forgot the words to the song.

3. Students must study before a hard test, or they will surely fail.

4. Tim did not study, and he failed.

5. Karen wished on a falling star, but hard work really earned her the job.

Activity 7

Correct the following run-on sentences. Remember the two easy methods. Either separate the sentences with periods and capital letters, or connect the sentences properly with a comma and a conjunction (and, but, or or).

1. Margie won the prize she really deserved it.

2. The music was loud he liked it that way.

3. The light was red the car roared through the crossing.

4. The basketball went through the hoop the Hawks won the game.

5. Lisa might choose the red tennis shoes she might choose the black ones with the white stripe on the toe.

Challenge

Rewrite the following paragraph correcting any sentence fragments or run-on sentences.

Ryan and Marcy wanted to visit the old man. Everyone said the old man was mean they decided to go anyway. The man lived in a rundown house on Oak Street. With his spotted dog. He always seemed so lonely. Ryan and Marcy knew he needed some friends. They took the man a box of candy. And some soda pop. They rang the old man's doorbell they were a little nervous. Then the old man came to the door. He smiled.

Writing With Style

Listen closely to people talking. They often use a lot of **ands** and **ums**. They use slang words, too—words like dude or heavy, man. When people talk, they use such words as filler to give themselves time to think. You don't need filler in your writing. Writing is not like everyday speech, unless you're writing dialogue.

Which of the following paragraphs is better? Why?

A. Last Saturday night turned out to be the most frightening night of my life. There was a terrible thunderstorm, and the power went out while I was watching *Nightmare on Elm Street* on television, and then I heard a scratching sound in the basement. Dude, it sounded like Freddy Krueger's metal glove. Well, I was so frightened that I ran to the phone to call for help, and the phone line was dead, which was heavy, man, and I knew I had to go downstairs and check on the noise. My heart was pounding as I shined the flashlight around the basement, and there sat my dog scratching his fleas. Like Freddy was nowhere.

B. Last Saturday night turned out to be the most frightening night of my life. There was a terrible thunderstorm. The power went out while I was watching *Nightmare on Elm Street* on television. Then I heard a scratching sound in the basement. It sounded like Freddy Krueger's metal glove scratching the floor. I ran to the phone to call for help. The phone line was dead! I knew I had to go downstairs and check on the noise. My heart pounded as I shined the flashlight around the basement. There sat my dog scratching his fleas. Freddy wasn't around. He's just a character in a movie that scared me. Real life is a dog with fleas.

Selection B is the better choice. Someone telling the story might be so excited that he or she would run the sentences together with *ands*. However, when writing the story, the narrator can take time to separate his or her thoughts. The writer has created suspense and scared the reader.

Vocabulary Builder

Choosing the Dictionary Definition

Often the dictionary will list several definitions for the same word. How do you know which definition is the one you want?

You must look at the word's context. How is that word used in the sentence? Which definition is best when the word is used in that context?

Look at this dictionary entry:

> boxer: noun *(1) a person who boxes, especially in competition, (2) any of a breed of large, short-haired dogs of the bulldog type, usually tan or brindled.*

Which definition would you choose for the word *boxer* in the following sentence?

> The boxer barked and showed his teeth when the stranger came near.

In each of the following sentences, one word is underlined. Look up that word in a dictionary. Copy the best meaning for the word as it is used in the sentence.

1. In addition to a rifle, the soldier carried a <u>club</u> as a weapon.

2. Sam decided to join the school drama <u>club</u>.

3. Close the window because a cold <u>draft</u> is coming into the room.

4. The first <u>draft</u> of his paper contained many mistakes.

5. The soldiers, knowing they had been beaten, planned their <u>retreat</u>.

6. Every weekend we go to our oceanside <u>retreat</u>.

Chapter Review

Chapter Summary

- ☐ A sentence fragment is not a complete thought. It can't stand on its own and shouldn't be punctuated like a sentence.

- ☐ Do not use sentence fragments in your writing.

- ☐ A run-on sentence occurs when sentences are not properly separated from each other.

- ☐ Run-on sentences make writing hard to follow. Be kind to your reader and make a good impression, too. Don't run your sentences together.

- ☐ Complete sentences should be separated with a period and a capital letter. They can also be joined by a comma and a conjunction.

Writing Practice

Choose an object you can see right now. Pretend you're that object. Write four sentences describing yourself. Write a fifth sentence telling what you are. Make sure each sentence is complete and is correctly punctuated. Make sure you do not write sentence fragments or run-on sentences.

example:

I am yellow.

Once I was very long, but now I am shorter.

I have a sharp end, and I have a flat end.

There is a number 2 printed on my side in black.

I am a pencil.

Chapter Quiz

A. Some of the items listed below are correct. Some contain sentence fragments. Some are run-on sentences. Number your paper from 1 to 10. If the sentence is correct, write a C by the number. If the item contains a fragment, write F by the number. If it's a run-on sentence, write RO by the number.

1. The bike skidded to a stop, it left black marks on the street.

2. The moon came out it turned the ocean golden.

3. Looked left and right then crossed the road.

4. The puppy barked and headed for home.

5. In case of fire.

6. All the tallest people in the class.

7. I liked the book it had an interesting plot.

8. How many pieces of cake.

9. We worked all afternoon, but we still did not have enough money.

10. The king put on his royal robe he sat on his throne.

B. Correct any sentence from the above exercise that you did not label with a C. Rewrite the new sentences on your own piece of paper.

Chapter 3

Writing Different Kinds of Sentences

Theodore Geisel, better known as Dr. Seuss, is a popular author and illustrator of rhymed children's stories. Although he started out to be an English teacher, his "doodling" soon became his whole career. Books such as The Cat in the Hat *and* Horton Hatches the Egg *have delighted children all over the world.*

Rhymed stories are fun to read aloud and fun to listen to.

Writers at Work: Theodore Geisel (1904–   )

Chapter Learning Objectives

- ☐ Identify and write a simple sentence.
- ☐ Identify compound subjects and predicates.
- ☐ Identify and write a compound sentence.
- ☐ Identify and write a complex sentence.
- ☐ Write a variety of sentence types and sentence lengths.

Words to Know

variety   many different forms or kinds of things

simple sentence   a group of words that expresses a complete thought and has one subject-predicate combination

example: Some people will pay $500 for one baseball card.

compound subject   two or more subjects with the same predicate

example: **Karen**, **Bill**, and **Jeff** worked at the ticket booth.

compound predicate   two or more predicates with the same subject

example: The alligators **opened** their jaws and **snapped** at the tourists.

compound sentence   two simple sentences joined by a comma and a coordinating conjunction (and, but, or)

example: Margo kept calling Ted's house, but no one answered.

subordinate clause   a clause that adds to the meaning of another clause but makes no sense by itself

example: **After she had exercised**, Linda was very sore.

independent clause   a clause that can stand alone as a complete sentence

example: **Mike scored two runs**, but Art did not score any.

complex sentence   a sentence with a subordinate clause and an independent clause.

example: Whenever it rains, the roof leaks.

subordinate conjunction   a conjunction that introduces a subordinate clause

example: The mountain climbers turned back **because** the snow was blinding.

The Simple Sentence

If you want people to read what you write, try to make your writing interesting. One way to do this is to use different kinds of sentences. Read the following paragraph:

The Mosquito
The mosquito is an amazing insect. The mosquito has forty-seven teeth. The mosquito is very small. It can carry twice its weight. The mosquito drinks blood. The mosquito lives in damp places. There are more than 2,000 kinds of mosquitoes. Scientists discover new kinds every year. Some mosquitoes carry disease. Humans look for ways to kill mosquitoes. They are very hard to kill.

What is wrong with the paragraph you just read?

One answer is that all the sentences are too much the same. They sound alike. It's almost as if you were just making a list of facts and not writing sentences. Or it is as if you were counting items! Read it aloud; doesn't it sound dull? Each sentence has one subject and one predicate. They are all just about the same length. Too many of them start with the same words.

If an ice cream store advertises 101 different varieties of ice cream, what does it mean? Why do people like variety in their lives?

The sentences about mosquitoes need more **variety**. In this chapter, you'll learn how to write different kinds of sentences to make your writing more interesting.

Most of the sentences you have worked with in chapters 1 and 2 have been **simple sentences.** That means they have just one subject-predicate combination.

This is a simple sentence:

> The rain splattered the windshield.

There is one subject, *rain.*

There is one predicate, *splattered.*

One way to vary simple sentences is to use **compound subjects** or **compound predicates.** This means there is more than one noun in the subject or more than one verb in the predicate.

> The dog and cat fought in the alley.

This sentence has a compound subject.

> The rabbit wiggled its nose and hopped across the cage.

This sentence has a compound predicate.

Look at a page in a newspaper or a magazine. See if you can find a sentence with a compound subject or a compound predicate.

> The boys and girls stood in the corners and giggled on the first day of dancing school.

This sentence has a compound subject and a compound predicate.

How could compound subjects or predicates help the paragraph about mosquitoes?

You might write:

> The mosquito drinks blood and lives in damp places. (compound predicate)

or

> The mosquito is very small but has forty-seven teeth. (compound predicate)

Even though many of the sentences you write will be simple sentences, they don't all have to be the same.

Activity 1

Number your paper from 1 to 10. Write CS by the numbers of sentences with compound subjects. Write CP by the numbers of sentences with compound predicates. If neither subject nor predicate is compound, leave a blank after the number.

1. Men and women played on the college volleyball team.
2. William and I brought peanut butter and banana sandwiches.
3. The driver of the car honked and waved.
4. Pizza and spaghetti were on the menu.
5. The skater twirled gracefully and bowed to the crowd.
6. Big drops of rain fell and ruined our picnic.
7. Most stores closed early for the holiday.
8. Will you stay here or go to the party?
9. The Tigers and the Bears played in Saturday's big game.
10. You should call and make an appointment.

Activity 2

Make each pair of sentences into one sentence by using a compound subject.

> example: Elvis Presley was a rock star.
>
> Buddy Holly was a rock star, too.
>
> Elvis Presley and Buddy Holly were rock stars.

1. Mr. Wonker wears suspenders.
   Mrs. Wonker wears suspenders, too.

2. New York is a big city.
   Chicago is also a big city.

3. The Wildcats are a top-rated team.
   The Bombers are also a top team.

4. Scott teased Ann.
   Brian teased her, too.

5. In the face of danger, Susan was very brave.
   Kevin was brave, too.

Activity 3

Make each pair of sentences into one sentence by using a compound predicate.

> example: The coach blew her whistle.
>
> She shouted to the team.
>
> The coach blew her whistle and shouted to the team.

1. The magician can saw a person in half.
   He can also make a rabbit disappear.

2. Many soldiers in the Spanish-American War got yellow fever.
   Many died from yellow fever.

3. Chris ran the 100-yard dash.
   Chris won a first-place medal.

4. The lion roared.
   He did not scare anyone. (Use *but* instead of *and*.)

5. Matt studied hard.
   He flunked the test anyway. (Use *but* instead of *and*.)

Compound subjects and compound predicates can help you say things in a different manner. They add variety and interest to your sentences.

Compound Sentences

In Chapter 2, you learned that you can join two complete sentences with a comma and a coordinating conjunction (usually *and*, *but*, or *or*). When you do this, you form what is called a **compound sentence**. Read the following example:

> Christine baked the cake, and Larry made the cookies.

In a compound sentence, there is a complete thought with a subject and a predicate on each side of the conjunction.

> Christine baked the cake, **and** Larry made the cookies.

Look at a page in a newspaper or a magazine. See if you can find a compound sentence.

Compound sentences are very useful. Use one sometimes instead of writing two short, simple sentences.

Warning!
Sometimes students confuse a simple sentence that has a compound subject or a compound predicate with a compound sentence. To tell the difference,

just look on both sides of the conjunction. Is there a subject and a predicate on each side? If so, the sentence is a compound sentence.

compound sentence: The wind howled, and the rain pounded.

simple sentence: The wind and rain pounded the coast. (no predicate on one side of the conjunction)

Activity 4

Number your paper from 1 to 10. Decide if each of the following sentences is simple or compound. Write S for simple or C for compound beside each number.

1. Spring and summer are her favorite seasons.
2. Carla likes snow skiing, but John likes water skiing.
3. Howard saved his money and bought a plane ticket to London.
4. Howard saved his money, and he bought a plane ticket to London.
5. The Boy Scouts saw Bigfoot, and they told everyone about it.
6. Eric did not believe in ghosts, but something had walked through his bedroom wall.
7. The snake crawled up on the rock and curled up in the sun.
8. The doorperson or the clerk will take your ticket.
9. Bars covered the windows, but the burglar got in anyway.
10. The play was held in the smallest theater, and some people had to stand.

Activity 5

Make each pair of sentences below into one compound sentence. Use the conjunctions *and, but,* and *or*.

> example: The table was all set. The guests did not arrive.

> The table was all set, but the guests did not arrive.

1. He was tired and hungry.
   The long trip had been worth the trouble.

2. She did not know where the interesting boy lived.
   She had his phone number.

3. You should be home by midnight.
   You might be locked out.

4. Mark Twain wrote a book called *The Adventures of Huckleberry Finn.*
   He wrote *The Adventures of Tom Sawyer.*

5. In the last inning, the Dodgers scored two runs.
   In the last inning, the Cubs made two errors.

Making Choices

And, but, and *or* each suggests a different meaning.

When two ideas are equally important, choose *and*.

> Bill washed the dishes, *and* Sue dried them.

When you want to show contrast between ideas, use *but*.

> He wanted chocolate, *but* he got vanilla.

When you join two ideas in a way that gives a choice between them, use *or*.

> You should answer the phone, *or* it will keep ringing.

Activity 6

Don't forget the comma before the conjunction in a compound sentence.

Write your own compound sentences.

> example: Last holiday season, I took a basket of food to a poor family, and my neighbor visited a children's hospital.

1. Tell about something you did during the last holiday season and something your friend did. (Use *and*.)

2. Tell about something you wanted to do last summer but didn't get to do. (Use *but*.)

3. Tell about your first choice for dinner tonight and your second choice. (Use *or*.)

Complex Sentences

You know that a sentence is a group of words with a subject and a predicate. You know that a sentence expresses a complete thought and can stand alone. Sometimes you will find a group of words with a subject and a predicate that cannot stand alone.

> after Sharon broke her date

The subject is *Sharon*.

The predicate is *broke*.

However, it doesn't make sense alone, does it? What happened after Sharon broke her date? Such a group of words is called a **subordinate clause**. A subordinate clause has a subject and a predicate but it cannot stand alone.

When you join a clause like this with an **independent clause,** you make a **complex sentence.**

> After Sharon broke her date, she stayed home and studied.

The part that can stand alone is called the independent clause:

> She stayed home and studied.

The part that cannot stand alone is called the subordinate clause:

> After Sharon broke her date

The words listed below often begin subordinate clauses. They are called **subordinate conjunctions.**

Some of these subordinate conjunctions indicate the time that something happened. Which subordinate conjunctions indicate time?

after	before	though
when	although	if
unless	whenever	because
since	until	while

This list is not complete. There are many more subordinate conjunctions.

You can vary your writing by using complex sentences.

> two simple sentences:
> The storm was coming. Tyler took out the boat.

> one complex sentence:
> Although the storm was coming, Tyler took out the boat.

Punctuation Note

A subordinate clause can appear at the beginning of a sentence or at the end. The placement of the subordinate clause determines the punctuation in the sentence. When the subordinate clause comes at the beginning of a sentence, it's followed by a comma. When the subordinate clause comes at the end of the sentence, no comma is needed.

> *If it rains,* take an umbrella. (subordinate clause at beginning)
>
> Take an umbrella *if it rains.* (subordinate clause at end)

Activity 7

Before you do this activity, review the "Punctuation Note" on page 38. When do you use a comma in a complex sentence?

Make each pair of sentences below into one complex sentence. Use the subordinate conjunctions listed on page 38. Try to use a different subordinate conjunction in each sentence.

> example: It is snowing.
>
> School might be canceled.
>
> Because it is snowing, school might be canceled.

1. Speed was important.
   Pony Express riders traveled all day and all night.

2. The department store closed.
   The shoppers stayed downtown.

3. A bodyguard always goes with the rock star.
   The rock star leaves the studio.

4. The clock struck one.
   The mouse ran down.

5. It rained.
   The baseball game was stopped.

Writing With Style

Using different kinds of sentences and different sentence lengths improves your writing. It makes your writing more interesting.

Which selection below is better writing? Why?

A. The mongoose is a small animal. It is very fierce. It lives in Africa and southern Asia. It eats all sorts of small creatures. It eats snakes. A mongoose will fight a deadly cobra. The mongoose moves very quickly. The cobra cannot strike it. Mongooses can be tamed. They are often kept around homes. They will drive away snakes.

B. The mongoose is a small, fierce animal that lives in Africa and southern Asia. It eats all sorts of small creatures, including snakes. A mongoose will even fight a deadly cobra. The mongoose moves very quickly, and the cobra cannot strike it. Since mongooses can be tamed, they are often kept around homes to drive away snakes.

If you chose B as the better example of good writing, you were correct. Selection B uses the variety of sentence types discussed in this chapter. Notice that it contains two simple sentences, one compound sentence, and two complex sentences. In selection A, all the sentences are simple, and the writing is choppy and less interesting.

Vocabulary Builder

Word Meaning and Parts of Speech
A word may have different meanings depending on how it's used in a sentence. The same word can be more than one part of speech. For example, if you see the word *sail* written all alone on a piece of paper, you can't give it any one definition. *Sail* can be used as a noun and a verb, can't it? The word must be used in a sentence before its meaning is clear.

Used as a noun, *sail* means a piece of fabric used to catch the wind, as in this sentence:

He bought a new boat with a yellow *sail*.

Used as a verb, *sail* means to move across water or to travel by water, as in this sentence:

We will *sail* to Hawaii in the spring.

Use the dictionary if you need help in writing the following sentences.

1. Write a sentence using *bowl* as a noun.

2. Write a sentence using *bowl* as a verb.

3. Write a sentence using *park* as a noun.

4. Write a sentence using *park* as a verb.

5. Write a sentence using *drive* as a noun.

6. Write a sentence using *drive* as a verb.

Chapter Review

Chapter Summary

☐ There are many different ways to get across the same ideas. Try to use different kinds of sentences when you write because it will make your writing more interesting.

☐ Simple sentences have one subject-predicate combination.

☐ Simple sentences can have a compound subject or a compound predicate.

☐ Compound sentences are formed by joining simple sentences with a comma and a coordinating conjunction.

☐ Complex sentences are formed by joining a subordinate clause to an independent clause with a subordinate conjunction.

Writing Practice

Look back at the selection called "The Mosquito" at the beginning of this chapter. Rewrite that selection. Make it more interesting by using a variety of sentence types. Use at least one simple sentence, one compound sentence, and one complex sentence.

Chapter Quiz

A. Some of the sentences below are simple sentences. Some of them are compound sentences, and some are complex sentences. Number your paper from 1 to 10. Decide which kind of sentence each item is. Then write **simple, compound,** or **complex** by each number.

1. Although the boat was old and shabby, it still stayed afloat.
2. Mr. Warren called the police and waited for them to arrive.
3. Mr. Warren called the police, and he waited for them to arrive.
4. After Mr. Warren called the police, he waited for them to arrive.
5. Mr. Warren waited for the police to arrive after he called them.
6. The hikers did not see the trail signs, and soon they were lost.
7. Although the mountain rumbled, a volcano did not erupt.
8. The store ran out of tire chains when the roads were icy.
9. Molly called and called, but her dog did not come home.
10. The students in the north wing and the students in the south wing met in the cafeteria.

B. Write one example for a simple sentence, a compound sentence, and a complex sentence.

Chapter 4

Writing Better Sentences

Piri Thomas began to write while serving a seven-year prison term. Like most good authors, he began writing about people and places he knew best. These are the Puerto Ricans and African Americans he grew up with in New York City. His most famous book is Down These Mean Streets. *It is a realistic story of how young people can be affected by life in the ghetto.*

Personal experience is a powerful source of writing ideas.

Writers at Work: Piri Thomas (1928–   )

Chapter Learning Objectives

☐ Add detail to sentences by using adjectives, adverbs, and prepositional phrases.

☐ Describe images and ideas clearly by using specific words.

☐ Choose interesting, vivid words.

Words to Know

adjective   a word that adds meaning to a noun or pronoun

> example: **Ten happy** campers set up their tents.

adverb   a word that adds meaning to a verb, an adjective, or another adverb

> example: The puppy howled **so sadly**.

preposition   a word that shows the relationship of a noun or pronoun to some other word in the sentence

> example: The grandfather clock stands **in** the corner.

object of the preposition   the noun or pronoun that follows the preposition in the prepositional phrase

> example: The star of the **show** walked angrily off the set.

prepositional phrase   the preposition and its object taken together

> example: The book **of poems** was **on the desk**.

details   all the small parts of something that make up the whole

> example: Tell us the **details** of your trip.

vivid   clear, distinct, colorful

connotation   idea or ideas associated with a word in addition to its actual meaning

synonym   a word with the same or nearly the same meaning as another word

> example: **Large** is a synonym for **big**.

Details Are the Key

In Chapters 1 through 3, you learned about writing sentences correctly. In this chapter, you will learn how to make those sentences even better. You will learn how to express your ideas in a clear and interesting manner.

Remember this **Key to Good Writing:**

You write to communicate. You have an image or an idea in your head. You want to give that image to your reader as exactly as possible.

Let's say you saw a strange-looking man on your way to class today. You can hardly wait to tell your friends about it. The man looked so suspicious.

"I saw a man today!" you say to your friends.

"Oh," one of them answers. Your friends don't seem very excited or interested. Why?

You didn't communicate your idea. You didn't present the image very clearly. This chapter will help you communicate more clearly. It will help you write sentences that present **vivid** pictures and ideas.

Using **details** is one key to good writing. Read some of your own writing over and ask yourself, "Is there anything more I could say to make the image or idea clearer to my reader?"

Activity 1

Look out a window or go outside. Focus on one thing you find interesting, beautiful, or ugly. Look at it long and hard. Now, write one sentence about it. Your goal is to make your reader see that thing just as you see it.

Using Adjectives and Adverbs

Certain kinds of words make the things you describe a lot clearer. For example, **adjectives** are words that describe nouns. They make your images clearer to your readers. They clarify your images and ideas by telling *what kind, which one,* or *how many.*

See Reference Guide, Grammar 34–38 for more information on adjectives.

She served the salad.

a. She served the **crisp, green** salad.

b. She served the **wilted, yellowed** salad.

After reading sentence a, you might be eager to eat. After reading sentence b, you might want to skip the salad.

Adjectives can make a difference!

Activity 2

Each of the following sentences is followed by a question. On your own paper, answer the question with an adjective. Then rewrite the original sentence, adding the adjective.

example: The dog barked at the visitor.

Was the dog vicious or friendly? *friendly*

rewrite: *The friendly dog barked at the visitor.*

1. The teacher told Sam to stand up in front of the class.

   Was the teacher angry or proud?_____

   rewrite:_____

2. Clouds filled the sky.

   Were they dark, threatening clouds or puffy, white clouds?_____

   rewrite: _____

3. She offered me the necklace.

   Was it a costly, diamond necklace or a cheap, plastic necklace? _____

   rewrite:_____

Adverbs describe verbs, adjectives, or other adverbs. Like adjectives, they make the things you describe clearer. Adverbs usually answer the questions *how, when, where, why,* or *to what extent.*

> She smiled.
>
> She smiled **coldly.**
>
> She smiled **warmly.**

See Reference Guide, Grammar 39–44 for more information on adverbs.

The adverbs in the sentences above tell how she smiled. Adverbs can really change the picture.

Activity 3

Each sentence below is followed by a question. On your own paper, answer the question with an adverb. Then rewrite the original sentence, adding the adverb.

> example: The patient rested.

Did the patient rest comfortably or uncomfortably? *comfortably*

rewrite: *The patient rested comfortably.*

1. He was hungry.

   Was he extremely hungry or slightly hungry?_____

   rewrite: _____

2. Paula wears lipstick.

   Does Paula wear lipstick often or never? _____

   rewrite: _____

3. The wind blew.

   Did the wind blow softly or fiercely?_____

   rewrite: _____

Activity 4

Number your paper from 1 to 5. Next to each number, list any adjectives or adverbs that appear in each of the sentences. Identify each word you list as an adjective or an adverb.

> example: The mad scientist laughed wildly.

mad—adjective

wildly—adverb

1. The graceful cheetah runs swiftly.
2. The fat man sang too loudly.
3. The terrible explosion happened suddenly.
4. The sick child sneezed constantly.
5. The carpenter skillfully sanded the beautiful, dark wood.

Activity 5

Write your own sentences, using adjectives and adverbs to make your images clearer. Use at least one adjective or adverb in each sentence. Underline the adjectives and adverbs that you use.

1. Write a sentence about some highway you have traveled.

Try using some compound subjects and predicates. Try writing some compound or complex sentences as well as simple sentences.

2. Write a sentence about a teacher you remember as being wonderful or terrible.

3. Write a sentence about spiders.

4. Write a sentence about a hat that you own or would like to own.

5. Write a sentence about an interesting relative.

Using Prepositional Phrases

*A **preposition** is a word that shows the relationship of a noun or pronoun to some other word in the sentence. A prepositional phrase begins with a preposition.*

Prepositional phrases can make your sentences clearer and more descriptive. A **prepositional phrase** works like an adjective or an adverb.

> The cake *on the table* looked stale.

The prepositional phrase, *on the table*, describes cake, a noun. That prepositional phrase works like an adjective.

> The burglar entered *through the basement window.*

The prepositional phrase, through the basement window, describes the verb, entered. That prepositional phrase works like an adverb.

Grammar Note
A prepositional phrase begins with a preposition and ends with a noun or a pronoun. That noun or pronoun is called the **object of the preposition.**

See Reference Guide, Grammar 48–53 for some more information on prepositional phrases.

> example: They crowded *into the room.*

Into the room is the prepositional phrase.

Into is the preposition.

Room is the object of the preposition.

Some common prepositions are listed in the *Reference Guide, Grammar 48.*

Activity 6

Each sentence below is followed by a question. On your own paper, rewrite the sentence, adding a prepositional phrase.

> example: The nervous student spoke.

Did the student speak to the principal or to the class? *to the principal.*

> *The nervous student spoke to the principal.*

1. The pitcher hurled the ball.

   Did the pitcher hurl the ball at the batter or at the crowd? _____

   rewrite: _____

2. The pot was filled.

   Was the pot filled with gold or with soup?_____

   rewrite: _____

3. I like ice cream.

   Do you like ice cream with chocolate syrup or with strawberries?_____

   rewrite: _____

Activity 7

Improve the following sentences by adding <u>at least one</u> prepositional phrase. (You can add adjectives and adverbs to the sentences, too.)

Sometimes it may seem hard to find enough to write. If you use more detail, you will find yourself writing longer sentences.

1. The woman fell.
2. The car skidded.
3. My uncle arrived.
4. The plane landed.
5. The creature appeared.

Challenge

Choose one of the sentences you have written. By using adjectives, adverbs, and prepositional phrases, expand that sentence even more. Really picture the thing you're describing. Make that sentence at least ten words long.

Using Better Words

You can improve your sentences by making general words more specific.

I took my **pet there**.

I took my **lizard to school**.

Which sentence creates a clearer picture? The second sentence is better because the word *lizard* is more specific than the word *pet*. The phrase *to school* is more specific than the word *there*.

Activity 8

On your own paper, rewrite each sentence below. Replace the underlined words with words that are more specific.

1. I will not eat that <u>food.</u>
2. The <u>vehicle</u> was parked in the road.
3. The <u>girl</u> is from <u>another country</u>.
4. Mike <u>put all his things</u> into his locker.
5. The <u>boat</u> sailed into the harbor.

Some words are more interesting than others. They're more interesting because they give a clearer picture, a more vivid or specific meaning.

> Mr. Smith walked into the room.

> Mr. Smith waddled into the room.

Name three animals that waddle. By saying that Mr. Smith waddled, you are giving him some of the characteristics of those animals.

Why is *waddled* a better word than *walked*?

Walked doesn't create much of a picture. Any Mr. Smith could walk. He could be thin or fat. He could be moving quickly or slowly. What kind of a Mr. Smith would *waddle*?

Make the words you use work for you. Use words that "color" your writing.

Activity 9

List all the verbs you can think of that could be used in place of *walked*. See how long you can make your list. When you're finished, circle the words you think are the most colorful and descriptive.

Notice that some of the **synonyms** for walk present a favorable picture. For example, the word *strolled* is a pleasant kind of walking.

Notice that some of the synonyms present a negative picture. Remember Mr. Smith waddling along? That is not a pretty sight!

Words also have **connotations**. They make people think of good things or bad things. For example, *fragrance* is a positive word for smell. *Stench* is quite a negative word. You can use word connotations to help get your message across to your reader.

Activity 10

A. On your own paper, write down the word or phrase with the most positive connotation in each group.

1. strange, odd, unique
2. chef, cook, kitchen helper
3. thin, skinny, slender
4. argue, discuss, quarrel
5. job, work, career

B. Write down the word or phrase with the most negative connotation in each group.

1. proud, conceited, snobbish
2. reproduction, fake, copy
3. shy, bashful, quiet
4. thrifty, economical, cheap
5. remind, nag, suggest

Challenge

The following sentences make Mabel sound pretty awful. Rewrite them, giving Mabel a better image. Just change the underlined words to words with more positive connotations.

Mabel screeched the words to the song. Her mouth opened wide in her skinny face, and her bony fingers clutched the song book. She peered at the audience.

Use a thesaurus from the library. How many different words can you find to call a "coat"? What other words might you use to describe an "ugly" sight?

The Thesaurus: A Book That Can Help You

A thesaurus is a special kind of book. It is a reference book that helps you find synonyms for words. Words are alphabetized in a thesaurus, just as they are in a dictionary. If you look up a word, you will find a list of other words that mean nearly the same thing (a list of synonyms). The thesaurus can help you find more interesting words for your writing. It can help you find a different word when you think you have used one particular word too many times.

For example, if you look up the word *color* in a thesaurus, you might find an entry like this:

color—noun: hue, tone, tint, cast, shade, tinge

verb: dye, tinge, stain, paint

A person might write: I chose the **color** for my bedroom, but I wanted a different **color** for the den.

After checking the thesaurus, that person might write: I chose the **color** for my bedroom, but I wanted a different **shade** for the den.

The thesaurus can help you find words you might not think of on your own.

Writing With Style

Successful writing means successful communication. The writer wants to show the reader some of the ideas, experiences, information, and images inside his or her head.

Compare the two selections below. Which selection presents a clearer image? Which selection lets the reader know more exactly what the writer experienced? Why is one selection better than the other?

A. I went out on my surfboard last Saturday. It was the first nice day of spring. I didn't surf much. I just lay on my board. It was pretty nice. I was happy. But then I saw what looked like a shark in the water.

B. Some articles had appeared in the paper about shark attacks just off the coast, but I wasn't thinking about those articles last Saturday. The sky was blue, and it was the first really warm day of spring. I paddled out over the foamy, white waves on my surfboard. I felt lazy that day. I was content just floating, letting the waves lift me up and down. The sun was warm on my back. The water was surprisingly warm, too. The sea salt stung my eyes a little, but it didn't matter. I was getting a head start on summer fun. Just then I saw it. The dark black fin cut through the water and raced toward me.

You probably shared the writer's experience more fully when you read selection B. What skills that you have read about in this book did the writer use?

Vocabulary Builder

Using Synonyms
A. Match the synonyms in each column by writing them in pairs on your paper.

example: 1. huge, tremendous

Column A   **Column B**

1. huge   wicked

2. call   snarl

3. evil   task

4. growl   tremendous

5. brag   summon

6. job   boast

B. Rewrite each sentence below using a synonym for the italicized word.

1. The roof collapsed, but no one was *hurt*.

2. The evil villain *laughed* as he sped away in the car.

3. He was a *rich* man after he won the lottery.

4. The old witch had an *ugly* nose.

5. Do you own that *strange*, spotted dog?

Chapter Review

Chapter Summary

- ☐ The purpose of writing is to communicate an idea or image as clearly as possible.

- ☐ Use specific details to present ideas clearly.

- ☐ Adjectives describe nouns or pronouns. They can make ideas clearer by telling *what kind, which one,* or *how many.*

- ☐ Adverbs describe verbs, adjectives, or other adverbs. They can make ideas clearer by telling *how, when, where, why,* or to *what extent.*

- ☐ Prepositional phrases work like adjectives or adverbs to make ideas clearer.

- ☐ Using specific words instead of general words improves sentences.

- ☐ Choose words carefully for the best meaning.

- ☐ Try to put yourself in your reader's place. Is your reader getting the picture you intended?

Writing Practice

Divide your paper into four columns headed **walked, said, ate,** and **big**.

Now list as many words as you can that mean nearly the same thing as the word heading each column. Think hard, and make your lists as long as possible.

Chapter Quiz

A. Make the sentences below more interesting and vivid. Fill in the blanks with adjectives, adverbs, and prepositional phrases as indicated. Use your own paper.

> *example: The _____(adj.) book _____(prep. phrase) is called* The Adventures of a _____(adj.) Creature.

> *The tattered book on the highest shelf is called* The Adventures of a Horrible Creature.

1. The _____(adj.) teacher walked _____(adv.) to her desk.
2. The _____(adj.) commercial advertised _____(adj.) dog food.
3. All the people _____(prep. phrase) laughed _____(adv.) when the _____(adj.) clown jumped _____(prep. phrase).
4. The _____(adj.) snack made her _____(adv.) sick.
5. Without his _____(adj.) wig, Mr. Glitch was _____(adv.) bald.

B. Replace each underlined word with a word that creates a more vivid image.

> example: The spotted monster <u>ate</u> the live chickens.

> The spotted monster **gobbled** the live chickens.

1. The spy <u>walked</u> into the dark, empty room.
2. The new student was very <u>nice</u>.
3. The fresh, hot pizza was <u>good</u>.
4. "Help me! I can't swim!" <u>said</u> Bill.
5. Linda would have driven farther, but she was <u>tired</u>.

The poetry of Gwendolyn Brooks explores the nature of greatness in very simple language. Her poems of dignity, caring, and hope increase our awareness of the beauty of the human spirit. In 1950, her sonnet-ballad "Annie Allen" won a Pulitzer Prize. She was the first black woman ever to win this prestigious award.

Simple language is often more powerful than complicated language.

Writers at Work: Gwendolyn Brooks (1917–   )

Chapter Learning Objectives

☐ Identify the subject of a sentence as either singular or plural.

☐ Write verbs that agree in number with their subjects.

☐ Write pronouns to replace some nouns.

☐ Write pronouns that agree with antecedents in gender and number.

Words to Know

singular   expressing only one

> example: I ate the banana.

plural   expressing more than one

> example: They ate the bananas.

pronoun   a word used in place of a noun

> example: He held it gently in his hand.

antecedent   the noun a pronoun replaces

> example: The man entered the room. All eyes turned toward him. (Man is the antecedent of him.)

gender   classification given to nouns and pronouns according to the sex of the person or thing described

> examples: **He** is masculine; **she** is feminine; **it** is neuter (has no sex distinction); **child** is common (can be either masculine or feminine)

Subject-Verb Agreement

Every sentence has a subject and a verb. The subject and the verb must match each other. If the subject is **singular** (only one), then the verb must be singular, too. If the subject is **plural** (more than one), then the verb must be plural, too. It will sound awkward if the subject and verb do not agree.

> Mary wears jeans.

> Mary wear jeans.

Which sentence is correct?

Does the second sentence sound awkward?

In the second sentence, the subject and verb do not agree. The subject, Mary, is singular. Wears is the singular form of the verb.

Grammar Note

We usually think of the letter s as a plural ending. However, an "s" on the end of a verb usually indicates the singular verb form.

Although plural nouns usually end in "s," the verbs that agree with singular nouns usually end in "s". (Of course, some irregular verbs are exceptions to that rule.) Read the following examples:

singular nouns	verbs that agree with singular nouns
dog	barks
duck	quacks
student	asks
doctor	examines

plural nouns	verbs that agree with plural nouns
dogs	bark
ducks	quack
students	ask
doctors	examine

irregular exception—singular	
child	is, was, has

irregular exception—plural	
children	are, were, have

The subject and verb must agree in number.

Activity 1

The verb *has* agrees with a singular noun.

The verb *have* agrees with a plural noun.

Look at the subject of each sentence below. On a separate piece of paper, write the correct verb (has or have).

1. Cats (has, have) eyes that glow in the dark.

2. Music students (has, have) tickets to the concert.

3. My teacher (has, have) the strictest rules.

4. Some animals (has, have) no teeth.

5. Oregon (has, have) more rain than California.

Sometimes subject-verb agreement is tricky. To write the correct verb, you must first recognize the correct subject. For example, the subject of a sentence is not found within a prepositional phrase.

> A. One [of the boys] was sick.

> B. All [of the boys] were sick.

In sentence A, the subject is one. The subject is not boys because boys comes within the prepositional phrase. The subject is singular.

In sentence B, the subject is all. All means more than one. The verb must agree with the plural subject.

Grammar Note
Certain words often appear before prepositional phrases.

These words are singular: one, either, neither, each.

These words are plural: both, many.

Activity 2

Write the subject of each of the following sentences. Then write the verb that agrees with each subject. You must decide if the subject is singular or plural. Remember, the subject will not be found within a prepositional phrase.

example: The boys in the back row (was, were) throwing popcorn.

answer: boys, were

(**Were** agrees with the subject, **boys**.)

1. One of the old-time radio programs (was, were) a show called "The Shadow."

2. Either of the pictures (looks, look) fine over the fireplace.

3. Both of those turkeys (worries, worry) about Thanksgiving.

4. Neither of his parents (was, were) at home.

5. The set of place mats (costs, cost) ten dollars.

6. Only one of the puppies (was, were) not sold.

7. The houses on the beach (was, were) flooded.

8. The chocolate in these cookies (is, are) delicious.

9. Both of the neighbors (is, are) willing to help.

10. A list of the team members (is, are) posted in the gym.

Should singular or plural verbs be used with compound subjects?

If you need to review compound subjects, see Chapter 3.

When the singular parts of the compound subject are joined with *or* or *nor*, the subject is considered singular.

Mike, Jill, or Ellen is going to pick you up for the party.

Neither William nor Andy is going to the party.

However, if the part of the subject nearest the verb is plural, then the verb must agree with the plural subject.

> Neither William nor his brothers are going to the party.

When the parts of the subject are joined by *and*, the subject is considered plural.

> The scissors and the glue are in the desk.

> The pilot and the flight attendant wear uniforms.

Activity 3

In each sentence below, write the form of the verb that agrees with the subject.

1. Mitts and Snowball (is, are) both Siamese cats.
2. Rain or darkness (cancels, cancel) baseball games.
3. *The Color Purple* and *Meridian* (is, are) books by Alice Walker.
4. John F. Kennedy and Abraham Lincoln (was, were) both killed while serving as president.
5. Either Sue or Ellen (is, are) fast enough to win the gold medal.
6. Six tablespoons of honey or five tablespoons of sugar (is, are) needed in the cookie dough.
7. Tacos and hamburgers (was, were) served at lunch.
8. Girls and boys (plays, play) on the championship soccer team.
9. Either the guitar player or the piano player (has, have) to leave the band.
10. The red sports car and the black sedan (go, goes) faster than the other cars.

A title is always singular.
For example:
My Life As a Dog *was a great movie.*
"Trees" is a poem by Joyce Kilmer.
The Old Man and the Sea *is a book by Ernest Hemingway.*

Warning!
There is one big exception to the rules you just learned. When the subject of a sentence is *you*, the plural verb form is used, even if that *you* is singular.

> wrong: You was the first one in line.

> right: You were the first one in line.

> wrong: You is the kindest man.

> right: You are the kindest man.

Most often, your ear will tell you if your subjects and verbs agree. Non-agreement doesn't sound right. However, when you are not sure which verb form is correct, look at the subject. Then decide if it is singular or plural.

Using Pronouns to Replace Nouns

> The creatures landed their spacecraft. The creatures climbed out onto Earth. The creatures' mission was to take over the bodies of some earthlings. The creatures planned to study the earthlings for six months. Then the creatures would give back the bodies and return to the creatures' own planet.

Something is wrong with the paragraph above. The word *creatures* is repeated too many times. **Pronouns** can replace those words. That is the job of pronouns. A pronoun replaces a noun.

> The creatures landed their spacecraft. <u>They</u> climbed out onto Earth. <u>Their</u> mission was to take over the bodies of some earthlings. The creatures planned to study the earthlings for six months. Then <u>they</u> would give back the bodies and return to <u>their</u> own planet.

The pronouns in the rewritten paragraph have been underlined. Notice that the word *creatures* was not replaced every time but just some of the time. The reader needs to be reminded occasionally of the original noun.

The noun the pronoun replaces is called its **antecedent.**

> The **creatures** landed their spacecraft.
>
> **They** climbed out onto the Earth.

Creatures is the antecedent for the pronoun *they.*

It must always be very clear to the reader just which word is the antecedent of the pronoun. Never use a pronoun unless you have named the antecedent first.

Activity 4

In the following story, the pronouns are <u>underlined</u>. Write down each pronoun, and next to it, write its antecedent.

Grammar 26 and 31 in the Reference Guide will give you lists of subject, object, and possessive forms of common personal pronouns.

You may have trouble when you get to the last sentence! But think the problem over carefully, and give it your best effort.

> example: Marie was happy. She was driving at last.
>
> pronoun: she; antecedent: Marie

At last Marie had turned sixteen. <u>She</u> could hardly wait to get a driver's license. Marie's mother had promised <u>her</u> the use of the family car. The car was a 1950 Chevrolet. <u>It</u> was red and white, and <u>it</u> was considered a classic. <u>She</u> loved that car!

Why did you have trouble with that last sentence? It was because the antecedent was not clear. Was the She in that last sentence referring to *Marie* or to *Marie's mother?* Watch out for this sort of thing in your own writing. The pronoun's antecedent must always be very clear.

Warning!

Sometimes writers use the pronoun *they* in writing without making the antecedent clear.

> **They** say that too much television is bad for children.
>
> Who are **they**?

Here are better ways to write the sentence:

> *The National Education Association* says that too much television is bad for children.
>
> *Some parents* say that too much television is bad for children.
>
> *Grade school teachers* say that too much television is bad for children.

Your reader will not get an accurate picture unless you make that picture very clear.

Using the Correct Pronoun

The pronoun you use must agree with its antecedent. It must agree in **gender** (masculine or feminine).

> Bill is a very funny fellow. He always makes jokes during English class. (masculine)
>
> Linda likes to tease Bill. She refuses to laugh at his jokes. (feminine)

The pronoun must agree with its antecedent in number (singular or plural).

> The beach ball was blue and red. It bounced lightly on the sand. (singular)

> The waves crashed on the shore. They carried little shellfish and seaweed. (plural)

Making Choices

How do you choose a pronoun when the antecedent has no particular gender (like the word student)? You have two choices. You can use the masculine pronoun, as in the following example:

> If a student cannot attend, *he* should call the office.

Or, you can use two pronouns, as in the following example:

> If a student cannot attend, *he or she* should call the office.

Sometimes you can avoid the problem by using a plural noun, as in the following example:

> If *students* cannot attend, *they* should call the office.

Activity 5

On a separate sheet of paper fill in the pronouns.

> example: The car was red. _____ (The car) was on sale for $12,000.

> answer: It

1. Bob bought Fran a bunch of roses. _____ (Bob) wanted to thank her for her help with the party.

2. The clouds moved in from the west. _____ (The clouds) brought rain.

3. Without Connie, the play would have been a flop. _____ (Connie) made _____ (the play) a success.

Writing With Style

Learn to use a variety of nouns and pronouns to refer to the subject of your writing. For example, if you're writing about tadpoles, think of other words to call them. (You could call them *baby frogs, they, tiny creatures,* and so on.) Compare the following two selections. One repeats the same words too many times. The other uses different terms for the same subject. Which selection do you think sounds better?

A. Baby frogs and baby toads are constantly changing creatures called *tadpoles. Tadpoles* have round heads that are usually the same size as their bodies. *Tadpoles* have long tails to help in swimming. *Tadpoles* are always changing in size and shape. First the *tadpole's* head begins to take shape. Then the *tadpole* begins to grow limbs and the *tadpole's* tail gets shorter. By the time the *tadpole* is a full-grown frog or toad, the *tadpole's* tail has disappeared.

B. Baby frogs and baby toads are constantly changing creatures called *tadpoles.* They have round heads that are usually the same size as their bodies. *Tadpoles* have long tails to help in swimming. These little animals are always changing in size and shape. First their heads begin to take shape. Then they begin to grow limbs, and their tails get shorter. By the time the *tadpole* is a full-grown frog or toad, its tail has disappeared.

How many times is a form of the word tadpole used in selection A? How many times is a form of the word tadpole used in selection B?

Which selection do you think sounds better? Why?

Notice that the word *tadpole* is repeated occasionally in selection B. From time to time, the writer needs to remind the reader of the subject.

Vocabulary Builder

Using Antonyms
A. Synonyms are words with similar meanings, and antonyms are words that have opposite meanings. Big and little are antonyms. Often and seldom are antonyms.

Match the antonyms in each column by writing them in pairs on your paper.

example: 1. inside, outside

Column A	Column B
1. inside	dry
2. clean	wide
3. wet	evening
4. narrow	outside
5. morning	alike
6. different	dirty

Words often have more than one antonym, just as they often have more than one synonym. *Sad* is an antonym for *happy*. *Sorrowful* and *gloomy* are antonyms for *happy*, too.

B. On a separate piece of paper, write an antonym for each of the following words.

example: whisper / shout

1. sharp / _____   4. adult / _____

2. heavy / _____   5. graceful / _____

3. fresh / _____   6. won / _____

Chapter Review

Chapter Summary

- ☐ The verb must always agree in number with its subject.

- ☐ To choose the correct verb, you must find the subject and decide if it is singular or plural.

- ☐ Most often, an incorrect verb form will sound awkward. Usually you will use the correct form automatically. When in doubt, read the problem sentence aloud. You'll usually "hear" an incorrect choice.

- ☐ Pronouns are used to replace nouns.

- ☐ Using pronouns prevents repetition of the same noun.

- ☐ Pronouns must always have a clear antecedent.

- ☐ A pronoun must agree with its antecedent in gender and in number.

Writing Practice

My _____(friend, neighbor, sister, father, and so on), _____(his or her name), has made a big difference in my life.

Fill in the blanks in the sentence above. You will be writing about somebody who has been important to you.

Now, write two more sentences describing this person and telling how he or she has changed your life. Use pronouns occasionally to avoid repeating the person's name. Describe both the person's physical looks and personality.

Chapter Quiz

A. There is a writing error in each of the following sentences. (The error is in subject-verb agreement or in pronoun usage.) Find the error. Rewrite the sentence correcting the error.

example: The fans is screaming for their hero.

corrected: The fans are screaming for their hero.

1. Cartoons is created by talented artists.

2. Fountain pens was first produced in America.

3. One of the dancers have a broken leg.

4. You was the first person in line.

5. Each of the young women held their baby tightly.

6. Each of the books on the library shelves have a number.

7. A ghost and a goblin dances under the moonlight.

8. The shoes were lost, but it were later found under the bed.

9. A spark from the forest fires have landed on his roof.

10. The teacher or the principal are calling Manuel's parents.

B. On your own piece of paper, rewrite the following sentences. Replace every underlined noun with the correct pronoun.

1. Sue was excited when she won the election.

2. Bob and Jim are best friends.

3. Lynn threw the letter in the trash.

4. Where did you hide the presents?

5. Give the papers to Sam and Jill.

Unit Review

A. Add words to each of the following sentence fragments to make a complete sentence. Write the complete new sentence on your own paper.

1. If I had only three days to live . . .

2. When it is very dark . . .

3. . . . tip-toed down the stairs.

B. Correct the following run-on sentence.

A heavy freeze came late in the spring it killed all the blossoms.

C. Expand each of the following sentences. Add adjectives, adverbs, and prepositional phrases to make ideas and images clearer.

1. The bird landed.   2. The door closed.

D. Find the mistakes in subject-verb agreement or in pronoun usage. Correctly rewrite the sentence on your paper.

1. Charles Lindbergh were the first pilot to fly solo across the Atlantic Ocean.

2. Men have never landed on the planet Pluto because he could not survive the cold.

3. Rebecca and Joan enjoyed her visit to the science museum.

Unit Two

Writing Paragraphs

6

What Is a Paragraph?

Dee Alexander Brown writes about the clash between Native Americans and white settlers on the American Frontier. Bury My Heart at Wounded Knee *is his most famous book. It tells about the American Indians' heartbreaking losses as the pioneers conquered the west.* Creek Mary's Blood *is another of Mr. Brown's well-known works.*

Skillful writing makes history as interesting as today's news.

Writers at Work: Dee Brown

Chapter Learning Objectives

- ☐ Identify sentences about one idea that belong together in a paragraph.
- ☐ Identify the topic sentence within a paragraph.
- ☐ Identify the supporting details within the body of a paragraph.
- ☐ Identify the concluding details within a paragraph.

Words to Know

paragraph   a group of sentences placed together because they all relate to the same idea

indented   set in from the margin

topic sentence   the sentence that states the main idea of the paragraph

support   to add strength to

example: Support your idea with facts.

body   main part

conclude   to bring to an end

summary   a short statement that brings the important points or details together

Understanding the Paragraph

Unit I discussed how to write good sentences. Usually, you need more than one sentence to explain or tell about something. Sentences are grouped together in paragraphs. Paragraphs make ideas clear and easy to follow. Just as there are skills to learn in writing sentences, so there are skills to learn about paragraphing. These skills are worth learning! Paragraphs are important tools in communication.

Usually people recognize a **paragraph** when they see one. They know it is a paragraph because it is **indented** at the beginning. They know the next paragraph begins at the next indentation.

However, it takes more than indenting to make a paragraph. How does the writer know when it's time to indent? Just what makes a paragraph a paragraph?

It's not a mystery! It's not something that only great writers understand. Paragraphing is simple and important. And once you understand what makes a paragraph, your writing will become easier, clearer, and more interesting.

Paragraphs help a writer divide a larger subject into smaller parts.

Refer to this sample paragraph as you read about paragraphs.

The Bermuda Triangle
The Bermuda Triangle is a mysterious place just off the coast of Florida. In 1945, five planes disappeared there. Another plane was sent to find them, but it disappeared, too. No one ever found the missing planes or any plane wrecks. Since then, many more planes and ships have disappeared in the same place. Scientists have studied the area, but they cannot find an answer to their questions. The Bermuda Triangle remains a mystery.

There are three basic parts to a paragraph. In fact, you will find that the number three is an important number to remember when you write. Watch for it as you read about English composition.

Paragraph part 1: topic sentence
A paragraph is defined as a group of sentences that are all about one idea. The writer identifies that idea in a paragraph, usually in the first sentence. The statement of that idea is called the **topic sentence.**

A good topic sentence lets the reader know right away what's going on. It also helps the writer stick to the point. In our sample paragraph, the topic sentence is "The Bermuda Triangle is a mysterious place just off the coast of Florida."

Paragraph part 2: supporting details (body of the paragraph)

Remember: A paragraph has three parts. The body of the paragraph should have at least three sentences.

A good paragraph has at least three sentences to **support** that topic sentence. All three sentences must back up the statement made in the topic sentence. In the sample paragraph, the job of the supporting sentences is to back up or to prove the statement that the Bermuda Triangle is a mysterious place.

Look at the sentences following the topic sentence in the sample paragraph. They make up the **body** of the paragraph. Do they all relate to the main idea? Do they all support the topic sentence?

Paragraph part 3: concluding sentence

The last sentence in a good paragraph should act as its **conclusion** or **summary.** A conclusion is especially necessary when the paragraph is not part of a larger piece of writing but is going to stand alone. Look at the sample paragraph. The last sentence in it restates the main idea.

The information you have read about paragraphing can be summed up with this diagram:

1　topic sentence

2　(1) sentence of support

　　　(2) sentence of support $\left.\vphantom{\begin{matrix}a\\a\\a\end{matrix}}\right\}$　　body

　　　(3) sentence of support

3　concluding sentence

Warning!

Paragraphs can be of different lengths, depending on the number off supporting sentences. An average paragraph has from five to seven sentences.

A good, strong paragraph should have at least three sentences of support. It may have more, but all sentences must support that topic sentence. If you can't find three things to say to support your topic sentence, you should probably come up with a different idea.

Activity 1

1. Name the three parts of a paragraph.
2. What does the topic sentence do?
3. The body of the paragraph should include at least how many sentences?
4. What do the sentences in the body of the paragraph do?

Congratulations!

You have just learned about a most important skill—paragraphing. Once you understand what makes a good paragraph, you are on your way to becoming a better writer.

Recognizing the Topic Sentence

The topic sentence expresses the main idea of the paragraph. The reader will expect that every other sentence in the paragraph relates to the topic sentence. When you're ready to write a sentence that doesn't relate to the topic sentence, it's time to begin a new paragraph.

A topic sentence usually appears at the beginning of the paragraph. Putting it first lets the reader know immediately what topic is going to be discussed.

> **Some kinds of mushrooms can be dangerous.** Each year, many people are poisoned when they pick and eat mushrooms they think are harmless. The "death cap" mushroom that grows in woods around the United States is one of the most deadly. Its poison works like the venom of a rattlesnake. The "death cap" looks very much like a common mushroom sold in grocery stores, but its poison can kill. Those who pick mushrooms to eat must be careful.

How do topic sentences help the writer? How do topic sentences help the reader?

The paragraph above has a clearly written topic sentence at the beginning. It lets the reader know just what the paragraph will be about. The topic sentence also helps the writer. It's important to be aware of your own topic sentences when you write. A topic sentence keeps you on track and helps you organize your thoughts.

Occasionally, a topic sentence will come at the end of a paragraph.

> He was only 5 feet 3 inches tall. He weighed 130 pounds. He could throw a 30-yard pass. He scored 12 touchdowns in one season. **Despite his size, Shorty Hernandez was one of the toughest football players at Mission High.**

Activity 2

Copy the topic sentence in each of the following paragraphs.

1. The new Riding High Amusement Park has some of the most thrilling rides in America. The giant roller coaster takes riders in a complete upside-down circle. Then it sends them flying toward the ground. The triple Ferris wheel is the tallest in the world. A ride called Elevator Shaft makes people feel as if they are falling down a dark hole. Visitors go home feeling thrilled and excited.

2. Spot was a dog hero. When Spot and his master, Steven, were lost in a snowstorm, Spot would not leave Steven's side. Spot's fine nose found the trail that led them down the mountainside. When Steven could go no farther, Spot barked and barked until someone heard him. By the time help arrived, Spot had lost his voice from barking so long. The local newspaper named Spot the "hero of the month."

3. The door creaks. Cobwebs hang from the ceiling. A rocking chair moves slowly, but no one is in it. A loud rattle comes from upstairs. Suddenly, a scream pierces the air. The haunted house on Mill Lane is a frightening place.

4. Termites are very destructive insects. They eat wood and paper. They tunnel their way through the woodwork of houses. They snack on books and furniture. Some figures show that termites cause as much property loss in the United States as fires. Homeowners consider termites dangerous pests.

Recognizing Supporting Details

Once you've written a topic sentence, you must find details to support it. Good, strong support means at least three sentences of details. Supporting details can give facts. They can give examples and make comparisons. They answer questions a person might ask about the topic sentence. The supporting details make up the body of the paragraph.

Later in this book, you will spend time writing your own supporting details. But for now, learn to recognize the supporting details in the body of a paragraph. Later on, when you're writing your own paragraphs, try to choose a topic you like. It will make it easier to find supporting details.

Activity 3

Remember that every sentence in the body of a paragraph must support the topic sentence. In the paragraphs below, one sentence doesn't support the topic sentence. Find that sentence and copy it on your paper.

A. The camel's ability to go without water is amazing. One way the camel survives without water is by turning some of the fat in its hump into liquid. Camels can drink gigantic amounts of water at one time. Since the camel doesn't sweat, it doesn't lose any of the water it drinks. Horses are also used for desert travel. The camel's ability to go without water makes it a perfect desert traveler.

B. Through the ages, people have had many beliefs about cats. Some people thought cats were unlucky. Others insisted that cats brought them good fortune. Many said dogs were man's best friend. In the Middle Ages, some people believed cats could speak and that witches talked to them. Sailors believed that a cat on board a ship would bring them a lucky trip. Something mysterious about cats makes people believe they have special powers.

Recognizing Concluding Sentences

Especially when a paragraph is going to stand alone (like those in the last exercise), it should have a concluding sentence. The concluding sentence helps the reader recognize that the writer has finished making his or her point. Usually, the concluding sentence summarizes information. It doesn't add new information. It simply repeats the main idea, using different words.

Look back at the two paragraphs in Activity 3. Each one has a concluding sentence. Notice that it is very much like the topic sentence. It repeats the main idea.

Activity 4

This chapter was written to help you recognize the parts of a paragraph. The next chapter will help you write paragraphs of your own.

Read each of the following paragraphs. Neither one has a concluding sentence. On your paper, write a concluding sentence for each paragraph.

A. Legends tell that Robin Hood was a kindly hero. Although he was an outlaw, he stole only from the rich, and he gave to the poor. He never bothered any group that included poor travelers or women. He never kept the money he stole. He always gave it to needy families.

B. Reading a book can be a wonderful way to pass time. A book can take its reader on adventures. It can introduce new friends or teach facts and information. A book can make a person forget problems of the real world for a little while.

Writing With Style

Read the following two paragraphs. One is a good paragraph with a topic sentence supported by sentences packed with detail. The other paragraph has sentences that don't support the topic sentence. Which is the good paragraph?

A. Paul Bunyan was a hero of American folk tales. Loggers in North American lumber camps once told stories of the giant lumberjack and his blue ox named Babe. According to the tales, Paul Bunyan carved out the Mississippi River and the Grand Canyon! He made the Rocky Mountains and the Old Faithful Geyser. These tales about Paul Bunyan are called "tall tales" because they are full of exaggerations. Paul Bunyan was a popular hero from 1850 to 1900, but stories about him are still told and retold today.

B. Pecos Bill was the cowboy hero of tales from the American Southwest. Cowboys once gathered around campfires to sing songs and tell stories about him. According to those stories, Bill was the strongest, smartest, toughest cowboy in the West. Some stories tell how he dug out the Grand Canyon one time when he was looking for gold. Casey Jones was a hero, too. He was a strong man who worked on the American railroads. Casey Jones was an engineer, but the black hero, John Henry, built the railroad lines. He drove steel rails into the ground faster than any man alive.

Can you see the differences between paragraph A and paragraph B? Paragraph A discusses only one topic, folk tales about Paul Bunyan. All of its sentences relate to that topic. The topic sentence of paragraph B suggests that it will discuss only Pecos Bill tales. But what happens in that paragraph? There are sentences in it that have nothing to do with Pecos Bill. Can you find these sentences? Why are the right details so important? Which paragraph was confusing and hard to follow? Why?

Vocabulary Builder

Using Antonyms to Make Comparisons

Antonyms are useful when discussing the differences between things. They can help you make comparisons. The following sentences are comparisons, and the antonyms have been underlined.

> Richard's job was <u>dull</u>, but my job was <u>exciting</u>.
>
> The character named Sam was <u>kind</u>, but William was an <u>evil</u> character.
>
> William was the <u>villain</u>, and Sam was the <u>hero</u>.

Use antonyms to make some comparisons. Underline the antonyms you use.

> example: Compare two animals.
>
> The dog is usually very <u>friendly</u>, but a wolf can be <u>fierce</u>.
>
> example: Compare two movies.
>
> The movie I saw <u>yesterday</u> made me <u>cry</u>. The one I saw <u>today</u> made me <u>laugh</u>.

1. Compare two friends.
2. Compare two teachers.
3. Compare two houses.
4. Compare two singers.
5. Compare two _____ (topic of your choice).

Chapter Review

Chapter Summary

☐ The first word in every paragraph is indented.

☐ A paragraph has these three parts:
1. the topic sentence
2. the body (at least three sentences of supporting details)
3. a concluding sentence

☐ The topic sentence is usually the first sentence in the paragraph.

☐ Every sentence in the paragraph must relate to the topic sentence. If not, that sentence doesn't belong in the paragraph.

Writing Practice

Remember that all the sentences in a paragraph should relate to one idea. Choose one of the topic sentences listed below. Complete the sentence by filling in the blank, and write that sentence at the top of your paper. Then list numbers 1 to 3. Write three sentences that deal with your topic sentence. You may write more than three sentences if you wish.

Topic Sentence 1: I would hate to work in a _____ restaurant.

Topic Sentence 2: I think _____ is the most dangerous career.

Topic Sentence 3: _____ is an exciting game to play.

Topic Sentence 4: _____ was the best movie of the year.

Chapter Quiz

Read the following paragraphs. Answer the questions below.

A. Mordecai Brown is an example of a man who overcame a handicap. Because of an accident when he was seven, Brown only had three fingers on his right hand. Despite his handicap, Brown became a major league baseball pitcher. He won more than 20 games in 1907 and again in 1908. And in both years he helped his team, the Chicago Cubs, win the World Series. Batters knew they could expect trouble from the curveball of "Three Finger Brown."

B. Two of the biggest sharks are the most harmless. The whale shark, the largest member of the shark family, eats only seaweed and small fish. Whale sharks have jaws wide enough to swallow a person, but they have no interest in harming human beings. The next-largest shark is the basking shark. It is found in the Arctic Ocean. This shark likes to come to the surface and "bask" in the sun. It is completely harmless. Many sharks are a danger to people, but these two huge fish are no threat.

C. The Hopi of Arizona do a strange dance. It is called the snake dance. The dancers carry live rattlesnakes in their mouths as they dance. The dancers handle the snakes very carefully and are rarely bitten. There are many kinds of snakes in the United States that aren't poisonous. The Hopi do the snake dance to ask for rain in the dry lands of Arizona.

1. What is the topic sentence in paragraph A?

2. What is the topic sentence in paragraph B?

3. What is the concluding sentence in paragraph A?

4. What is the concluding sentence in paragraph B?

5. What is the sentence that doesn't belong in paragraph C?

Chapter 7 Writing Good Paragraphs

Ernie Pyle wrote about World War II from the frontlines. His widely read newspaper columns told the story of the ordinary soldiers, the G.I. Joes. He wrote with honesty and warmth about their heroism and humor in the face of war's hardships. He was with his beloved G.I.'s when he was killed by enemy gunfire on a small Pacific island.

Reporting from the scene of the action sometimes calls for courage.

Writers at Work: Ernie Pyle (1900–1945)

Chapter Learning Objectives

☐ Write clear topic sentences for paragraphs.

☐ Write paragraphs that contain three parts: topic sentence, supporting details, and concluding sentence.

☐ Use different types of support for topics: facts, figures, examples, details and description.

☐ Put supporting details in logical order.

Words to Know

fact   something known to be true

figure   a number

description   a picture in words; the details that create a picture of something

logical   something that is reasonable, or makes sense

example: It is logical to take an umbrella when it looks like rain.

chronological order   events arranged in the order they happened

Writing a Topic Sentence

Remember from the last chapter that the topic sentence expresses the main idea of a paragraph. It is usually the first sentence of the paragraph. The topic sentence is underlined in the following paragraph:

People shouldn't be afraid of spiders. Spiders can be helpful. They eat many harmful insects. Without spiders, these insects would destroy many fruits, grains, and vegetables. Spiders seldom bite people. Most spider bites are not dangerous anyway. Spiders provide beauty, too. Their silken webs are works of art. Humans shouldn't be too quick to kill the helpful spider.

Now write some topic sentences of your own.

Activity 1

Each of the following paragraphs has a body (supporting details) and a conclusion. But there is no sentence that expresses the main idea of the paragraph. Write a topic sentence for each paragraph.

A. There were no street lights on 45th Street. The buildings were run-down, and many of them were empty. The only people on the street at night were the homeless and police officers. Most of the stores had gone out of business. Those that were left had bars on the windows. It wasn't a good place to live.

B. Westlake High School's star basketball player is seven feet tall. He plays center and will probably lead the team to the state championship. Westlake's whole team is fast and skillful. Most of the players are terrific shots. The coach has led many winning teams. So far this season, Westlake has won every game.

Writing a topic sentence helps you limit your subject so that you can cover it in one paragraph. You cannot, for example, tell everything you know about music in one paragraph. That subject is too big. A topic sentence narrows the larger subject to a topic you can cover in one paragraph.

If the subject were music, these would be some possible topic sentences:

> In the 1960s, the Supremes popularized the Motown Sound.
>
> Rap music always has a message and delivers it with style.
>
> Some people think record albums should be rated just like films are.

Activity 2

The subjects listed below are too broad and general for one paragraph. Choose one of the subjects and write it on your paper. Under it, write three topic sentences on that subject. You should be able to use each of these topic sentences to begin a paragraph.

movies	relatives	clothes
the beach	feeling lonely	science
dogs	winning contests	teachers

Review: The Three Parts of the Paragraph

Keep this diagram in mind when you're writing.

1 topic sentence

2 (1) sentence of support ⎫

  (2) sentence of support ⎬   body

  (3) sentence of support ⎭

3 concluding sentence

Writing Supporting Details

Once you have written a topic sentence, your paragraphing job is clear. You must support that topic sentence. You can use different types of sentences for support. You can support your topic sentence with **facts** and **figures**, with examples, and with details and **description.** The paragraph below has been developed using facts and figures.

Supporting your topic sentence means proving or explaining why it's true. How do the details in this paragraph prove Alaska was a good buy?

Many people laughed when the United States bought Alaska in 1867, but it turned out to be a good buy. Today Alaska sends gas and oil to other parts of the United States. Fishing is another important Alaskan industry. Alaska is also rich in timber, with over 100 million acres of forested lands. In addition, there is gold in Alaska, and water to provide electric power. Alaska is not a frozen wasteland as people once thought. It's a land with plenty to offer.

The writer supported the paragraph about Alaska with facts and figures.

Now you try it.

Activity 3

Write a paragraph that supports its topic sentence by using facts and figures. Use the list of facts and figures given below to write a complete paragraph. You will need to write a topic sentence first.

Babe Ruth played 21 seasons in baseball's American Baseball League.

In 1927, he set an all-time record of 60 home runs.

Babe Ruth holds 76 major league records.

In his career, he hit 714 home runs.

Ruth batted in 2,209 runs.

He played in 10 World Series.

The paragraph below has been developed with an example.

> Mountain climbers should always consider the weather before they begin a climb. Last May, five high school students went on a climb when the weather looked bad. They didn't listen to warnings of an approaching storm and were caught in a blizzard. They were forced to dig a snow cave where they lay huddled all through the night. At last, rescuers found them and dug them out. All the climbers were badly frostbitten. Three of them lost toes and fingers. They learned that it can be deadly to climb when the weather looks bad.

Do you see how the topic sentence has been supported by the story of one climb? That is called a paragraph developed by example.

Now you try it.

Activity 4

Chapter 4 talked about creating an image for your reader. Your goal as a writer is to make the reader see what you see. Using details and description as supporting sentences helps create that image.

Choose one of the topic sentences below. Write a complete paragraph supporting the sentence with one or more examples.

Motorists should never drive over the speed limit.

Gymnastics (or any sport you choose) can be very dangerous.

It is not easy to sew (or anything else you choose).

My aunt (or any relative you choose) is a funny person.

I am sure that cats can think.

Saturday nights are really boring in my town.

Sometimes you might want to use details and description to develop a paragraph. The following paragraph does just that.

Some people think the junkyard is ugly, but I think it's beautiful. In the spring, tiny wildflowers grow up between the twisted metal of old cars. In the summer, the sun sparkles off hundreds of pieces of broken glass. Gentle breezes blow scraps of colored cloth and paper across the ground. In the winter, the whole place is covered with a blanket of snow, and silver icicles glitter everywhere. The junkyard has its own special kind of beauty.

Can you picture the junkyard described in this paragraph?

Do you see how the writer picked very specific details and descriptions to make a point?

Now you try it.

Activity 5

Write your own paragraph. Use details and description to develop one of the following topic sentences.

> In the middle of the night, my apartment can be noisy (or lonely or peaceful).
>
> I will never forget seeing Michael Jackson (or any performer you choose) in concert.
>
> Sports fans can be fanatics.
>
> The view from the top was worth the climb.
>
> It is never boring in English class.
>
> It was a dance to remember.

Activity 6

Five topic sentences are listed below. Decide how each would best be developed. Number your paper from 1 to 5. Write facts and figures, examples, or details and description by each number. (Sometimes a topic sentence can be developed in more than one way.)

1. The United States produces much of its own energy.

2. Writing paragraphs requires concentration.

3. George Michael (or a singer you choose) is a great rhythm and blues singer.

4. "Roseanne" (or a show you choose) is the funniest show on television.

5. Birds may look small and delicate, but they're really very strong.

Challenge

Write your own paragraph. Develop the topic sentence you chose in Activity 6. Use the method you decided was best.

Putting Details in Order

In many paragraphs, the order of the details isn't so important. Sometimes writers will begin with the least important detail and move to the most important. Often they save the most interesting, detail for last.

A clearly written paragraph presents supporting details in a **logical** order. One way to organize details is by time. This order is called **chronological order.** And, in fact, certain kinds of paragraphs must be written in chronological order. For example, if you're telling your readers how to do something, it is important to tell them at the beginning of your paragraph what they should do first. Tell them the rest of the steps in chronological order.

In paragraphs that describe what happened, chronological order is easiest to follow. Most likely, you will tell the details in the order they took place. A description of a full day at the beach would probably begin in the morning and end in the evening.

Read the following paragraph. Its details are arranged in chronological order.

The old man almost met with a terrible accident. He was standing on the corner waiting for the light to change. When the light turned green, he stepped off the curb. He did not look left or right but started across the street. The old man must have been hard of hearing because he did not turn when the truck came rumbling around the corner. The truck driver slammed on his brakes just in time to avoid hitting the old man.

Notice the sequence of events: (1) the old man waits for the light, (2) he steps off the curb, (3) he starts across the street, (4) the truck comes, (5) the truck driver slams on the brakes. The events are presented in chronological order.

Now you try it.

Activity 7

The following details are out of order. Use these sentences to write a paragraph, but put the details in chronological order.

Here is your topic sentence: Ed's try at home repair ended in disaster.

1. He got the ladder from the garage and leaned it against the house.

2. Suddenly the ladder began to tip.

3. The next thing Ed knew, he was lying on the ground.

4. Ed decided it was time to patch the gutters.

5. As Ed climbed to the top, he felt dizzy.

Writing With Style

It's very important to limit your topic to a size you can really support. If your topic is too big, it's impossible to say anything meaningful in one paragraph. Read the following paragraphs. Paragraph A has a topic sentence that presents too broad a topic. Paragraph B has a topic sentence that limits the topic to a good size.

A. Cars were an important invention. Henry Ford made one of the earliest cars. Cars are used mainly for transportation. They can get people places quickly. One popular new car is the Firewing GL. Most American families own at least one car. Without cars, Americans' lives would surely be different.

B. This year's Firewing GL has turned out to be a very popular car. It is a racy-looking sports sedan that can go up to 180 miles per hour. The Firewing is great looking and fast. It uses much less fuel than similar models. It can comfortably carry five passengers and a trunk full of luggage. Best of all, the Firewing GL has an amazingly low price.

Cars was just too big a topic. By limiting the topic to one type of car, the writer was able to present specific details. These details provided focus and made the point.

Vocabulary Builder

Base Words
A base word is a word on which other words are built.
Sometimes word parts are added to the beginning or end of
base words. For example, *place* is a base word. You could add
mis to the beginning of the base word to make *misplace*. You
could add *ment* to the end of the base word to make
placement.

Understanding base words can help you increase your
vocabulary. You can change the meaning of base words by
adding parts to the beginning or to the end.

A. Write the word in each group that is a base word.

   1. hopeful, hopeless, hope

   2. open, reopen, opened

   3. helpful, help, helpless

   4. take, taken, mistake

   5. comfortable, discomfort, comfort

B. Write the base word of each of the following words.
   examples: unused = use
   asleep = sleep   healthy = health

   1. remove   6. remake

   2. secretly   7. interesting

   3. visitor   8. looked

   4. distrust   9. cheerful

   5. truthful   10. discount

Chapter Review

Chapter Summary

☐ Remember the three parts of a well-developed paragraph: topic sentence, body of supporting sentences (at least three), and concluding sentence.

☐ Make sure your topic sentence expresses the main idea of your paragraph.

☐ Topic sentences should narrow the subject to a topic that can be covered in one paragraph.

☐ Supporting details can be facts and figures, examples, or details and descriptions.

☐ In paragraphs that tell "how-to" or "what happened," it is best to arrange supporting details in chronological order.

Writing Practice

You're on your own now. It's time to write your own paragraph. Remember what you have learned. You may use one of the suggested ideas or come up with your own idea.

Topic suggestions:

• Tell about a time when you felt lonely.

• Describe a dream for the future.

• Review a movie.

• Describe your favorite meal.

When you're finished, read over your paragraph. Compare it to the three parts of the paragraph diagrammed on page 93.

Chapter Quiz

A. Write a topic sentence for each of the following subjects. Make sure the sentence narrows the topic enough so that you could write about it in just one paragraph.

1. strange creatures

2. insects

3. music

4. holidays

5. movie stars

B. Decide how you would develop each of the following topic sentences. Write facts and figures, examples, or details and descriptions by each sentence number.

1. The shoreline was littered with amazing things after the storm.

2. My Aunt Esther has had some strange experiences.

3. Foreign made automobiles are very popular in the United States.

4. Americans like to win in sporting events.

5. No one would buy a house that looked like that!

Chapter 8

Writing Better Paragraphs

In 1988 Toni Morrison won the Pulitzer Prize for her novel Beloved. *For the most part, her stories are centered on the lives of African Americans living in small towns. Her work is celebrated for its interesting characters and lively dialogue.* Tar Baby *and* Song of Solomon *are two more of her best-selling novels.*

Writing believable dialogue takes a good "ear" for speech patterns.

Writers at Work: Toni Morrison (1931–   )

Chapter Learning Objectives

☐ Write topic sentences that make the reader want to read the rest of the paragraph.

☐ Write topic sentences that get to the point.

☐ Write sentences in the body of the paragraph that support the topic sentence.

☐ Use transitional words to show the connection between sentences.

Words to Know

transition   the act of moving from one thing to another

transitional words   words that help a reader move from one idea to another. They show how one idea relates to and connects with another idea.

Writing Interesting Topic Sentences

Of course, all writers want to make their writing as clear and as interesting as possible. Here are some ways to improve your paragraphs.

You know that the topic sentence expresses the main idea in a paragraph. Your reader needs a topic sentence. It shows where the paragraph is going; it tells the reader what to expect. But the topic sentence can serve another purpose. A good topic sentence should interest your reader in your subject. It should make the reader want to read on, to find out what you have to share.

How can you make your topic sentences more lively and interesting? First, get right to the point. Don't waste words. Present your topic clearly and without any unnecessary words.

Don't write: I am going to write about the way buffaloes are disappearing in America.

Do write: American buffaloes are disappearing.

Don't write: I want to tell you some of the reasons why I never eat in the school cafeteria.

Do write: I avoid eating in the school cafeteria.

Activity 1

On a separate sheet of paper, number from 1 to 5. Then read each pair of topic sentences. Write the letter of the better topic sentence from each pair. Be ready to explain your choice.

1. a. My paragraph is about hamsters.

   b. Hamsters make friendly, lively pets.

2. a. I am supposed to write about a city I like, so I will write about my birthplace.

   b. I think my birthplace is the most beautiful town in the world.

3. a. It's hard to catch a gopher, but it can be done.

   b. There are many ways to catch a gopher, and I am going to tell you about some of them.

4. a. Well, last Saturday night I saw a movie, and it was frightening.

   b. *Aliens* was a frightening movie.

5. a. Grace Whipfelter is as unusual as her name.

   b. Grace Whipfelter is an unusual girl, so I am going to write about her.

Remember, the topic sentence should make your reader want to read your paragraph. Make that sentence so interesting your reader has to go on.

One way to add interest to your topic sentence is to express an opinion or state a choice.

> Uninteresting topic sentence: The beagle is a type of dog.

> More interesting topic sentence: The beagle isn't for just anybody.

A topic sentence should give the reader just enough information to tempt her or him into staying with you.

Which of the following topic sentences would make you most eager to read the paragraph?

1. A scary thing happened to me last night.

2. The sky was dark, the wind was howling, and I was about to have the scariest night of my life.

3. I never thought I could scream in terror, but I did last night.

You probably chose sentence 2 or sentence 3. Both those topic sentences give more detail than sentence 1. They give the reader enough information to become interested in the topic.

Look at the first page of some novels that you have read. Do the first lines make you want to read on? How did the authors catch your interest?

Activity 2

On a separate sheet of paper, number from 1 to 5. Then read each pair of topic sentences. Write the letter of the better sentence. Be ready to explain your choice.

1. a. Once somebody took some candlesticks from our house.

   b. We called it the mystery of the missing candlesticks.

2. a. Mr. Cooper is my teacher.

   b. Leonard A. Cooper is the kindest teacher I have ever had.

3. a. Jose Canseco plays baseball.

   b. Jose Canseco is a terrific baseball player but a bad driver.

4. a. The zoo is a good place to visit.

   b. Roaring tigers, deadly snakes, poisonous spiders, and all of them safe to be around—but only at the zoo.

5. a. "Star Trek" was a television show.

   b. The television show "Star Trek" took viewers on exciting adventures.

Activity 3

The following five topic sentences are poorly written. Rewrite each one, improving it. Make sure you state the topic directly and that you provide enough information to make it interesting.

1. I want to tell you about my Uncle Ralph (use any relative's name).

2. It happened a long time ago, and I really don't remember very well, but I'll try to tell you something about my first day of school.

3. I don't know too much about it, but this is how to build a swimming pool in your backyard.

4. This paragraph is about stamp collecting.

5. There are many reasons that children shouldn't play with matches, and I am going to tell you some of them.

Helpful Hint #1
Unless you are giving directions, avoid using the word *you*. Don't talk directly to your reader. Notice all the *you*'s in the sentences in Activity 3. These sentences are really better off without them.

Helpful Hint #2
Look at sentence number 3 in Activity 3.
Never tell the reader that you don't know
what you're talking about! If you don't
know, find out before you begin to write.
You don't want to lose your reader's trust
and confidence right from the start.

Making Every Sentence of Support Count

In Chapter 7, you learned to use facts and figures,
examples, and details and description to develop
your topic sentence. Make sure that every sentence
you write in the body of your paragraph counts.
Avoid sentences that really do nothing to support
your point. Avoid sentences that repeat or restate an
idea already presented in another sentence.

The underlined sentences in the following
paragraph repeat information. They add no new
support and should be left out of the paragraph.

Chimpanzees may be the most intelligent
animals in the world. They are very smart.
There are chimps who have been trained to ride
bicycles and to eat with forks. They are clever
enough to invent all kinds of ways to get to
their food. Chimps have been known to pile
boxes on top of each other to reach food left in
high places. Even though they are just animals,
they are really very intelligent. Some
chimpanzees have been taught to communicate
with people by hand signals. Chimpanzees
often surprise humans with their ability to
learn.

Activity 4

Read the following paragraph. Find the sentences that repeat ideas and don't add support to the topic. Write down those sentences.

> The Great Mirando made it easy to believe in magic. He came onto the stage dressed in a purple robe that sparkled mysteriously. He made a bowl full of fish disappear. Then he made a rabbit wearing a baseball cap appear. Mirando's tricks definitely looked real. When he waved his wand, he rose from the ground. Then he floated above the stage. Maybe it was a trick, but it certainly looked real. When the act ended, Mirando simply clapped his hands and disappeared.

Using Transitional Words

Transition means moving or changing from one thing to another. When you're writing a paragraph, you're moving from one sentence to another. You need to make this movement smooth and easy to follow. One of the easiest ways to link your sentences smoothly is through the use of transitional words.

*When you graduate from high school you are making a **transition** in your life.*

Transitional words show the connection between one sentence and another. They serve as guides for your reader as he or she reads your paragraph.

Look at the transitional words and phrases on the next page. Notice that these transitional words all deal with time. They help your reader understand how your sentences fit together chronologically.

at first	a little later
then	finally
next	afterward
meanwhile	later
at last	soon
before long	after that
at the same time	as

The transitional words in this paragraph help the reader keep track of time:

> The beginning of our vacation was full of disasters. <u>First</u> our car wouldn't start when we were ready to leave. It took a full hour to fix the problem. <u>Then</u> we discovered that the dog had disappeared. <u>After</u> looking around the neighborhood, we found him under the house. <u>At last,</u> we pulled out onto the highway. <u>Before long,</u> we heard a siren screaming behind us. A police officer pulled us over and told us that we were speeding. <u>Finally,</u> with a sixty-dollar speeding ticket and a late start on our vacation, we were on our way.

Note
You will not want to use a transitional word or phrase in every sentence. Too many transitional words can sound awkward and strange.

Activity 5

Rewrite the following paragraph. Add some transitional words that will help the reader follow the chronological order. The list above will help you think of some transitional words.

Everyone knew the tornado was coming. The sky grew very dark. The air got warm and strangely still. The birds stopped singing. My dog ran and hid in the basement. The wind began to howl and whistle. A garbage can rolled down the street, and traffic signals danced crazily on their wires. A voice on the radio warned everyone to take cover.

What does it mean if a person calls a job a "transitional job"? Cut an interesting article out of the newspaper. Underline any transitional words and phrases you find in that article.

Other kinds of transitional words show how one idea in your paragraph relates to another idea. These transitional words help link your ideas together. They make your sentences flow smoothly. Transitional words make your ideas clearer to your reader, and that is one of the goals of good writing.

Notice that the following transitional words show how one idea would relate to another idea. They can link sentences together.

for example	also
on the other hand	in conclusion
for this reason	even so
in addition	in comparison
however	although
as a result	indeed
most importantly	furthermore
another	in fact

In the following example, transitional words show the relationships between ideas.

Some people love oysters and others hate them. For some people oysters are a rare treat. They consider a really fresh oyster one of the tastiest items in the world. These people eat oysters fried, grilled, and in soups and stews. They even make oyster dressing for their turkeys. <u>In fact,</u> some oyster-lovers eat their oysters raw. <u>On the other hand,</u> others find oysters disgusting. These people think oysters are strange and slimy and salty. <u>Also,</u> they dislike the strange, dark-colored insides of the oyster. <u>Indeed,</u> although many oyster-haters admit that oysters are a healthful food, most would never eat one.

Activity 6

Find the transitional words and phrases in the following paragraph. List them on your paper.

The strangest creatures can be friends. For example, the giant rhinoceros and the tiny tick-bird are the best of pals. Indeed, they help each other survive. The little bird rides around on the rhinoceros's back. The bird eats ticks off the rhino. Thus, the rhino provides the tick-bird with food. In turn, the tick-bird helps keep the rhinoceros clean and comfortable. Furthermore, when the near-sighted rhinoceros fails to see an enemy coming, the tick bird chirps a warning. The rhino and the tick-bird are as different as can be. However, they are best friends.

Challenge

Write a paragraph about a day you spent with one of your good friends. Use transitional words to arrange what you did chronologically. Also use them to move smoothly from one sentence to the next.

Writing With Style

Transitions can make a difference. Look at the same paragraph written first without transitions and then with transitions.

Without transitions:

> Many people think rabbits and hares are the same animals, but that isn't true. The animal often called a jack rabbit is really not a rabbit at all. It is a hare. Hares have always lived in all parts of the world. Rabbits were at one time found only in Europe. Rabbits are smaller than hares. They have shorter legs and ears. Rabbits dig burrows in the ground. Hares do not have burrows. Hares are much faster than rabbits. The confusion between rabbits and hares raises one question. Is the Easter Bunny a rabbit or a hare?

With transitions:

> Many people think rabbits and hares are the same animals, but that isn't true. For example, the animal often called a jack rabbit is not a rabbit at all. It's a hare. Hares have always lived in all parts of the world. Rabbits, on the other hand, were once found only in Europe. Rabbits are smaller than hares. Also, they have shorter legs and ears. Although rabbits dig burrows in the ground, hares don't build burrows. Furthermore, hares are much faster than rabbits. Indeed, the confusion between rabbits and hares raises one question. Is the Easter Bunny a rabbit or a hare?

Can you find the transitional words and phrases in the second paragraph? How do these words improve the paragraph?

Vocabulary Builder

Prefixes

A *prefix* is a group of letters added at the beginning of a word. A prefix changes the meaning of the word. For example, the prefix *re* means *again*. So, to *recheck* something is to check it again. Here are some common prefixes and their meanings.

Prefix	Meaning	Prefix	Meaning
bi, duo	two	multi	many
tri	three	pre	before
non	not	co	with, together
re	again	anti	against
trans	across	dis	opposite

A. Use the list of prefixes above to write the word described by each definition. The first one has been done as an example.

1. to make again   remake

2. three-wheeled cycle   _____

3. against war   _____

4. having many purposes   _____

5. not poisonous   _____

B. Write a word beginning with each of the prefixes listed in the box.

Chapter Review

Chapter Summary

☐ Avoid using unnecessary words in your topic sentences. Don't say, "I am going to write about . . ." or "My paragraph is about . . ."

☐ Write topic sentences that encourage your reader to read on. Use enough information and words to express an opinion.

☐ Make sure every sentence in the body of the paragraph adds to the support of your topic sentence. Don't include sentences in the body that merely repeat a detail or restate the topic sentence.

☐ Transitional words and phrases help readers understand the time order of your paragraph. They also show the relationships between sentences.

Writing Practice

Write a paragraph describing a day you remember. Write the paragraph in **chronological order**. Use **transitional** words and phrases to guide your reader and to keep the time order clear.

Remember what you have learned. Write a topic sentence that is direct and makes the reader want to read about your day. Make each sentence of support add to the main idea. Write a concluding sentence to let your reader know your paragraph is ending.

Write about a day you that you'll never forget. Was that your happiest day, scariest night, or funniest moment?

Chapter Quiz

A. Read the paragraph below. On your own paper, do the following things:

1. Rewrite and improve the topic sentence.

2. Copy the one sentence in the body that should be left out.

3. List any transitional words and phrases.

> I am going to tell you about the day the lion escaped from the zoo. My house is only three blocks from the city zoo. Therefore, I was especially interested when I heard that a lion had somehow escaped from its cage. It was a hot summer day, all the doors and windows in my house were open, and I suddenly pictured a giant lion strolling into my kitchen. First, I closed and locked the doors and windows. Then, I stared nervously outside. I was worried. Before long, I saw something with yellow fur moving in the bushes. I quickly dialed the city's emergency number. Soon the zoo truck arrived. I saw two men hurry to the edge of the yard and go into the bushes. In a moment, they came out. They were carrying a very small, very harmless lion cub.

B. Find a copy of a newspaper. Write down four topic sentences that were used to begin paragraphs.

Unit Review

A. Write your answers in complete sentences on your own paper.

   1. What are the three main parts of a paragraph?

   2. At least how many sentences should be included in the body of the paragraph?

   3. What is the purpose of a topic sentence?

   4. Name three different ways you can support your topic sentence.

B. Write a topic sentence for the following list of supporting details.

   a. There are many kinds of rattlesnakes, but the diamondback rattler of the southeastern United States is the most poisonous.

   b. An angry snake strikes with lightning speed.

   c. The bite of a large rattlesnake can kill a person.

C. Write at least three sentences of support for the following topic sentence. Then tell if you used an example, facts and figures, or details and description.

topic sentence: *The storm passed, leaving terrible damage behind it.*

Unit Three

Writing Paragraphs with a Purpose

Chapter 9 · Writing to Explain, Inform, or Tell a Story

Jim Murray has been writing sports stories for newspapers for nearly 30 years. His columns in the Los Angeles Times *are known for their humor and wit. He does more than just report what happens in the world of sports. He shares his personal views with his readers by relating sports events to the world at large.*

Newspaper writers must work quickly to meet deadlines.

Writers at Work: Jim Murray (1919–   )

Chapter Learning Objectives

- ☐ Write an explanatory paragraph.
- ☐ Write an informative paragraph.
- ☐ Write a narrative paragraph.

Words to Know

explanatory paragraph   a paragraph that explains clarifies, and gives details

informative paragraph   a paragraph that gives information and shares knowledge

narrative paragraph   a paragraph that tells of events and experiences

anecdote   a short, interesting story about an event or a person

fiction   imaginative writing; something made up or invented

nonfiction   writing based on real people and events

Writing How-To Paragraphs

An **explanatory paragraph** often tells how to do something or how to make something. If you wrote a paragraph giving someone directions to your house, that would be an explanatory paragraph.

There are certain points to remember when you write an explanatory paragraph.

- Remember your goal.

    You want to teach your reader something.

- Remember to make it clear.

    Write simply. Don't use technical words that the reader won't understand.

- Remember to make it easy to follow.

    Use chronological order in a how-to paragraph
    Use transitional words to guide the reader.

Read this sample explanatory paragraph.

One of the easiest tricks to teach a dog is how to sit. To begin the training, stand your dog on your left side. Hold it firmly on a short leash. Then, in a clear, confident voice, command the dog to "sit." As you give the command, pull up slightly on the leash. At the same time, push down on the dog's rear end. Once your dog is sitting, repeat the word "sit" several times. Don't let it stand up or lie down. Then praise your dog cheerfully and heartily. Soon your dog will learn what you expect when you give the command to "sit." Before long, the dog will be sitting on command without the leash or the tap on the rear end.

Activity 1

On your paper, list the transitional words and phrases you find in the explanatory paragraph above.

Notice that the paragraph was written about a very limited subject. A writer couldn't do a good paragraph on "How to Train a Dog." That topic is too big. You couldn't begin to cover all the points in one paragraph. By limiting the topic to "How to Teach a Dog to Sit," the writer was able to write a full, detailed explanation.

Activity 2

Some of the following topics are too broad to be fully covered in a single paragraph. Others would be fine topics for one explanatory paragraph. List the topics that would be good choices for an explanatory paragraph.

How to cook	How to maintain a car
How to make brownies	How to change a tire
How to play basketball	How to shop
How to shoot a free throw	How to buy the right stereo

Activity 3

Think about things you know how to do well. Think about things you do around the house (for example, iron a shirt, make a bed, care for house plants, wash windows, set up an aquarium). Think about things you do for fun (for example, swing a golf club, do a back dive, maintain a bicycle, learn a new dance step, plan a party).

Choose a topic to explain. Make sure the topic is not too broad. (You couldn't tell how to make a dress. There would be too much to cover. You could, however, tell how to sew on a button.)

List the necessary steps involved in the task.

Use that list to write an explanatory paragraph telling your reader how to do something or how to make something.

Writing Paragraphs That Give Information

Often, your purpose in writing will be to tell your reader about something you know. You will be sharing information. Such paragraphs will be developed with details and with facts and figures.

Suppose you know about the life of the Apache chief, Geronimo. Writing a paragraph about Geronimo would be writing an **informative paragraph.** Read the following example.

> Geronimo was a famous Apache chief. He lived from 1829 until 1909, and he is remembered as an angry warrior. Geronimo wanted to drive all white people out of the Southwest. He led raids against white settlers in New Mexico and Arizona. Geronimo's bloody raids made the white people fear all Apaches. Geronimo was finally captured in 1886, but he escaped. He was recaptured, and he died in prison in 1909. Geronimo was one of the last chiefs to refuse to make peace with the white settlers.

An informative paragraph often begins with a topic sentence that is really a definition of something or someone. Who was Geronimo? He was a famous Apache chief.

Read these definitions. Each one could be the topic sentence of an informative paragraph.

> Chow mein is an interesting Chinese dish.
>
> The Siberian husky is a sturdy, swift sled dog.
>
> Marian Anderson was an opera star.
>
> Jupiter is the largest of the planets.

Activity 4

Write a definition for five of the following topics. Those definitions could serve as topic sentences for informative paragraphs.

hurricane	an electric guitar	a cobra
the Chicago Bears	compact disks	a tidal wave
Maya Angelou	the latest dance	

Challenge

Write an informative paragraph. Use one of the definitions you wrote in Activity 4 as your topic sentence. You may want to use the dictionary and an encyclopedia to find details, facts, and figures to support your topic. Or you may know enough already to write a good paragraph.

A Paragraph That Tells a Story

A paragraph that tells a story is called a **narrative paragraph.** Such a paragraph answers the question, "What happened?" Narratives can be different lengths. They can be many pages long, or they can be just one paragraph. A very short narrative is called an **anecdote.** An anecdote usually describes one incident.

Your story about the traffic accident you saw is an anecdote.

A narrative can be **nonfiction** (true) or **fiction** (imaginary). Narratives are usually told in chronological order. A narrative that is interesting usually describes some sort of problem. The end of the story comes when that problem is solved.

When you write a paragraph you think of as a story, ask yourself these questions: What is the problem in this story? How is that problem solved? If you can't answer those questions, you really don't have much of a story.

When planning your narrative paragraph, you can come up with details by asking yourself a few questions. Whether your story is true or imaginary, ask yourself these questions: Who? What? Where? When? Why? How?

Here are some examples:

> Topic sentence: Sue and I almost drowned on our last trip to the beach.
>
> **Who?** Sue and I
>
> **What?** almost drowned when we were caught by the outgoing tide
>
> **When?** late in the afternoon, after the lifeguards had gone off duty.
>
> **Where?** Seaside Beach
>
> **Why?** We were caught by the outgoing tide.
>
> **How?** The water was quite warm, and we went out too far.

Choose an interesting news article. Use the information in that article to answer the questions who, what, when, where, why, and how.

Once you have come up with your list of details, you can write your narrative paragraph. Read the paragraph below based on the details about the incident at the beach.

> Sue and I almost drowned on our last trip to the beach. We had gone into the ocean at Seaside Beach very late one afternoon. Although it was a cloudy day, the water was quite warm. The beach was nearly empty. Everyone, including the lifeguards, had gone home for dinner. We were laughing and splashing. Then, suddenly, our laughs turned to screams of fear. We realized we were caught by the outgoing tide and couldn't get back to shore. Neither Sue nor I was strong enough to fight the tide alone. We were beginning to panic when a group of women came walking up the beach. When they saw us waving our arms, they swam out to help us. They were strong swimmers, and soon we were safe on shore.

What was the problem in the sample paragraph on page 126?

How was that problem solved?

Activity 5

How would you answer the who, what, when, where, why, and how questions for one of the following topic sentences? This will be fiction, so you will have to use your imagination to come up with the details. Choose a topic sentence, then answer these questions: Who? What? When? Where? Why? How?

> The brave dog, Rover, had to struggle to find his way home.
>
> Teresa and I know we saw a flying saucer that night.
>
> Ed and Tonio thought they would never find their way out of the forest.
>
> The babysitting job turned into a nightmare.
>
> Finding my lost wallet turned out to be an adventure.
>
> Beth Sanchez became a hero in one day.

Activity 6

Write a narrative paragraph. Use one of the topics from Activity 4, or choose a topic of your own. The paragraph may be fiction or nonfiction.

If you use a new topic, you should answer the who, what, when, where, why, and how questions before you begin. Also, before you begin to write, answer these two questions: What is the problem of my story? How will that problem be solved?

Writing With Style

When writing an explanatory paragraph, you need to think through the process you're going to describe. List the necessary steps. Ask yourself, "Could I do this task if I were given these instructions?" Then write your paragraph, using your list as a guide.

The writer of paragraph A didn't think through the process before writing. Could you follow the instructions?

A. You can turn plain popcorn into a special treat by making caramel corn. You just need to mix some caramel with some popcorn. The caramel is made of butter, brown sugar, corn syrup, and salt. It makes the popcorn taste really good. You put the popcorn and the other ingredients together and cook it. Oh yes, you also need to add soda and vanilla. Don't forget to stir it often. It's delicious, but it's a lot more fattening than plain popcorn.

You probably decided that the directions in paragraph A were fairly hard to follow. Now look at paragraph B. These directions are complete, detailed, and presented in chronological order. They provide enough information for the reader to actually make caramel corn. That means the paragraph is a success.

B. You can turn plain popcorn into a special treat by making caramel corn. First pop about 6 quarts of popcorn and keep it in a warm oven. Then begin the caramel syrup by melting 2 sticks of butter. Next stir into the butter 2 cups brown sugar, 1/2 cup corn syrup, and 1 teaspoon salt. Bring this mixture to a boil. Then remove the mixture from the heat and add 1/2 teaspoon soda and 1 teaspoon vanilla. Pour the caramel syrup slowly over the popped corn. Mix it well with a fork. Bake the popcorn-caramel mixture at 250 degrees for one hour. Open the oven and stir the mixture every 15 minutes. When the caramel corn is done, it will smell sweet and delicious. You will want to snack on it right away, but wait until it cools.

Vocabulary Builder

Number Prefixes
Knowing about number prefixes can often help you understand unfamiliar words. If you know what the prefix means, you can often figure out what the whole word means. Use the chart below to answer the questions. Write your answers on a separate piece of paper.

mono, uni = one	quad = four	sept = seven
bi = two	quint, penta = five	oct = eight
tri = three	sex, hexa = six	deca = ten

1. What is a unicycle?

2. How often is biweekly?

3. How many babies are there if a mother has triplets?

4. How many feet does an animal have if it's called a quadruped?

5. How many singers are in a quintet?

6. How many sides are in a hexagon?

7. What do you call an eight-sided figure?

8. How many events are in an athletic contest called a decathlon?

Chapter Review

Chapter Summary

- ☐ An explanatory paragraph tells how to do something or how to make something.

- ☐ Write details in chronological order in an explanatory paragraph.

- ☐ Use transitional words to guide the reader and keep time order clear.

- ☐ Make sure the subject is narrow enough to explain fully in one paragraph.

- ☐ An informative paragraph gives details, facts, and figures about a topic.

- ☐ The topic sentence of an informative paragraph is often like a definition.

- ☐ A narrative paragraph tells the story of an incident or a person.

- ☐ A narrative paragraph should present some type of problem and end with that problem's solution.

Writing Practice

Think of a person in history whom you admire. It might be Abraham Lincoln, John Kennedy, Harriet Tubman, or Chief Joseph. Choose anyone you think did something really worthwhile. Find out more about that person by looking in an encyclopedia or other reference book. Make some notes, listing some of the things the person accomplished. Then use those notes to write an informative paragraph.

Chapter Quiz

Read each of the following paragraphs. Tell if it is an explanatory paragraph, an informative paragraph, or a narrative paragraph. Then choose which paragraph you liked best and write a paragraph telling why you liked it.

A. The evil-looking Mr. Smith turned out to be the nicest man in my neighborhood. Once all the kids on my block were afraid of Mr. Smith. He sat on his porch in the summer and stared at us as we played. In the winter he watched out of his front window as we walked to school. He never smiled. He just glared and frowned, and we were sure he was thinking of terrible things to do to us. Then one day in cold December my puppy, Pogo, was hit by a car. No one was around but me, and I could see my dog needed help quickly. I had to get him to the pet hospital! Suddenly I felt a hand on my shoulder. It was Mr. Smith. He gently lifted Pogo and carried him to his car. Then Mr. Smith smiled. He told me my dog would be OK. Together we took Pogo to the pet hospital. Pogo pulled through, and I knew it was all thanks to my good neighbor.

B.   A kayak is a light canoe made of animal skins. The skins are stretched over a frame of bone or wood. Kayaks are sometimes 20 feet long, but they are never more than 20 inches wide. The top of a kayak is covered with skin except for one small opening. The person paddling the kayak climbs in through that opening. He or she closes a flap to make the boat watertight. A paddler can turn the kayak completely over in the water. Since the kayak is watertight, it will pop back right side up again. Many Eskimos in Alaska use kayaks for fishing, hunting, and traveling.

Chapter *10* Writing to Persuade

Jane Addams is best known as a social reformer. Her main concerns were with the welfare of women, children, and the elderly. Her writing skill helped earn money and respect for her projects. Twenty Years at Hull House is her most famous book. It tells the story of the settlement house she founded in Chicago.

Powerful writing about a good cause can persuade readers to help.

Writers at Work: Jane Addams (1860–1935)

Chapter Learning Objectives

☐ Write a persuasive paragraph.
☐ Write specific reasons, facts, and figures.
☐ Identify facts and opinions.
☐ Use qualifying words and phrases.

Words to Know

> **opinion**   a belief, an attitude, or a viewpoint
>
> **persuade**   to get someone to do something or believe something; to convince
>
> **qualify**   to limit, make less strong
>
> > example: *In my opinion*, ice cream is better than cake.

Stating Your Opinion

Sometimes you write to give your **opinion** on a subject. Your goal then is to present enough reasons and facts to convince the reader that you're right. For example, you might want to convince your reader that teenagers are good drivers. You will aim to **persuade** your reader to accept your opinion.

The first sentence of a persuasive paragraph should present your opinion. It will serve as a topic sentence for the rest of the paragraph.

Your topic must (1) be a clearly stated opinion, (2) be something you care about, (3) be something you know enough about to provide at least three solid statements of support.

The topic *television* isn't suitable for a persuasive paragraph. It doesn't state an opinion. However, you could narrow the topic and say what you think about television.

Either of these two sentences would be a good topic sentence for a persuasive paragraph:

> I think Americans watch too much television.

or

> In my opinion, television teaches people about the world.

Activity 1

On a separate sheet of paper, finish each of the following sentences by stating an opinion. Each opinion could serve as a topic sentence for a persuasive paragraph.

Most people have opinions on quite a few subjects. What are some things you feel strongly about?

1. I think the food in the school cafeteria _____ .

2. I feel this city needs _____ .

3. In my opinion, _____ was America's best president.

4. I think that _____ is a waste of time.

5. I believe that people under age twenty-five are _____ drivers.

6. There are several reasons that people should not buy a _____ .

Supporting Your Opinion

Your opinion is of little value if you can't support it. Once you've written your topic sentence, your job is to convince your reader that your opinion is right. Sometimes you have enough reasons and facts in your head to be persuasive. Sometimes you must do a little research to come up with enough convincing arguments.

In the body of your persuasive paragraph, give specific reasons that support your opinion.

Some topics can be supported using what you already know. Read the following examples:

Would you want to hire this person as a waiter? Why or why not?

> I believe I should be hired as a waiter in your restaurant. Because I worked as a waiter last summer in Ann's Diner in Seattle, I have had the necessary experience. In fact, before I left Ann's Diner to return to school, I was chosen "Outstanding Employee" of the month. Both the owner, Jill Johnson, and her customers stated that I was a friendly, speedy worker. I never missed a day of work and always arrived on the job early. I enjoy waiter work and believe I could do an excellent job in your restaurant.

Certain topics might require a little research if you need to come up with facts and figures. Some of the information in the following paragraph came from *The World Almanac.*

> It seems that one of the safest ways a person can travel is by train. Trains cannot fall from the sky like airplanes. Cars fairly often run into each other, but a train is very unlikely to run into other trains. Unlike buses, trains don't have to fight traffic on crowded highways. Trains are driven by well-schooled engineers and serviced by skilled mechanics. Figures show that trains are one of the safest ways to travel. In 1987 in the United States, 23,587 passengers were killed in automobiles and taxis, 50 died on buses, and 252 were killed in airplane crashes. Only 16 people died on passenger trains. The train seems to be a very safe way to get from one place to another.

Note
Often the supporting details in a persuasive paragraph are listed in order of importance. The most important, persuasive detail is left for last. That way, readers are left with the best evidence in their minds. For example, the paragraph on train safety used the most convincing fact (that only 16 people were killed on trains in one year) as the last detail of the paragraph.

Activity 2

Use the list of details given below to write a persuasive paragraph. The paragraph should prove that the neighborhood needs a new park.

Are there things you would like to see changed in your neighborhood? Learn to state your opinions clearly and to support those opinions with details. Those are the first steps to getting what you want!

Remember to do the following things:

• First write a topic sentence clearly stating the opinion.

• Then write sentences of support.

• Use transitional words.

• Save the most impressive detail for last.

• Write a strong conclusion restating your opinion.
    a. Children are forced to play ball in the street.
    b. There are no parks for ten miles in either direction.
    c. Studies show that children who have places to play are less likely to get into trouble.
    d. Everyone, young and old alike, can enjoy the beauty of trees, flowers, and grass.
    e. There are several acres of land available to the city for a reasonable price.

Challenge

Write your own persuasive paragraph. Choose one of the topics listed below. Before you begin the paragraph, make some notes listing at least three details that support your topic.

Who was your best teacher

Why students should/should not be required to attend school

Why movie stars deserve/do not deserve such high salaries

Why the store should take back an item you're returning

Why teenagers should take drivers' education before they get their drivers' licenses

Fact or Opinion

There are two kinds of statements. A statement of fact is not the same as a statement of opinion. A statement of fact is something that can be proven right or wrong.

> The Empire State Building is in New York City.

This is a statement of fact. It can be proven true by observing that the building is, indeed, in New York City. Everyone would agree it's true.

> It's fun to climb the steps of the Empire State Building.

This is a statement of opinion. The writer may think it's true, but certainly not everyone would agree.

When you write, it's very important to recognize if you're writing facts or opinions.

- A statement of fact can be proven true or false.

- A statement of opinion can't be proven true or false.

- Certain words act as signals that a statement is an opinion. Words that show approval or disapproval are words of opinion.

- Some opinion words are *better, good, bad, pleasant, unpleasant, best, poor,* and *great.*

  Ralph is a *better* dog than Spot.
  (That is someone's opinion.)

- Statements that say what is desirable are statements of opinion. Words like *should, ought to,* and *must* are opinion words.

  Linda *should* ask Stan to the dance.
  (That is someone's opinion.)

- Predictions are another kind of opinion. Words and phrases like *will, shall,* and *is going to* signal a prediction. Any statement that predicts what will happen in the future is an opinion.

  It *is going to* rain this afternoon.
  (That is someone's opinion.)

No one knows for sure what will happen in the future. You can say, "I am going to buy a new television tomorrow." But how do you know for sure that it's going to happen? Something could come up and prevent it. That's why any prediction is a statement of opinion.

Activity 3

Decide if each of the following sentences is a statement of fact or a statement of opinion. Number you paper from 1 to 9. Write F for fact or O for opinion by each number.

1. Mark Twain was a writer.

2. Mark Twain was a good writer.

3. Speeding is against the law.

4. Carrots are better than celery.

5. Tomorrow I'll visit Aunt Millie.

6. Dogs are more fun than cats.

7. There are more girls in this class than boys.

8. The Jets will win the Super Bowl.

9. Astronauts have landed on the moon.

Using Qualifying Words

When you write statements of fact you can present them just as they are. However, when you write a statement of opinion, you must make it clear that it isn't a fact. You must *qualify* it.

> Don't say: Mrs. Estevez is a terrible boss.

> Do say: *In my opinion*, Mrs. Estevez is a terrible boss.

In my opinion qualifies the statement. It lets the reader know that you understand that the statement is your opinion and not a fact.

Sometimes writers make statements that are too general.

> Don't say: Teenagers are safe drivers.
> (You can't prove that all teenagers are safe drivers.)

> Do say: *Many* teenagers are safe drivers.
> (You could prove that statement true.)

Many is a qualifying word.

Unqualified statements	Qualified statements
It will rain tomorrow.	It will *probably* rain tomorrow.
Dogs bark at cars.	*Many* dogs bark at cars.
Teachers give too much homework.	*Some* teachers give too much homework.

This chart lists some qualifying words:

some	apparently	seems to
several	probably	in my opinion
many	almost	I think
most	usually	often
may	sometimes	it seems
might	supposedly	

Unqualified statements are often unfair. Which of these statements is fair?
1. "Today's parents don't understand their children."
2. "Some of today's parents don't understand their children."

Activity 4

A. On a separate sheet of paper, write the numbers of the statements you think need to be qualified. (Hint: You should write seven numbers.)

1. Police officers don't smile.

2. The car is in the garage.

3. You will need to replace that car in five years.

4. People who have had hard lives write the best stories.

5. Portland is the largest city in Oregon.

6. Women love ballet.

7. She will make a good lawyer someday.

8. Cruncho Crispos is a cereal.

9. Everyone loves Cruncho Crispos.

10. Dogs hate mail carriers.

B. Rewrite the seven statements you selected, using qualifying words to make them better sentences.

The Great Persuaders

Advertisers are some of the greatest masters of persuasion. Ads make us want things we never knew we wanted before. That is because we are persuaded that a product will somehow improve our lives.

Sometimes the advertiser will not come out and say, "Buy this; it will make life better." Instead, the ad will suggest that idea. For example, an advertisement might picture a beautiful, happy woman with her arms around a handsome man. Such an ad might suggest that a certain kind of perfume will make a woman attractive and bring her romance.

Another ad could picture a man with three children smiling at him as he cooks with a certain brand of barbecue sauce. This ad would suggest that a father who uses that sauce will have a happy family.

Try this for fun!

Cut three ads out of a newspaper or magazine. Write down some of the reasons given for buying each product. Remember, the reasons might be stated in the ad or suggested by the picture.

Writing With Style

If you really want your writing to persuade readers, you must avoid being too emotional. Calm, detailed information is more persuasive than heated, emotional opinion. Which paragraph would be more likely to convince a state legislature to pass a seat belt law?

A. I feel that this state should require automobile drivers and passengers to wear seat belts. It's so dangerous to drive without belts. People can be killed! People just don't realize how stupid it is to ride in a car without a belt. There is absolutely no reason to travel in an automobile without a seat belt. Some people say it wrinkles their clothes, but that's crazy. It all comes down to one thing: seat belts save lives!

B. I feel this state should require automobile drivers and passengers to wear seat belts. Safety tests prove that people are less likely to be badly hurt in an auto accident if they're wearing seat belts. Thirty-two states have already passed laws requiring people to wear seat belts. Those seat belt laws have, indeed, reduced traffic deaths. Some people may say that seat belts are uncomfortable or a bother. That is, I think, a small price to pay for added safety. It all comes down to one thing: seat belts save lives!

Notice how paragraph A insults the reader by using words like stupid and crazy. Paragraph B avoids name-calling and provides some facts and figures.

Vocabulary Builder

Using Euphemisms
Euphemisms are words or phrases that make unpleasant things seem better. Euphemisms are often used to persuade people that things aren't really so bad. Sometimes people feel they're being polite when they use a euphemism. For example, instead of saying somebody "died," they might say that person has "passed away." That term sounds less harsh. Instead of calling someone an "old person," people sometimes use the term "senior citizen."

Euphemisms can be used to hide ugly truths. A city government, instead of admitting there are slums, might say it has an "underprivileged area." During World War II, Japanese-Americans were put into American concentration camps. These places were called "relocation centers."

Don't be fooled by euphemisms. What do the euphemisms below *really* mean? Write your answers on a separate piece of paper.

1. stretching the truth = _____

2. news delivery agent = _____

3. visually handicapped = _____

4. rest room = _____

5. house of correction = _____

6. sanitation engineer = _____

7. between engagements = _____

8. the Selective Service = _____

9. recycled automobile = _____

10. misguided youth = _____

Chapter Review

Chapter Summary

☐ The topic sentence of a persuasive paragraph should state your opinion.

☐ Your goal in a persuasive paragraph is to convince your reader that your opinion is the right one.

☐ Provide at least three strong details supporting your opinion.

☐ Save the most important detail for the last supporting sentence you write.

☐ Write a concluding sentence that restates your opinion in other words.

☐ Be sure statements you present as facts are accurate.

☐ Qualify broad statements with words like "some," "might," and "probably."

Writing Practice

There are two sides to most issues. The statements of opinion written below present both sides of one issue. Choose one side of the issue listed. Make a list of details that would support your side. Then write a complete persuasive paragraph. Include a topic sentence, at least three good sentences of support, and a concluding sentence.

In my opinion,

a. Too much television confuses people about what's real and what's not.

b. Television has made Americans smarter and more aware.

Chapter Quiz

A. Write a sentence expressing an opinion on each of the following subjects.

> example: homework
>
> In my opinion, teachers should never give homework on weekends.

1. tanning salons

2. women's rights

3. television

4. fast food restaurants

5. the speed limits

B. The opinion below has three reasons to support it. However, the reasons aren't very convincing. They aren't specific and don't give enough information. Copy the opinion on your paper. Then rewrite each reason so that it serves as better support for that opinion. Sometimes you may need to turn one reason into several sentences.

> People should not drive when they have been drinking alcohol.
>
> a. It is dangerous.
>
> b. You could get into trouble.
>
> c. It is not a smart thing to do.

C. Rewrite the following sentences. Use qualifying words to change them into statements of fact.

1. Tornadoes are more damaging than earthquakes.

2. Advertisements are full of lies.

3. Good students study three hours a day.

Chapter *11* Writing to Describe

Lillian Hellman was a talented American playwright. Her most famous play The Little Foxes *showed the terrible influence of greed on an American family. One of her short stories based on a true incident, was made into the popular movie* Julia. *She also wrote two autobiographical books,* An Unfinished Woman *and* Scoundrel Time.

All powerful drama is based on universal human emotions.

Writers at Work: Lillian Hellman (1905-1984)

Chapter Learning Objectives

☐ Write a descriptive paragraph with specific details to create a picture for the reader.

☐ Write descriptions that appeal to all the senses.

☐ Write character descriptions that include physical appearance and personality.

☐ Identify and write similes and metaphors.

Words to Know

senses   the faculties of sight, hearing, smell, taste, and touch

figure of speech   an expression in which words suggest an image that is different from the literal meaning of words

literal   actual, real, exactly as things are

exaggeration   something stretched beyond the truth; something made larger or greater than it really is

simile   a figure of speech in which two things are compared by using the word *like* or *as*

example: *She sang like a bird.*

metaphor   a figure of speech in which one thing is compared with another by suggesting a likeness between the two

example: *His heart is an iceberg.*

implies   suggests in an indirect way

moderation   the opposite of exaggeration; neither too much nor too little

precision   saying exactly what a thing is; every detail accurately described

Organizing a Descriptive Paragraph

In Chapter 4 you read about one of a writer's primary goals. That goal was to take images and ideas from the writer's own head and put them, as exactly as possible, into the reader's head. When writing a *descriptive* paragraph, you must remember that goal. You will be trying to describe something to a reader as clearly as possible.

A descriptive paragraph is organized just like the other types of paragraphs described in this book.

Do you recognize this diagram from earlier chapters?

1   topic sentence

    1. sentence of support
2   2. sentence of support   body
    3. sentence of support

3   concluding sentence

1. The topic sentence will tell the reader what you're describing. Read this example:

   The grandfather clock was very old and very valuable, but best of all, it recalled memories of my grandparents' house.

2. The body of the descriptive paragraph will provide details for your reader. It should give enough details for the reader to picture and experience what you're describing. Read this example:

   The clock was much taller than I was as a ten-year-old boy. It was made of fine, smooth, dark brown wood. The wood was perfect except for two scratches. Those two long, light-colored scratches ran down the left side of the clock. They showed where the cat had tried to climb up the side. The clock had a bright, white face painted with gold numbers. I always called them "fancy numbers" because of their curly ends. Two heavy brass balls hung on chains down the front of the clock. I would stare at the balls through the clock's glass door. They were, I decided, just about the size of grapefruits. My favorite part of the magnificent clock was its sound. The clock had loud, strong, even ticks that echoed through the room. Then, each hour, came the long, mellow tones of the striking chimes.

3. The concluding sentence should summarize the topic and may express your feelings about it. Read this example:

I loved that old clock because it was a part of my childhood.

When writing a descriptive paragraph, remember your purpose. Your purpose now is to give your reader an image that is as exact as possible. You want to describe something as it really appeared to you.

Note
Be sure to limit your topic. You can't write a complete description if your topic is too broad. For example, it would be hard to fully describe your town in one paragraph. However, you could describe one street corner or one bus stop or one house.

Using All Your Senses

When we experience things, we do not only see them. Our other **senses** are involved, too. What other sense does the writer of the clock paragraph use in the description?

The sense of hearing is used when the writer describes the sounds the clock makes.

Of course, not every experience involves all the senses. The writer would not be likely to describe how the clock tasted or smelled. However, when you write to describe, you should use as many of your senses as you can.

Which senses would you use to describe your classroom?

The Senses

seeing   tasting   hearing

touching   smelling

Activity 1

Choose an item from the list below. Write *sight, sound, smell, taste,* and *touch* on your paper. Under each sense, list as many details as possible to describe the object you chose.

a pizza   a gym locker room

the ocean   a wet dog

a rose   a baby

Activity 2

Imagine that you've lost your sense of sight. Write a paragraph describing something by using only your four other senses. Here are some suggestions, but you may write about any other topic that interests you:

a summer day   a busy street corner

going to a movie   a church   a date

a gym during a basketball game

Challenge

> Close your eyes. Listen for a while, and then list the sounds you hear. Now write a paragraph describing those sounds and how they make you feel.

It Takes More Than Adjectives

When people think about describing something, they often think first of using adjectives. For example, if someone were describing a dog, that person might write, "It was a *big, brown, shaggy* dog with *ugly, long, sharp, white* teeth." All the words in italics are adjectives, or words that describe nouns. However, long lists of adjectives can bore your reader. Try it for yourself. Read the sample sentence aloud—how does it sound to you? Adjectives are useful in a description, but it's not a good idea to use too many.

There are other ways you can describe your subject. For example, verbs can also be descriptive. Let the verbs you use paint a picture for your reader. For example, a dog that *howls* is different from a dog that *whines*. A dog that *growls* is different from a dog that *yaps*.

The nouns you use can also be descriptive. If you call a dog a *hound*, it changes the image. If you call the dog a *beast*, the reader will get a much different picture than if you call it a *pup*. What other nouns can you think of to use in place of dog?

Activity 3

For each of the following words, list at least three other words that present a clearer picture and have a more specific meaning. Write your answers on a separate piece of paper.

1. talk

    talk loudly:

    talk quietly:

    talk angrily:

2. boat

    big, ocean-going boat:

    little boat with oars:

    luxury boat:

3. trip

    long, hard trip:

    short, holiday trip:

    trip on the ocean:

What's in a Name?
Names have different connotations. Why might a person called Bobby as a child decide to go by Robert as an adult? Does a woman named Bertha have a different image than a woman named Tammy? If you are describing an imaginary character, you can create a picture in your reader's mind just by choosing a certain name.

Try this for fun!

What kind of person do you picture from the following names? Try to write a one-sentence description for each name. Compare your descriptions with those of others in your class. Are any of your descriptions similar?

Billy	Winston
Gertrude	Rachel
Chudney	Elizabeth
Wilbur	Mario

Many famous people, especially movie stars and other entertainers, take new names. Here are some examples:

Bo Derek was Cathleen Collins.

Judy Garland was Frances Gumm.

James Garner was James Baumgardner.

Pee-Wee Herman was Paul Rubenfeld.

Rock Hudson was Roy Scherer, Jr.

Marilyn Monroe was Norma Jean Mortenson.

Tony Randall was Leonard Rosenberg.

Ringo Starr was Richard Starkey.

Tina Turner was Annie Mae Bullock.

John Wayne was Marion Morrison.

Natalie Wood was Natasha Gurdin.

Stevie Wonder was Stevland Morris.

Why do you imagine some movie stars take new names?

Describing Characters

Occasionally you may write a description of a person. You may be asked to describe a character from a book, or you may be describing a real person you know. When describing a character, you need to think about more than just what that character looks like. You also must think about the character's personality.

Activity 4

A. Think of a person about whom you feel strongly. The person can be real or fictional. Then use the categories listed below to work up a characterization of that person. Use as many descriptive words as you can for each item.

Make sure each paragraph has the following items:
(1) topic sentence
(2) body
(3) concluding sentence

Hair: Ears:

Eyes: Mouth:

Nose: Skin:

Height, weight, and shape:

Usual clothing:

What he or she likes to do:

What he or she doesn't like to do:

How he or she acts around other people:

What kind of mood he or she is usually in:

Any unusual characteristics he or she has:

Something he or she might say:

B. Use the notes you made in Part A to write two descriptive paragraphs. In the first paragraph, describe the person's physical appearance. In the second paragraph, describe what the person is like.

Figures of Speech: Using Similes and Metaphors

Would you be using a simile if you said, "Mary is a doll?"

A **figure of speech** is an expression that is not meant **literally**. The expression, "He is as wide as a barn," doesn't mean that the person really measures the same distance across as a barn. The expression is a figure of speech. There are different kinds of figures of speech. One is **exaggeration,** as in this example: "I'm so hungry I could eat a horse."

Another commonly used figure of speech is the simile. A **simile** is a comparison between two different things saying one is like the other. A simile must use the word *like* or *as* to make the comparison. "He is as wide as a barn" is a simile. (It's also an exaggeration, isn't it?) It compares a man to a barn. The qualities being compared are their widths.

Sometimes writers use similes when they're describing something. A carefully thought out simile can help the reader get a much clearer picture. The reader can imagine exactly how something looks or tastes or feels.

Here are a few more similes:

The water tasted like boiled sweat socks.

The shirt was as soft as a baby's skin.

He acted as playful as a kitten with a ball of string.

Activity 5

A. Copy these sentences on your paper. <u>Underline</u> the two items being compared in each simile.

1. The snowflakes were like cotton balls.

2. His tears fell as heavily as rain.

3. His stomach looked like a big watermelon.

4. My math teacher has a neck like a giraffe's.

5. The house was as silent as a graveyard.

Compare yourself to an animal by completing the following sentence: "Today I feel like a _____." What qualities of that animal do you have?

B. Now write some similes of your own by completing the following sentences on your own paper.

1. The rain on the roof sounded like_____ .

2. The sun sparkled on the water like _____ .

3. Maria is as tall as _____ .

4. Larry chatters like _____ .

5. Donna is as thin as _____ .

6. The baby's skin was as soft as _____ .

A **metaphor** is another figure of speech. It **implies** a comparison of unlike things without using the word *like* or *as*. A metaphor simply calls one thing another or gives one thing the characteristics of another thing.

> example: *My father is a bear when he wakes up in the morning.*

That metaphor calls the father a bear. It does not use the word *like* or *as*.

Activity 6

A. Copy the following sentences on your paper. <u>Underline</u> the two items being compared in each metaphor.

1. The sun was a golden giant.

2. Happiness is a chocolate ice cream cone.

3. Joy is the morning of a first snowfall.

4. The wind was a howling animal.

5. The ice turned the tree branches into bent fingers.

B. Write your own "Happiness is . . ." metaphor.

Writing With Style

Figures of speech can give style to your writing. They help the reader see what you're seeing and understand exactly what you mean. Which of the sentences in each pair below creates a clearer picture?

1. a. Her hat had lots of colorful feathers and was very fancy.

   b. Her hat was as brilliant as a peacock's tail.

2. a. The night was very dark.

   b. The night was as dark as the inside of a deep cave.

3. a. The boy was very shy.

   b. The boy was a shy little rabbit hiding in the corner.

4. a. The wind howled.

   b. The wind howled like a mournful ghost searching for a place to rest.

5. a. Their new quarterback is very, very big.

   b. Their new quarterback is built like a brick shed.

You probably chose the *b* sentences as the better ones. The *b* sentences all contained *figures of speech*. Of course, you don't want to use figures of speech in every sentence you write. You don't even want to use them in every paragraph. But once in a while, they can really help you create a more vivid, precise picture for your reader. You've probably figured out by now that the key words in descriptive writing are **moderation** and **precision.**

Vocabulary Builder

Suffixes

A suffix is a group of letters added at the end of a word. A suffix changes the meaning of a word. Often, it also changes the word's part of speech. When *ly* is added to the end of an adjective, it makes the adjective an adverb. For example, when *ly* is added to the adjective *weird*, it becomes the adverb *weirdly*.

A. On your own paper, use the suffix *ly* to make the word in parentheses into the adverb that would fit into the sentence. The first one has been done as an example.

1. The ball hit him (sudden) from behind.   suddenly

2. She (quick) hid the money in her purse.

3. She laughed (wicked) after she played the trick on him.

4. There was (most) junk at the garage sale.

5. He shook his head (sad) and left the room.

B. Add the suffix *ly* to each of the following adjectives. Then use each adverb in a sentence.

1. swift

2. loud

3. clear

4. strange

5. tight

Chapter Review

Chapter Summary

☐ A descriptive paragraph is organized like other paragraphs. It has a topic sentence, a body of sentences of support, and a concluding sentence.

☐ Your purpose in writing a descriptive paragraph is to give the reader an image that is as exact as possible.

☐ Use as many senses (sight, sound, smell, taste, and touch) as you can when describing something.

☐ Use colorful, specific verbs, nouns, and adjectives.

☐ Tell about personality as well as physical appearance when describing people.

☐ Use figures of speech sometimes for clearer images.

☐ One type of figure of speech is the simile (comparisons using like or as).

☐ Another figure of speech is the metaphor (comparisons implying that one thing is another).

Writing Practice

Write a descriptive paragraph. Use at least one figure of speech in your paragraph. In the description, appeal to at least one other sense in addition to the sense of sight.

Check to make sure your topic sentence presents the thing you're describing. Also make sure your paragraph has at least three good supporting sentences and a concluding sentence.

Chapter Quiz

A. List the five senses.

B. Write the word in each pair that presents the clearest, most specific picture.

1. talk chatter

2. horse stallion

3. hut house

4. shattered broken

5. fell crashed

C. Decide if each of the following sentences is a simile, a metaphor, or not a figure of speech at all. Number your paper from 1 to 10. By each number, write **S** if it's a simile, **M** if it's a metaphor, or **NFS** if it's not a figure of speech.

1. The cat was fat.

2. The cat was as fat as a marshmallow.

3. The railroad tracks were silver threads sewn into the landscape.

4. The dark sky looked mysterious.

5. The panther was as black as the night.

6. The airplane was a silver bullet speeding through the sky.

7. The tornado hit the city like a bomb.

8. Her hair was as golden as autumn wheatfields.

9. The ocean was blue with flecks of gold where the sun shone on it.

10. The whitecaps were like little hands waving at the shore.

Chapter 12 Writing to Compare

Amy Tan was born soon after her parents moved from China to California. Her first novel The Joy Luck Club *was a best seller. It tells how a young American woman, like herself, learns to appreciate her Chinese heritage. This change comes about through the warm and humorous tales told at club meetings by her mother and her mother's friends.*

Comparing one generation with another can show interesting similarities and differences.

Writers at Work: Amy Tan (1952-   )

Chapter Learning Objectives

☐ Write a paragraph of comparison.

☐ Write transitional words within that paragraph.

☐ Identify similarities and differences in a paragraph of comparison.

Words to Know

comparison   the act of noting the likenesses and differences of things

similarities   points of likeness: the state of being close to the same

differences   points that are not alike

characteristics   distinguishing features; features that make something or someone special and individual

What Is a Paragraph of Comparison?

Making a **comparison** is often a good way to develop a topic. When you have two things with definite similarities and/or differences, you can write a paragraph of comparison. You can compare books, people, places, animals—almost anything.

These are examples of comparisons. To compare means to point out how two things are alike or how they are different.

        black—white
        tall—taller
        green—yellow
        happy—sad
        fast—slow
        fast—faster
        friendly—unfriendly

A paragraph of comparison takes two subjects and points out how they are alike and how they are different.

The lists below show two subjects suitable for discussion through comparison. There are enough differences to make a well-developed paragraph.

Subject #1	Subject #2
Modern Automobiles	Early Automobiles
start quickly with key	crank to start
go fast—up to 100 mph	went slow—30 mph
reliable	broke down all the time
comfortable	cold, wet
purpose: transportation	purpose: transportation

The paragraph of comparison is developed the same way as any other paragraph. It has the same three main parts.

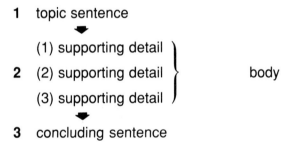

1 topic sentence

(1) supporting detail

2 (2) supporting detail   body

(3) supporting detail

3 concluding sentence

1. The topic sentence presents the subjects and sets up the comparison.

   Modern automobiles are surely an improvement over the earliest models.

2. The body presents details that support the topic sentence. The details prove the topic sentence is true.

   In the early days of the automobile, drivers had to spend time and energy cranking up the car just to get it going. Today a turn of the key makes the engine roar. It certainly took longer for yesterday's motorist to get somewhere. Although many modern autos can easily go 100 miles an hour, the early cars were racing at 30! When today's drivers start a trip, they expect to get where they're going. However, the pioneers of motoring never knew for sure if their new invention would make it all the way. Another important feature of today's cars is comfort. Now drivers expect heaters and air conditioners. In contrast, drivers long ago had to carry heavy blankets to keep warm. And, as the cars were open to the weather, people got wet when it rained.

3. The concluding sentence restates the subjects of the comparison.

Despite the differences, both today's automobiles and yesterday's got people where they were going.

When do you write paragraphs of comparison?
You will find many times when a paragraph of comparison is appropriate.

Could you compare yourself with a character in a book or movie? How are you like that character? How are you different?

You might want to compare two characters in a book.

You might want to compare two books written by the same author.

You might want to compare two friends, two cities, two teachers—the list can go on.

Comparison is a good way to develop a paragraph.

Activity 1

To begin thinking in terms of comparisons, write some sentences that compare. Use the topics suggested on the next page to get you going.

example: *Compare two sports.*

Basketball provides more physical exercise than golf.

(Hint: Don't just say one is better or worse than the other. Mention some qualities of the subjects of your sentence.)

1. Compare two animals.

2. Compare boys and girls.

3. Compare summer and winter.

4. Compare roller skates and ice skates.

5. Compare two brands of tennis shoes.

Note

Sometimes in a comparison you will want to prove that one thing is *better* than another. At other times, you will just want to show that they are different or that they are alike. You will write about the **similarities** and **differences** between the two things.

Activity 2

Which of the following topic sentences suggests that the writer is going to use comparison to develop the paragraph? On your own paper, write the numbers of the sentences that suggest comparisons.

1. The Greeks and the Romans had many things in common.

2. I like Saturdays better than Sundays.

3. Last summer I saw Prince in concert.

4. My favorite book is *The Twenty-One Balloons.*

5. *The Call of the Wild* and *White Fang* are books about dogs in the frozen North.

6. I think that today's teenagers have to make more decisions than teenagers of the last generation.

7. A new city park is more important than a new baseball stadium.

8. Students at Westside Middle School are very bright.

9. Doritos taste better than Ruffles potato chips.

10. Thousands of people are homeless.

Using Transitional Words in Comparisons

Do you remember learning about transitional words and phrases in Chapter 8? Transitional words show the connection between one sentence and another. They guide the reader through the paragraph.

The transitional words in the box below are especially useful in a paragraph of comparison.

Which of these transitional words would introduce differences? Which would introduce similarities?

however	unlike
on the other hand	but
in comparison	then
although	now
on the contrary	similarly
in like manner	in the same way

Read the following sentences to see how some of those transitional words can be used.

Patrick is kind. *However,* his brother can be quite mean.

Last spring was warm and dry. *In comparison,* this spring was rainy and cool.

Unlike stuck-up Cecil, Mike is very friendly.

Unlike dogs, cats can keep people from feeling lonely.

Centerville is a crowded, noisy city, *but* Springfield is still a peaceful, sleepy town.

Activity 3

Read the following paragraph of comparison.

A. Tell what two things are being compared.

B. List the transitional words and phrases used in the paragraph. You should find three of them.

> Wonder World and The Great Getaway are both big amusement parks, but each draws a very different crowd. Wonder World is a park built for those who love to dream and to imagine. Walking into Wonder World is like walking into a different universe. It's a land full of elves and princesses and storybook characters. But on the other hand, The Great Getaway is a place for the daring. Wonder World offers a boat trip through a fantasy land, but the Great Getaway offers a hair-raising trip on the world's largest roller coaster. Visitors to Wonder World come away saying, "Wasn't that cute!" In comparison, when visitors to The Great Getaway leave, they're barely able to speak at all.

Writing Your Own Paragraph of Comparison

Activity 4

To do this activity, first think of two people you know. They might be two friends, two teachers, two relatives, two television stars, or two writers.

A. Divide your paper into two columns. Head each column with the name of one of the people. Under each name, list **characteristics** of that person. Include at least five items on each list.

example: *My friend, Ronda Jones*	*My friend, Estella Perez*
tall	*short*
smart	*also smart*
likes reading, music, tennis, movies	*likes outdoors, camping, hiking, football*
is an excellent student	*is a good athlete*
is always cheerful	*is rather moody*

B. Use the information from your lists to write a paragraph of comparison. Remember, the topic sentence will introduce the comparison. You might want to reread the sample paragraph about automobiles on pages 164–165 as a model paragraph.

C. When you finish your paragraph of comparison, go through this checklist. Put a check mark by each item you find in your paragraph.

- A topic sentence that states the subjects compared
- At least three sentences of supporting details
- Some transitional words
- A concluding sentence

Writing With Style

By now, you have learned that very different paragraphs can be written on the same subject. The two paragraphs below were written on the same topic: the safety of a new car called the Superbo 6000. Each paragraph shows a different method of development.

A. developed using examples

The Superbo 6000 has brought great improvements to the area of auto safety. A new, secret body material has made the car almost crash proof. When it first came out, the Superbo was put through some pretty amazing tests. It was crashed head-on into a solid brick wall. The Superbo was rolled over and over. In every test, both robot driver and car came through without serious harm. However, the most impressive example of the Superbo's safety came on the open road. In a real highway accident, a family of five riding in a Superbo was hit by a large pickup truck. The truck was traveling at 50 miles per hour! The Superbo 6000 had some minor damage, but the people were unharmed. Indeed, the Superbo 6000 begins a new era in auto safety.

B. developed using comparison

The Superbo 6000 is safer than other cars on the market today. Most cars still have steel or fiber glass bodies, but the Superbo is built from a new secret material. Harder than steel, almost impossible to dent, the material also has a give and bounce that absorbs shocks. The Superbo 6000 also is equipped with tires wider than those on most other automobiles. These wider tires give a more stable ride on slick roads. Although the Superbo 6000 costs a bit more than many other cars, its safety record makes it today's best automobile.

Give Your Opinion
Both methods (example and comparison) developed good, strong paragraphs. Which method of development do you think worked best? Why?

Vocabulary Builder

Suffixes That Make Nouns
Adding a suffix (word ending) to a base word can change the part of speech. The suffix *ness* can change an adjective into a noun. When *ness* is added, the adjective *weird* becomes the noun *weirdness*.

A. Add *ness* to each of the words in parentheses to change them into nouns. Rewrite the sentences on a separate piece of paper.

1. Her (quick) saved him from drowning.
2. The (sudden) of the rainstorm caught everyone without umbrellas.
3. He giggled and stuttered, showing his (nervous).
4. A terrible (sore) spread through all her muscles after the track meet.
5. After his dog died, he was left with a feeling of (sad).

You can also use suffixes to make verbs into nouns. Here are some of the common noun suffixes: *ion, ist, or, er, al,* and *ant.*

For example, the verb *act* can be turned into the noun *action.* The verb *write* can become the noun *writer.*

B. The words in parentheses are missing suffixes. Decide which of the suffixes listed above to add to the words. Write the word with its proper suffix.

1. The doctor told her that she needed an (operate).
2. The boss said that the job was so big that they must hire another (work).
3. The traffic officer kept the cars moving in the right (direct).
4. She needed help on the project, so she hired an (assist).
5. The (act) came on stage and read his part.

Chapter Review

Chapter Summary

- ☐ A paragraph of comparison tells how two subjects are alike and how they are different.

- ☐ A paragraph of comparison has the same three basic parts as any paragraph (topic sentence, body, conclusion).

- ☐ The topic sentence names the subjects and sets up the comparison.

- ☐ The body presents details to support the topic sentence.

- ☐ The concluding sentence restates the subjects of the comparison.

- ☐ Certain transitional words help the reader understand that things are being compared.

Writing Practice

Practice making comparisons by writing a paragraph about yourself. Use the examples below, or make up your own.

Topic: I would rather _____ than _____ .

Some suggestions to fill in the blanks:

be a lawyer than a police officer

be a student than a teacher

be a horse than a cow

play violin than drums

Chapter Quiz

A. Answer the following questions. Write your answers in complete sentences on a separate sheet of paper.

1. What is the purpose of a paragraph of comparison?

2. What does the topic sentence do in a paragraph of comparison?

3. Write a sentence that makes a comparison.

4. What are three good transitional words to use to show differences between things?

5. What are two good transitional words to use to show similarities between things?

B. Write three sentences that show the differences between things. Use the three transitional words you listed in exercise A above. Write your sentences on a separate sheet of paper.

C. Write two sentences that show the similarities between things. Use the two transitional words you listed in exercise A above. Write your sentences on a separate sheet of paper.

Unit Review

A. Write an answer for each of the following questions. Write your answers in complete sentences on your own paper.

1. What is a writer's goal in an explanatory paragraph?

2. What is the purpose of an informative paragraph?

3. What does a narrative paragraph do?

4. Explain the difference between a fact and an opinion.

B. Picture each object below. Then list descriptive words and phrases that would appeal to each of the senses.

a rose   an orange   an old tennis shoe

C. Figures of Speech

Write three similes describing that rose, orange, and old tennis shoe.

example: *The red rose smelled like the breath of summer.*

Unit Four

Writing an Essay

Chapter *13* What Is an Essay?

Writers at Work: Alice Walker (1944-   )

Alice Walker is a novelist, poet, and essayist. Her third novel The Color Purple *earned her the Pulitzer Prize. It was also made into an award-winning movie. Her collection of essays* In Search of Our Mothers' Gardens *also explores the destructive effects of sexism and racism in American life.*

Good writing connects one person's life experience to the lives of many others.

Chapter Learning Objectives

- ☐ Identify an essay as a group of paragraphs dealing with one idea.
- ☐ Identify the three basic parts of an essay: introduction, body, and conclusion.
- ☐ Tell what a thesis statement is.
- ☐ Identify a thesis statement in context.

Words to Know

essay   a short piece of writing about a particular subject

composition   an essay

thesis statement   a sentence that presents the idea that the essay will support

The Basic Essay

An **essay** is a group of paragraphs (at least five) dealing with one idea. Sometimes essays are called **compositions.** In much the same way you learned to develop a paragraph, you will learn to develop a whole essay.

An essay is built very much like a paragraph. A paragraph is made of sentences, and an essay is made of paragraphs. Ideas that are too long to be covered in one paragraph become topics for essays.

Remember the diagram of the paragraph? Study this diagram of the paragraph again for review.

1   topic sentence

    (1) sentence of support

2   (2) sentence of support   }   body

    (3) sentence of support

3   concluding sentence

Now take a look at the diagram of an essay.

1   introductory paragraph

(1) paragraph of support
2   (2) paragraph of support   } body
(3) paragraph of support

3   concluding paragraph

Notice that the diagram of an essay is very much like that of a paragraph. The only difference is that the parts of the essay diagram are paragraphs instead of sentences.

Do you believe in any superstitions? Will you walk under a ladder? Do you worry about bad luck if you break a mirror? Do you have a lucky charm?

A basic essay includes the following elements:

1. An introductory paragraph

Some people won't walk under ladders. Others worry if black cats cross their paths. These people act as they do because of superstitions. Superstitions are beliefs that have no basis in fact. However, many people believe that these superstitions are true.

2. A body of at least three supporting paragraphs

Throughout the ages, there have been superstitions about salt. People once thought that salt had magic powers because it could keep things from decaying. The ancient Sumerians began the custom of throwing a pinch of salt over the left shoulder. They believed it would keep bad luck away. Several cultures considered spilled salt a sign of bad luck. Indeed, many people still toss a pinch of spilled salt over their shoulders, just to be on the safe side.

Even today, many people believe in signs of bad luck. Some feel they can control their futures by avoiding such signs. The superstitious never open umbrellas indoors because that is thought to bring misfortune. They never step on cracks in the sidewalks. Most avoid anything having to do with the number thirteen, believing that number is a bad luck sign. Some hotels avoid having a room number thirteen, going right from twelve to fourteen. Some buildings have no thirteenth floor. Even though these superstitions have no basis in fact, they certainly affect people's actions.

Never write, "I am going to tell you about . . ." or "My paper is about . . ." as an introduction.

Just as there are signs of bad luck, so are there signs of good luck. Some people believe a four-leaf clover will bring luck. Others look to a horseshoe or a rabbit's foot as a symbol of good fortune. Superstitions say that picking up a pin or a penny will mean a bright tomorrow. Perhaps these good luck charms have always been around because they make people feel better about the future.

3. A concluding paragraph

As people become better educated and learn more about the real world, they believe less in superstitions. However, a large number of people in the world will still toss salt over their shoulders or go out of their ways to avoid walking under ladders. Many people cling to superstitions because they're a bit afraid that the beliefs might, indeed, be true.

Look carefully at this essay about superstitions.

Notice that the <u>introduction</u> states the essay's topic. The reader knows the essay will be about people who are superstitious.

Notice the three paragraphs that make up the <u>body</u> of the essay.

Paragraph 1: superstitions about salt

Paragraph 2: superstitions about bad luck signs

Paragraph 3: superstitions about good luck charms

Notice that each of the paragraphs in the body has a topic sentence, a body, and a concluding sentence.

Notice that the last paragraph of the essay serves as a conclusion. It is a summary that restates the topic.

Activity 1

Number your paper from 1 to 8. Write words from the box that would complete each sentence. Some words will be used more than once.

essay	conclusion	three
introduction	paragraphs	five
body		

An essay is a group of (1) _____ dealing with the same subject.

The three parts of the basic essay are the (2) _____ , (3) _____ , and (4) _____ .

The topic of the essay is stated in the (5) _____ .

The topic is supported in the (6) _____ of the essay.

There must be at least (7) _____ supporting paragraphs in a well-developed essay.

A basic essay would be at least (8) _____ paragraphs long.

Activity 2

Number your paper from 1 to 5. Write **P** next to the number if the topic could be covered in just one paragraph. Write **E** if you think the topic requires an essay.

1. How to iron a shirt

2. Ways to enjoy the summer

3. Famous dancers

4. Why I like ice cream

5. All about myself

The Introduction

The introductory paragraph of an essay is different from other paragraphs you have written in these lessons. It doesn't follow the usual pattern. It has its own special pattern and purpose. The purpose is to let the reader know the topic of the essay and to interest the reader in that topic.

The introductory paragraph makes a point. The rest of the essay must support that point.

One sentence in the introduction must clearly state the topic. That sentence is called the **thesis statement.** The thesis statement is the most important sentence in the introduction. Everything else in the essay works to support it. The thesis statement will usually be the last sentence of the introductory paragraph.

The introductory paragraph in the sample essay on superstitions had this thesis statement:

> However, many people believe that these superstitions are true.

That statement lets the reader know what to expect from the rest of the essay. The reader will assume that the essay will support that thesis. In short, the essay will prove the thesis.

Your introductory paragraph must have a thesis statement. The thesis statement expresses the point of the essay. Once you have written a clear thesis statement, you're on your way to a good essay. You know exactly what your point is, and you know your job is to prove that point. Every sentence you write will support the thesis statement.

Read this thesis statement:

> *There are several reasons I like being my age.*

After making that statement, the writer knows exactly what to do. The writer must prove the statement, give the reasons, and discuss them. Each reason will be stated in a topic sentence and developed in a paragraph.

Activity 3

On your own paper, copy the thesis statement from each of the following introductory paragraphs.

1. The turkey is on the table. It's brown and crisp and juicy. The air is filled with smells of cinnamon and cranberries and sage dressing. The family is gathered around the table. Thanksgiving is my favorite holiday.

2. Animals can't talk. They can't tell people what is on their minds. Their eyes, however, show feeling. They seem happy sometimes, and at other times they seem quite sad. There is no doubt in my mind. I believe that animals, just like people, can think.

3. Students come to Ridgeview School every weekday for nine months of the year. They spend six hours of each day in Ridgeview's halls and classrooms. Because students spend so much time there, the school should be a better place. I think Ridgeview School could be improved in several ways.

4. The sun was shining. Soccer fans filled the stands. The two best teams were facing each other on the field. It was going to be an exciting game.

5. Not long ago, most people believed a heavy machine could never stay up in the air. Today, airplanes fly across the country in a few hours. Two brothers, Wilbur and Orville Wright, made the dream of flight come true.

Developing a thesis statement takes a little thought. You must look at the subject from different angles. How do you feel about the subject? Try to look at just one small part of a subject.

Given the broad subject of *movies,* one writer made this thesis statement:

> *The movie* Invasion of the Body Snatchers *is the most frightening film I have ever seen.*

Given the broad subject of *your city,* another writer came up with this thesis statement:

> *My city needs more recreational activities for teenagers.*

Now you try it.

Activity 4

Choose three of the subjects listed below. For each subject you choose, write a sentence that could serve as a thesis statement for an essay.

Automobiles	Rock music
Summer jobs	Food
Friends	Pets
Dislikes	Loneliness

The Body

Compare the body of an essay with the body of a paragraph. There is that number 3 again. Both paragraphs and essays need at least three supporting details.

Body = at least three paragraphs of support for the thesis

Having written the thesis statement, the writer goes on to develop the body of the essay. A strong essay should have a body of at least three paragraphs of support. Look back at the body of the essay on superstitions on pages 178-179.

What is the topic sentence of the first supporting paragraph?

Throughout the ages, there have been superstitions about salt.

What is the topic sentence of the second supporting paragraph?

Even today, many people believe in signs of bad luck.

What is the topic sentence of the third supporting paragraph?

Just as there are signs of bad luck, so are there signs of good luck.

Notice how each of these topic sentences supports the thesis statement that many people today are still superstitious.

Activity 5

Practice writing topic sentences to support a thesis statement. On your paper, write topic sentences that could develop each of the thesis statements below.

1. **Thesis statement**: If I found a magic lamp, I know what my three wishes would be.

   topic sentence 1: I would wish that I would always be healthy.

   topic sentence 2: _____

   topic sentence 3: _____

2. **Thesis statement**: There are several reasons that _____ is my favorite relative.

   topic sentence 1: _____

   topic sentence 2: _____

   topic sentence 3: _____

3. **Thesis statement**: My life would be quite different if I had been born a hundred years ago.

   topic sentence 1: _____

   topic sentence 2: _____

   topic sentence 3: _____

Look at the topic sentences you've written. Think about how you would develop each of them into a supporting paragraph.

The Conclusion

The purpose of the concluding paragraph is to wrap up your essay and let your reader know the end has come. You shouldn't introduce any new ideas in the conclusion. Just summarize the material you've already presented and restate the thesis statement, using different words.

Sometimes in the conclusion a writer will repeat a few key points or give an opinion. The concluding paragraph, like the introductory paragraph, is not developed in the same way as other paragraphs. And it's usually shorter than supporting paragraphs.

Read the concluding paragraph from the essay on superstitions on page 179.

Never write, "That is the end of my paper" or "That is all I have to say" as a conclusion.

> As people become better educated and learn more about the real world, they believe less in superstitions. However, a large number of people in the world will still toss salt over their shoulders or go out of their ways to avoid walking under ladders. Many people cling to superstitions because they're a bit afraid that the beliefs might, indeed, be true.

Notice how the paragraph restates some of the points mentioned in the body of the essay (throwing salt over the shoulder, not walking under ladders). Notice that the last sentence of the conclusion really restates the thesis of the essay, that many people still believe in superstitions.

Activity 6

Read each conclusion below. If it's a good conclusion, write **Good** on your own paper. If it's a bad conclusion, one that introduces another idea, write **Bad**.

1. Indeed, Ridgeview School must improve, or some students will stop going to class there. Changes should be made before it's too late. Next year I'll graduate and go on to college.

2. I'm glad that we celebrate the day the Pilgrims feasted at Plymouth Colony. I'll always look forward to the sights, the smells, and the warm feelings of Thanksgiving.

Writing With Style

It's most important that the introductory paragraph clearly states the main idea of the essay. Both the writer and the reader need to be sure just what point the essay will make. If the writer doesn't have a clear thesis statement, the essay will probably go off the track. It could end up being confusing and rambling.

One of the introductions below has a clear thesis statement. The other introduction would leave a reader (and the writer) wondering what the essay is about. Which introduction do you think is better?

A. I was nervous. I worried about my appearance, and I worried about what I would say. Would they like me? Would I do things correctly? I was right to worry because the first day of my new job was a disaster.

B. I was glad to have a job. They could have hired a lot of different people, but they chose me. My parents were really glad that I was working. It would be great to have some money to spend. Things didn't go very well the first day, but I know I can learn to do the job right. I get a week's vacation after I have worked for six months.

You probably chose introduction A as the better one because it limits the topic and presents a clear thesis statement. Unfortunately, introduction B rambles on about all sorts of things and never really comes to the point. What do you expect the essay following introduction A will be about?

Can you tell exactly what the essay following introduction B will be about?

Vocabulary Builder

Suffixes That Make Verbs
You can use some suffixes to turn nouns and adjectives into verbs. Two common suffixes are *ify* and *ize*. For example, with these suffixes the noun *terror* becomes the verbs *terrify* and *terrorize*. When you add a suffix, the end of the root word often gets cut off. A dictionary will show you how much of the root word to keep.

harmony + ize = <u>harmonize</u>   special + ize = <u>specialize</u>

horror + ify = <u>horrify</u>   note + ify = <u>notify</u>

Choose one of the underlined words above to fill in each blank. Rewrite the sentences on a separate sheet of paper.

1. The singers in the trio tried to _____ .

2. The scary music and the headless ghosts will _____ visitors at the Halloween haunted house.

3. If you move, be sure to_____ the post office.

4. The college student decided to _____ in foreign languages.

Chapter Review

Chapter Summary

☐ An essay is a group of paragraphs dealing with one idea.

☐ An essay has a paragraph of introduction, at least three paragraphs of supporting details (the body), and a concluding paragraph. A basic essay, therefore, is at least five paragraphs long.

☐ The introductory paragraph should have a thesis statement, which is a sentence that tells the main point of the essay.

☐ Everything in the essay should support the thesis statement.

☐ Each supporting paragraph of the body should be developed as you learned in Unit III: with a topic sentence, a body, and a concluding sentence.

☐ The concluding paragraph sums up the main points and restates the thesis, using different words.

Writing Practice

Choose one of the topics below. Write an introductory paragraph for an essay about that topic. The paragraph need only be a few sentences long, but remember your purposes: (1) let the reader know the point of the essay in a thesis statement and (2) get your reader's interest.

A ghost I would like to meet

Dress codes in schools

The best movie I ever saw

Why people should visit my state

Chapter Quiz

A. Identify the three parts of an essay. Explain how each part is used. Write your answers on a separate sheet of paper.

B. Use the following nouns and adjectives in a sentence. Then use the suffixes *ify* and *ize* to create verbs. Use the new verbs in a sentence. Use a dictionary if you need to check spelling. Write your sentences on a separate sheet of paper.

beauty   magnet   summary   memory

C. Choose three of the subjects below. Write a sentence for each that could be used as a thesis statement for an essay. Write your sentences on a separate sheet of paper.

School   Movies

Television   Hobbies

Sports   Drugs

Chapter *14* Writing Your Own Essay

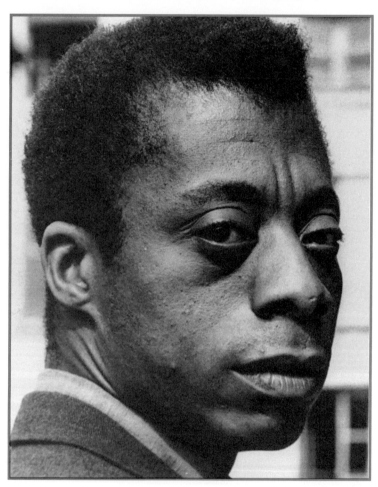

James Baldwin grew up in Harlem during the Depression. The frustration and hopelessness he saw all around him gave him much material for his novels and essays. In books such as The Fire Next Time, *he presents a vivid picture of life as he knew it.*

A personal essay often states the writer's deepest beliefs.

Writers at Work: James Baldwin (1924-1987)

Chapter Learning Objectives

☐ Write a list of possible essay topics.

☐ Write a simple outline for an essay.

☐ Write a short essay from your own outline.

Words to Know

outline   a plan that lays out the main part, but not all the details

rough draft   the first, unpolished copy of a piece of writing

Choosing a Topic

"The hardest part of writing," some people say, "is deciding what to write about." Actually, if you give it a little thought, you'll probably discover a lot of topics for your essays. Here are some suggestions:

Tell what happened

Have any funny, embarrassing, or frightening things happened to you? Perhaps you know about something really interesting or exciting that happened to someone else. Have you had any adventures on a job, at school, or on vacation? Sometimes even small situations can make good essays.

Keep a notebook with a list of possible topics for writing assignments. If you read or hear about something that makes you angry or pleased or confused, write down your feelings on the subject. These could be future essay topics.

Tell about people or places

People you know or people you just know about can be good subjects for essays. Do you know of someone who is an example of courage? Of wisdom? Of artistry? Do you know about someone unusual? Someone who has an unusual career or way of living?

Have you visited, lived in, or read about any interesting places? Even ordinary places like a deserted graveyard or a colorful neighborhood can make wonderful essay topics.

Explain how to do something or how to make something

Just as you wrote how-to paragraphs, so can you write a how-to essay. Do you know how to do something that might interest others? Perhaps you have a hobby that gives you experience and skills you can share. You might tell your readers how to make a dress or how to improve their tennis game.

After doing a little research, you could write a how-to paper on a subject that is new to you. You might tell how a jet engine works or how some of the planets were named.

Give your opinion and persuade others

Everyone has opinions. You can use your ideas to convince your readers just how right your opinions are. Do you have an opinion on problems in the schools, about laws involving teenagers, about the way minority groups are treated in your city? You can find ideas for essays of opinion in the newspapers, on television, and in movies.

Activity 1

Copy the headings below on a separate sheet of paper. Under each heading, write as many essay topics as you can. Write at least three for each heading.

example: *Things that happened*

- Six teenagers were lost in a mountain blizzard.
- A winter storm knocked out electricity for five days.
- I almost drowned when a storm came up on the lake.
- My dog found its way home after being lost for a week.
- I went to a winter survival camp in the mountains.

Now you try it.

1. Things that happened
   a.
   b.
   c.

2. Interesting people
   a.
   b.
   c.

3. Interesting places
   a.
   b.
   c.

4. How to do something

   a.

   b.

   c.

5. Things I believe in and could persuade others to believe

   a.

   b.

   c.

Choose topics that are broad enough

When you choose a topic, remember that you must have enough to say about it. Recall from Chapter 13 that you'll need to write at least three paragraphs in the body of your essay. And remember that each paragraph will discuss a different point. As you consider a topic, ask yourself, "Can I think of three important points about this topic?"

If you can't think of three important points, choose another topic.

Don't choose a topic that is too broad

Very often, people choose topics that are too big. Don't pick a topic so broad you can't cover it in a basic essay. For example, you wouldn't want to write one short essay on "Trees of America." The topic is so big that all you would be able to do is list the trees. You couldn't possibly discuss all the different kinds of trees, their uses, where they grow, how they are cared for, and so on. But when you limit your topic to "How Americans Depend on Trees," you could easily write a paper that makes a point and is of the right length.

Activity 2

Number your paper from 1 to 10. Read each suggested essay topic and decide if it's suitable for a short essay. Write *too limited*, *too broad*, or *good* next to each number. (Hint: Five of the listings would be good essay topics.)

1. My plan to make a million dollars g d
2. Equal rights for all Americans b
3. The history of the state of New Jersey b
4. My favorite Ohio vacation spot G
5. How to make shrimp and avocado salad L
6. My eccentric Uncle Harvey G
7. Romance novels B
8. Pollution B
9. The ugliest place I have ever been G
10. One day at the mall G

Planning Your Essay

Some people think the quickest, easiest way to get an essay written is to just start writing. They ask, "Why waste time outlining my plans?" They're wrong. If you begin writing without planning ahead, you may find yourself rambling. You may even get lost halfway through the essay. You may find yourself confused. And if you're confused, your reader will surely be!

At this point, you may get discouraged and give up. But why let that happen? Give yourself a helping hand. It doesn't take that long to plan your essay in a simple **outline.**

And once that outline is complete, the task of writing the essay becomes quite manageable, even enjoyable! After all, writing can be a pleasurable, exciting activity.

Now to plan an essay, just fill in the basic essay diagram:

1. Introduction

Write your thesis statement. (Be sure you write a complete sentence.)

There are several reasons

I like being my age

2. Supporting paragraph 1

Write the topic sentence presenting your first idea of support. (Write a complete sentence.)

At the age of 16 I can

learn to drive a car

    Summarize detail 1 to support topic sentence.

    Summarize detail 2 to support topic sentence.

    Summarize detail 3 to support topic sentence.

3. Supporting paragraph 2

Write the topic sentence presenting your second idea of support. (Write a complete sentence.)

    Summarize detail 1 to support topic sentence.

    Summarize detail 2 to support topic sentence.

    Summarize detail 3 to support topic sentence.

4. Supporting paragraph 3

Write the topic sentence presenting your third idea of support. (Write a complete sentence.)

Summarize detail 1 to support topic sentence.

Summarize detail 2 to support topic sentence.

Summarize detail 3 to support topic sentence.

5. Conclusion

You can develop the conclusion as you write your essay.

Use this outlining guide when you plan an essay. You'll find that once it's completed, the hardest part of your job is over.

Read the following example of an essay outline.

Topic: Some ways to spend a rainy Sunday afternoon

1. Introduction

Thesis statement:

There are several ways to put a rainy Sunday afternoon to good use.

2. Supporting paragraph 1

Most people's homes could use some cleaning.

- Clean closets. (Give old clothes to the needy.)
- Wash the inside windows so they sparkle when the sun shines.
- Clean out the refrigerator.
- Clean the basement or the attic.

Do you have any good ideas for a rainy Sunday? Maybe that's an essay topic for you.

3. Supporting paragraph 2

There might be an old friend or a distant relative who would be surprised and pleased by a phone call or letter.

- Call up someone who was a friend long ago.
- Write letters to relatives.
- Call or visit an elderly person who might be lonely.
- Write thank-you notes, birthday cards, or get well wishes.

4. Supporting paragraph 3

- A lazy, rainy Sunday is a perfect time to curl up and read.
- Visit a far-off land just by opening a novel.
- Read a book that teaches something new.
- Spend a few hours reading the Sunday paper.
- Do the crossword puzzle and read sections you normally skip.

5. Conclusion

Activity 3

Now it's time to really get writing! You'll make your own outline for a basic essay.

First, choose a topic
Look back at the list of topics you wrote in Activity 1. You might want to use one of them. You might also choose from the topics listed on the next page. Choose something that interests you, and make sure it's neither too broad nor too limited.

Suggested topics:

- The great (or terrible) part about having a brother (or sister)
- The great (or terrible) part about being an only child
- What I hope to be doing when I'm sixty
- My unusual family
- Mistakes parents often make
- Some very effective TV commercials
- A terrifying airplane flight
- A day I would like to forget
- How to prevent bicycle accidents

Write your topic at the top of your paper.

Now complete the planning outline following the diagram on pages 198–199.

Writing Your Complete Essay

Congratulations! If you've gotten this far, it means you have completed the planning outline for your essay. The hardest work is done. Now, with that planning outline in hand, it's time to write the complete essay.

Activity 4

Using your planning outline from Activity 3, write your own essay.

Hints:

Introduction: You'll need to write two or three sentences that lead up to your thesis statement. You might try a brief description or story that leads to the thesis.

> example:
>
> It was raining hard. The clouds were so thick, it was almost like night at midday. It was Sunday, I was home alone with nothing to do, and I was bored. However, I soon discovered that there are ways to put a rainy Sunday to good use.

Do you recognize the thesis statement from the sample planning outline at the end of the introduction?

Supporting paragraphs: As you begin writing your supporting paragraphs, recall everything you learned in Units II and III about writing good paragraphs. You can use examples for support. You can use facts and figures. You can use details. Just take it one paragraph at a time and always use your planning outline as your guide. This approach will ensure that you don't become confused and that your last paragraph is as strong as your first paragraph.

If you begin to have trouble, return to Units II and III and give yourself a quick review. Then go on. It's important to keep writing and thinking. You have all the tools you really need. So just keep on using what you already know.

Here is an example of a completed supporting paragraph developed from the sample planning outline:

> Like most people, I live in a house that could always use a Sunday's worth of cleaning. My

closets were bulging with clothes I never wore. There were needy people who could use those old clothes. As I watched the rain, I realized that my windows as well as my closets needed attention. It was raining that Sunday, but one day the sun would shine in on all that dirt. Last of all, I turned to a really big job, the attic. Cleaning the attic was a dusty, dirty chore, but it meant finding wonderful, old treasures. I used that rainy Sunday to make my house sparkle.

Conclusion: You'll need to write a short paragraph of conclusion. Your job here is to summarize your points and let the reader know your paper has come to an end. You'll also restate your thesis using different words.

You can restate main points:

Cleaning the house, renewing old friendships, and catching up on reading are all good ways to spend time. A rainy Sunday became a chance to do things that there never before seemed time to do.

You can find a lesson in what you have said:

Don't let time pass by without making it count. I found that a rainy Sunday afternoon doesn't have to be boring at all. Because I used my time wisely, that Sunday turned out to be a most worthwhile day.

With the conclusion comes the end of the **rough draft** of your essay. If you followed the planning outline, you should have written a well organized, easy-to-follow essay that presents a point and supports it. You should feel your essay is clear and well developed. Your readers should find your paper easy to read and easy to understand.

Writing With Style

The two paragraphs below could both serve as supporting paragraphs in an essay with the following thesis statement:

There are often some interesting characters in a bus station.

On your own paper, answer the questions below.

A. While I waited for my cousin to arrive on a bus from Kansas, I saw the strangest family. There were four of them—a man, a woman, and two little girls. They all wore black from head to toe. The man, a tall, thin fellow, wore a wide-brimmed, black hat. The woman and the girls wore long, black capes with tight-fitting hoods. Not only was their clothing strange, but their faces were, too. Not one of them smiled the whole hour I waited. They stood like statues, looking grim and serious. When the loudspeaker announced that the next bus to Massachusetts was leaving, the strange family picked up their bags. Without a word, they headed for the station exit.

B. While I waited for my cousin to arrive on a bus from Kansas, I saw the strangest family. There were four of them. There was a man. There was a woman. There were two little girls. They all wore black. They wore strange clothing. They looked very serious. They stood very still. I had to wait at the bus station for my cousin because my dad had to work. When the loudspeaker announced the next bus, the strange family left.

You probably chose paragraph A as the better paragraph, but why?

1. Which paragraph uses description and detail?

2. Can you find any similes in paragraphs A or B?

3. Are sentences of varying complexity and length?

4. Are there any sentences that don't stick to the topic?

Vocabulary Builder

Have Some Fun with Illustrated Words
Show that you understand what words mean. On your own
paper, write a synonym for each of the words below. Then
either draw a picture that illustrates the meaning of the word
or cut out a picture from a newspaper or magazine.
Advertisements will be a good source of pictures.

1. scowl

2. blissful

3. forlorn

4. daring

5. hilarious

6. gigantic

7. boulevard

8. banquet

9. delicate

10. cinema

Chapter Review

Chapter Summary

☐ Choose a clear essay topic that is neither too broad nor too limited.

☐ Understand your own purpose: do you intend to tell what happened, tell about a person or a place, explain how to do something, or persuade your reader that your opinion is correct?

☐ Always make a planning outline before you write your essay.

☐ Take one paragraph at a time, and follow your planning outline to write a clear, well-organized essay.

Writing Practice

An essay should have a title. The title should be brief. It should suggest your topic but not tell everything about it. It's important that your title be correctly written. Follow these rules:

1. Always capitalize the first and last words in the title.

2. Capitalize all important words (nouns, pronouns, verbs, adjectives, adverbs, and all prepositions of more than four letters).

3. Do not use a period after a title.

4. Do not put the title in quotation marks.

Write three possible titles for your essay from Activity 4. Circle the title you like best.

Chapter Quiz

From each of the following groups, choose the one item that could be used as a topic for a whole essay. Then, indented under it, list the other items as possible paragraph topics.

> example: dresses oddly, likes animals better than people, my unusual sister, keeps strange hours, laughs more than anyone I know

> my unusual sister
>   dresses oddly
>   likes animals better than people
>   keeps strange hours
>   laughs more than anyone I know

1. Amelia Earhart, Charles Lindbergh, pioneers in aviation, Orville and Wilbur Wright

2. mowing lawns, babysitting, working at fast food restaurants, ways for teenagers to make money, walking dogs

3. watch too much television, things children do to annoy their parents, stay out late, argue about rules, eat junk food

4. a perfect date, kind and considerate, good-looking, good sense of humor

5. taking the boat out from the dock, fishing all day, noticing storm clouds rising, being unable to get back to shore as the waves came up, having the coast guard boat rescue us, our adventure on the lake

Chapter 15 Writing Better Essays

Joan Didion is a widely read essayist as well as a best-selling novelist. Slouching Towards Bethlehem, *one collection of her essays, paints a moving portrait of American life in the 1960s. Her work points out how difficult it is to make wise choices in a complex society.* A Book of Common Prayer *is one of her widely read novels.*

Essays reflect personal opinion as well as objective reality.

Writers at Work: Joan Didion (1934-   )

Chapter Learning Objectives

☐ Proofread and edit the rough draft of an essay.

☐ Define and identify in context first-person, second-person, and third-person points of view.

☐ Identify past and present verb tenses.

☐ Identify transitional words that link paragraphs.

☐ Write a final copy of an essay.

Words to Know

proofread   to read over a piece of writing to find and mark any mistakes in mechanics

mechanics   the spelling and punctuation of a piece of writing

edit   to prepare a piece of writing for the final copy by finding and correcting any mistakes in facts, point of view, and style

content   the ideas in a piece of writing

narrator   the one telling the details

personal   of one's own; for example, a *personal* experience is a person's own experience

point of view   the eyes through which something is written; the way in which something is viewed

first person   the personal point of view; uses the pronoun *I*

third person   the point of view of a narrator who stays outside the writing and tells about the subject; uses the pronouns *he, she,* and *they*

second person   the point of view of a narrator who speaks to the reader; uses the pronoun *you*

The Final Copy

Before you write the final copy of your essay, you should **proofread** and **edit** your rough draft. Remember, your goal in writing is to get your ideas across to your reader as clearly as possible. Check for misspelled words, missing punctuation, and unrelated details in your paper. They will make your paper hard to read and understand. Your ideas won't be clear. In this chapter, you'll write the final copy of the essay you began in Chapter 14. Make good use of the hints in this chapter. Then that final copy should be a clear, well-developed piece of writing.

The final copy is the last step in writing your essay. Before you write it, you should carefully proofread your rough draft and correct any errors in punctuation and spelling (**mechanics**). Then, check for errors in factual material and style. This process is called editing. This is a time to look for any errors in grammar (such as run-on sentences, sentence fragments, and mistakes in subject-verb agreement).

In addition, the edit stage is a time to decide if you wrote everything the best way you could. Have you said everything you wanted to say? Have you tried to keep your reader in mind? Did you enjoy yourself? If not, why not? What was hard? What will you do differently the next time? See how you feel at this point, reading over your essay. If you're feeling like "Maybe it could've been better," remember it's not too late. You still have time to make changes in the final draft of your essay.

Use the following checklist to edit your paper.

<u>Check content:</u>

Introduction:

☐ Does the essay have a thesis sentence?

☐ Is the thesis sentence clear?

Supporting paragraphs:

☐ Are there at least three supporting paragraphs?

☐ Is there a topic sentence in each supporting paragraph?

☐ Does each sentence in the paragraph support that topic sentence?

☐ Are there enough (at least three) sentences of detail in each paragraph?

☐ Are there any sentences that don't relate to the topic sentence and should be removed?

☐ Are some transitional words used?

Conclusion:

☐ Does the essay have a conclusion?

☐ Does the conclusion use different words to restate the thesis?

<u>Check mechanics:</u>

☐ spelling   ☐ capitalization

☐ apostrophes in contractions and possessives

☐ run-on sentences

☐ fragments   ☐ subject-verb agreement

☐ commas in compound sentences

☐ commas in complex sentences

☐ sentence end marks

Read this example of an edited paragraph.

Why was the sentence about the albatross removed from the paragraph?

The penguin is an unusu*a*el bird from the icy antarctic. Some people say penguins look like fat little men wearing tuxedos. Penguins stand up on short legs⊙They walk with a waddle. Although they are birds they can't fly. ~~A bird called the Albatross lives in the antarctic two.~~ Their strange walk and unusu*a*el appearance make penguins quite amusing creatures.

Now you try it.

Activity 1

Proofread the following paragraph. On a separate sheet of paper, list any changes and corrections you feel are necessary. Look for spelling errors, missing commas, capitalization errors, sentence fragments, and sentences that don't belong in the paragraph.

You might want to have someone else check over your rough draft, too. Another reader might catch some errors that you missed.

The old house on elm street is most certainly haunted. When the moon is full, strange noises come from the top floor of the house. On such a night neighbors have heard sad cries and terribel moans. Dim lights have flickered on and off in upstairs rooms and the front door has been known to swing open suddenly. Then closed again. The old house is probably worth a lot of money. Strangers to the neighborhood say that the lights and noises are just the people who live their playing tricks. That cant be the case. No one has lived in the old house for over thirty years.

Activity 2

At this point, proofread the essay you wrote for Activity 4, Chapter 14. Use the editing checklist provided in this chapter. Take your time. You can catch errors only by reading slowly and carefully. Sometimes it helps to read your essay aloud.

Make any necessary corrections on your rough draft, but don't recopy your essay until the end of this chapter.

Checking Point of View

What is the major difference between the following two paragraphs?

A. I love to go to the beach. I love the smell of the salt water and the sound of the waves breaking on the shore. It makes me feel good to watch children running and laughing with the fresh wind blowing in their hair. Food tastes especially good at the beach. I sleep better at night at the beach. Most of all, I love to look at the ocean stretched as far westward as I can see. The ocean makes this world seem so big and mysterious and exciting.

B. The beach is a wonderful place. The air smells of salt water, and the waves make a gentle sound as they break on the shore. Children run and laugh, and the fresh wind blows in their hair. A day at the beach can make a person hungry and tired, ready to eat well and to sleep well. The great ocean stretches far, far westward. It takes a big, mysterious world to hold such an ocean.

First-person point of view

You probably noticed paragraph A uses the word *I* many times. The **narrator** is a part of the essay. The essay is written from a **personal** point of view. Writing that uses the pronoun *I*, with the narrator appearing in the essay, is written from the first-person point of view. The **point of view** is the way the writer sees things.

The "I" in a first-person essay can really be you, the writer. The narrator in paragraph A was probably the writer of the essay describing a personal experience. But the I can also be imaginary. If you're writing a fictional account, you might still choose to tell the story in the first person. For example, *I will never forget the night I found the space creatures in my garage.* Using the first person is a good way to make a fictional event seem more believable.

Third-person point of view

Paragraph B is a less personal description of the beach. The beach is not seen through one person's eyes; rather, it is described by a narrator who stays out of the account. This is called the third-person point of view. When the third-person point of view is used, the account is told by a narrator who sees, hears, and knows everything. The pronouns *they, he,* and *she* are used. When you write, you should be aware of the point of view you're using.

Activity 3

Number your paper from 1 to 5. Tell whether each sentence below is written from the first-person point of view or the third-person point of view.

1. I can't remember a day when my little brother didn't get into some kind of trouble.
2. Some people just can't get along with their brothers and sisters.
3. Kirk Gibson is becoming a baseball legend.
4. I love to hear Aretha Franklin sing.
5. A red car sped down Main Street and raced around the corner.

Second-person point of view

There is also a second-person point of view. The second person point of view uses the pronoun *you* in the essay. When you use the second-person point of view, you talk directly to the reader. The only time the second-person point of view should be used is in a how-to essay, one that gives directions or instructions.

Correct:

Building a children's playhouse is not a difficult task. You must first gather the necessary tools for the job. You will probably need a hammer, a saw, some screwdrivers, and some screws and nails. A trip to the local lumberyard should provide you with the wood for the house.

The second-person point of view was used correctly in the paragraph above because the writer was giving directions to the reader. The writer intended to talk directly to the reader. However, the use of the second-person point of view in the next paragraph is not correct.

Incorrect:

You never saw anything funnier than the monkeys in the zoo. They are very much like human beings. They watch you out of wise, little eyes. If you offer them a peanut, they will often take the food with their little humanlike hands. You will love the way the mother monkeys hug and cuddle their babies. Sometimes the monkeys seem so human, it almost makes you shiver.

The pronoun *you* should not be used in the paragraph on monkeys. The reader wasn't at the zoo. The reader didn't offer the monkeys a peanut. The writer does not know that the humanlike monkeys make the reader shiver. The pronoun *you* is incorrectly used.

The paragraph reads much better written in the third person:

> The monkeys in the zoo are very much like human beings. They watch the zoo visitors out of wise, little eyes. If a person offers a peanut, a monkey will often take the food with its little humanlike hands. The mother monkeys hug and cuddle their babies much as human mothers do. Sometimes the monkeys seem so human that it's almost frightening.

Activity 4

Rewrite the following items on your own paper. Change from the second-person point of view to the first- or third-person point of view.

example:

People should never drive a car after drinking alcohol. You could cause a terrible accident.

rewritten:

People should never drive a car after drinking alcohol. They could cause terrible accidents.

1. The cafeteria serves surprisingly good food. You can get homemade soups and delicious, freshly baked pies.

2. The rattlesnake is a dangerous snake. You can die from its bite.

3. Teenagers should try to understand their parents. You should give your parents a chance to explain their feelings.

4. My grandmother lives in a cozy apartment. You can sip tea from her beautiful china cups while you watch the rain through white lace curtains.

5. Some people are quite cruel to animals. I think you should realize that animals have feelings.

Activity 5

Take out the essay you edited in Activity 2. Read it over, checking point of view. Ask yourself the following questions:

- Is this a how-to essay? If not, is it written from the first- or third-person point of view?

- If it is a how-to essay, have I used the second-person point of view?

Checking Verb Tense

What is the major difference between the following two paragraphs?

A. The sun set, and I began my night in the wilderness. I snuggled down in my sleeping bag and watched the stars twinkle in the black sky. Then I heard the long howl of a wolf somewhere in the darkness. I pulled the sleeping bag around my head. It was going to be a long night.

B. The sun sets, and I begin my night in the wilderness. I snuggle down in my sleeping bag and watch the stars twinkle in the black sky. Then I hear the long howl of a wolf somewhere in the darkness. I pull the sleeping bag around my head. It's going to be a long night.

*What do you think **future tense** means?*
This is a sentence written in the future tense:
I will probably buy a new car.
Can you write an example of a sentence written in the future tense?

Paragraph A is written in the past tense. It's describing something that happened in the past. Past-tense verbs like snuggled, watched, and heard are used. The writer uses past-tense verbs throughout the paragraph.

Paragraph B is written in the present tense. It's describing something as it happens. Present-tense verbs like snuggle, watch, and hear are used. The writer uses present-tense verbs throughout the paragraph.

You should avoid shifting tenses within an essay. Decide if you will write in the past tense or present tense, and then stick to that choice.

Notice that the paragraph below changes verb tenses:

> The elevator *stopped* between the second and third floors. The three people inside the elevator *looked* worried. One man <u>pushes</u> the buttons nervously. The other man <u>tries</u> to open the elevator door. The woman on the elevator *banged* on the door. Then the trapped trio *yelled* for help.

The verbs in italic print are past-tense verbs. The underlined verbs are present-tense verbs. All the verbs should have been in either past tense or present tense.

Activity 6

Rewrite the paragraph above so that all the verbs are in either past or present tense.

Activity 7

Read the rough draft of your essay. Correct any errors in verb tense. Ask yourself the following questions:

- Is the essay written in the past or present tense?

- Is that verb tense used consistently throughout the essay?

Linking Paragraphs with Transitional Words

You have already learned how transitional words link sentences within a paragraph. You should also use transitional words to show the links between your paragraphs. For example, transitional words that show time can guide your reader through your essay. Read the following example:

The parade began early in the morning. The air was still cool, and the marchers were in good spirits. The bands played loudly, and the baton twirlers threw their batons high into the air. The flowers on the horse-drawn floats were fresh and colorful. It was a beautiful sight.

Several hours later, the mood of the parade changed. The temperature soared to ninety-eight degrees, and the marchers were hot! The band members had unbuttoned their high collars, and the dancers were dragging their feet. The flowers on the floats had wilted and faded. Even the horses seemed hot, tired, and in need of water. Luckily, the end of the parade route was near.

The transitional words (in bold print) show the relationship between the second paragraph and the first. They help the reader recognize the passage of time. Such transitional words are often used at the beginning of a paragraph.

Review the transitional words listed in Chapter 8. The same transitional words can be used at the beginning of paragraphs to link the paragraphs themselves.

Notice in the following paragraphs how transition takes the reader from one idea to the next:

> The mountain lion is a large, wild animal. It belongs to the cat family. Throughout the history of the Americas, the mountain lion has given people cause for alarm.
>
> **For example,** the early settlers of North America hated to hear the wail of the mountain lion. They thought it sounded like a person in terrible pain. They knew that cry meant the lion was hunting. They knew their sheep, their calves, and their ponies were not safe.

When you write, you already know the steps you will be taking to develop your ideas. Your reader though, does not have your writing outline in front of him. If your writing is not clear, you will confuse your reader.

Use transitional words to guide your reader. That way he will not become confused by your writing.

Transitional words can also cue your reader that the conclusion has come. You might begin a concluding paragraph with a transitional expression such as, "In conclusion," "Thus," or "Therefore."

Transitions act as bridges between ideas. Use them to bridge the ideas between sentences, and then between whole paragraphs.

Activity 8

Read the rough draft of your essay. Have you used any transitional words or phrases to begin your paragraphs? Try adding some transitions to show connections between paragraphs.

Writing With Style

Writing a rough draft and then a final copy is a necessary part of developing your essay. Don't try to save time by skipping a step in the essay-writing process.

The second copy is bound to be more polished than the first copy. Even the most experienced writers find mistakes in their first drafts.

Paragraph A below is a first draft. Paragraph B is a final copy. What changes did the writer make?

A. The planet mars is more like earth than any other planet. Mars has polar caps that probably are of ice and snow. The caps get larger in the winter and slowly melt away in the summer. Scientists thinks that Mars has an atmosphere. It is denser than Earth's atmosphere. The planet Venus has an atmosphere too. During the day, the surface of Mars would be comfortably warm but at night it became bitterly cold. There are no oceans! There is much less water on Mars than on Earth. The humidity of Mars is about the same as that of a desert on Earth. Living beings exactly like humans couldn't live on Mars. However, scientist believe there is plant life on the planet.

B. The planet Mars is more like the Earth than any other planet. Like the Earth, Mars has polar caps that probably are of ice and snow. Those caps get larger in the winter and slowly melt away in the summer. Scientists think that Mars has an atmosphere. However, that atmosphere is denser than the Earth's. During the day, the surface of Mars would be comfortably warm, but at night it becomes bitterly cold. There are no oceans on Mars. In fact, there is much less water on Mars than on Earth. The humidity of Mars is about the same as that of a desert on Earth. Although living beings exactly like humans couldn't live on Mars, scientists believe there is plant life on the planet.

Vocabulary Builder

Commonly Confused Words

Writers often confuse certain words because those words look or sound so much alike. When you use these words in your writing, be careful. Make sure you are writing the word you mean.

Decide which word in each pair below would properly complete each sentence. Use a dictionary if you need help deciding which word is correct. Write your answers on a separate sheet of paper.

1. Everyone came to the meeting (except, accept) Jill.

2. The bus (past, passed) him by without stopping.

3. I really (wonder, wander) if the sun will ever shine again.

4. Which team do you think will (loose, lose) Saturday's game?

5. Mr. Clemson (quiet, quite, quit) his job as a chicken plucker.

6. He loves to eat chocolate-covered bananas for (desert, dessert).

7. He can eat more chocolate-covered bananas (then, than) anyone I know.

8. She broke the (led, lead) on her pencil by pressing too hard.

9. The teacher insisted on Sylvia's (presence, presents) in English class.

10. (They're, Their, There) tickets were being held at the box office.

Chapter Review

Chapter Summary

- ☐ Use the checklist on pages 210–211 to edit your essays. Always check content and mechanics.

- ☐ An essay written from the first-person point of view uses the pronoun *I*. It's a personal account with the narrator appearing in the essay.

- ☐ An essay written from the third-person point of view uses pronouns like *he, she,* and *they.* The narrator is not directly inside the essay but tells about the subject.

- ☐ An essay written from the second-person point of view uses the pronoun *you.* The narrator talks directly to the reader. The second-person point of view is usually only used in how-to essays.

- ☐ As a writer, be aware of the verb tense you're using.

- ☐ Is your essay written in the past tense or in the present tense?

- ☐ Transitional words link paragraphs and make the relationships between paragraphs clear.

Writing Practice

It's time to write the final copy of your essay. You should now have an edited rough draft of the essay. Copy that essay over. Be sure to include any changes and corrections. Write the title of your essay at the top of the first page. If you followed all the steps for a well-developed essay then your essay is something you can be proud of.

Chapter Quiz

A. <u>Point of View:</u> Identify the point of view in each of the following sentences. (Is it first person, second person, or third person?)

> example: I will never forget the day I cut my sister's hair. = first person

1. I wanted to earn enough money to buy that red sports car.

2. The dancers came out onto the stage.

3. As Sam watched the rain fall, he could feel tears running down his face.

4. When training your dog, you must speak firmly and clearly.

5. I sat down in the last row of the movie theater.

B. <u>Verb Tense:</u> Rewrite each of the following sentences so that all verbs within each sentence match (are either past or present tense). The verbs have been <u>underlined</u> for you.

> example: *Horse racing <u>is</u> one of the oldest sports and <u>dated</u> back to the early days of Greece and Rome.*
>
> corrected: *Horse racing is one of the oldest sports and dates back to the early days of Greece and Rome.*

1. Mrs. Williams <u>called</u> her son Johnny, and Johnny <u>comes</u> *came* running home.

2. Because the party <u>was</u> boring, Julio and his friends <u>decide</u> to leave.

3. The monkey <u>screams</u> *cried* and <u>shook</u> the bars of its cage.

4. When the sun <u>shines</u>, people <u>smiled</u> and <u>was</u> happy.

5. The crowd <u>stood</u>, <u>cheered</u>, and then <u>leaves</u> the stands.

Unit Review

A. Write your answers to the following questions in complete sentences on your own paper.

1. How are an essay and a paragraph alike?

2. What is the thesis statement of an essay?

3. What is the difference between a thesis statement and a topic sentence?

B. Write one possible essay topic from each of the following categories. (Please write your topics in sentence form.)

example: Things that happened: A strange guest came for a week-long visit.

1. Things that happened

2. Interesting people

3. How to do something

4. My opinion about

C. For each sentence below, write the letters of all descriptions that apply.

a. past tense   d. second person

b. present tense   e. third person

c. first person   f. contains transitional words

example: *An hour later, the rooster flew to the top of the barn and crowed loudly.*   a, e, f

1. I want to ask my boss for a raise, but I'm afraid.

2. Father blamed the youngest child for the broken window.

Unit Five

Practical Writing

Virginia Woolf was a novelist, essayist, and letter writer. Much of her work is based on her own life experience. Her novel To The Lighthouse *reflects her own childhood.* Three Guineas *and* A Room of One's Own *reflect her strong interest in feminism. Most of her novels are set in London, where she lived and worked most of her life.*

A good writer observes the world with a close eye for details.

Writers at Work: Virginia Woolf (1882-1941)

Chapter Learning Objectives

☐ Write a correct, interesting friendly letter.

☐ Properly address an envelope.

☐ Write a formal business letter.

Words to Know

format   the plan, style, or layout of something

abbreviation   a shortened form of a word

zip code   a postal code designed to speed up mail service by assigning special numbers to each area of the country

Writing a Friendly Letter

Perhaps you have friends or relatives who live far away. One way to keep in touch with them is by writing a letter. A friendly letter is one written to someone you know. A friendly letter does the following things:

1. lets someone know you're thinking of him or her

2. allows you to tell the person what has been happening to you

3. lets the person know that you would like to hear from him or her, too

As with any other form of writing, a letter should express your thoughts clearly to your reader.

Write it correctly!
People expect letters to be written in a certain way. Even friendly letters have a proper **format** that should be followed.

The Parts of a Friendly Letter

215 S. E. Forty-ninth Street
Portland, OR 97215
January 8, 1989

} heading

} salutation

Dear Terry,

Let your friends know you're thinking of them.

I hope you're happy with your new job in California. You certainly sounded excited in your last letter. We all miss you here, but we're glad you like your new home.

Tell them what has been happening to you.

I have some news for you. I finally got my driver's license. Yes, I know I had to take that test five times, but I passed it last week. Those driving lessons that you suggested really paid off. Believe it or not, I can even back out of the driveway without hitting anything. When you come for a visit, I'll take you for a ride.

} body

I'm still working at the Burger Barn. Last week they made all the employees dress up in animal costumes. Did I ever feel silly! You should've seen me dressed up like a chicken.

Encourage them to write.

I would love to hear all about your new home and your new job. Have you met any interesting people? Don't forget to write.

Your friend,

Carol

} closing

} signature

When you look at the sample of the friendly letter, you can see it has five parts.

1. The Heading

The heading tells where you are and when you're writing. It usually appears in the upper right corner of the page and has three lines. The first two lines give your address, and the third line gives the date. Notice correct capitalization and punctuation in the sample.

Sometimes, if your letter is very informal, you can leave off the address in the heading. Always be sure, however, to include the date.

2. The Salutation

The salutation is a greeting. It begins on the left side of the paper. In a friendly letter, the salutation is followed by a comma. Be sure to capitalize the first letter of the salutation.

"Dear _____," is the most common greeting. However, in a friendly letter, you can use any greeting you wish (for example, "My dearest Susan," or "Hi, Jill,").

3. The Body

In this part of the letter you talk to your friend. Remember your paragraphing skills here. Just like any other time, you should be writing in good paragraphs.

4. The Closing

The closing is the way you sign off. It's written in the middle of the page below the body of your letter. It begins with a capital letter and is followed by a comma. You may use any closing you like in a friendly letter. These are some commonly used closings:

Sincerely,	Love,
Sincerely yours,	As always,
Yours truly,	Your friend,

5. The Signature

The signature ends your letter. Use only your first name if it is a letter to a very close friend. Otherwise, it is best to write both your first and last names so there is no question about who wrote the letter.

Activity 1

Each of the following pairs shows the same part of a friendly letter. One item has been written correctly. The other item has errors. On your paper, write the letter of the correct item.

---

1. a. 555 Elm Street
   Lakeview, WA 74003
   August 1, 1989

   b. 555 Elm Street
   Lakeview WA 74003
   August 1 1989

2. a. Sincerely yours,
   Lynn

   b. sincerely yours!
   Lynn

3. a. dear Uncle Elmer:

   b. Dear Uncle Elmer,

4. a. February 5, 1989
   4141 Black Hawk Drive
   Sunnyside, AZ 49201

   b. 4141 Black Hawk Drive
   Sunnyside, AZ 49201
   February 5, 1989

5. a. Yours truly,
   Jan

   b. Yours Truly, Jan

Activity 2

Show that you know the format of a friendly letter. Pretend you're writing a letter to Aunt Ruth. On a blank piece of paper write the following items:

1. the heading

2. the salutation

3. the body (You don't have to write the letter now. Just draw lines to represent the body.)

4. the closing

5. the signature

Challenge

Actually write the body of the letter to Aunt Ruth. Pretend that you just started a new job at the Wonderworld Amusement Park. Tell her about the things you do, an interesting person you work with, and how you like your job. Be sure to write in paragraphs, and follow the format of the sample letter.

Writing a Business Letter

Have you ever ordered something through the mail?

Have you ever written to request information (perhaps for a school report)?

You will probably do business by mail many times. Perhaps you'll order a product or complain about a product to a manufacturer. Perhaps you'll write to a business as a part of your job or write to request information.

A business letter should be businesslike. That means it should be neat and typed if possible. A business letter is formal and so it must follow a specific format.

When writing a business letter, follow these guidelines:

1. Use standard-sized (8 1/2" by 11") paper.

2. Type the letter if possible (if not possible, write neatly in blue or black ink).

3. Write on only one side of the paper.

4. Follow the format shown.

The Six Parts of a Business Letter

heading {

215 Oakwood Avenue
Portland, OR 97215
January 8, 1989

inside address {

The Athlete's Closet
444 Westlake Drive
Mytown, PA 67221

salutation {

Dear Sir or Madam:

body {

   I need some information on your new Waterfun skin diving equipment. Please send me the Spring 1989 Waterfun catalog.

   I am enclosing a money order for $3.75 to cover the cost of the catalog ($3.00) and postage ($.75).

closing {

Sincerely,

Christine Collins

signature {

Christine Collins

A business letter can also be done in block style as shown below. Use block style only when the letter is typed. In block style, all parts of the business letter begin at the left margin. The paragraphs aren't indented. There is a double space between paragraphs.

Block Style Business Letter

The Athlete's Closet
444 Westlake Drive
Mytown, PA 67221
January 15, 1989

Ms. Christine Collins
215 Oakwood Avenue
Portland, OR 97215

Dear Ms. Collins:

We're happy to send you the Spring 1989 Waterfun catalog. We're also enclosing an order blank so you can order more products.

You will also be receiving, free of charge, a copy of the new book for skin divers called *Underwater Adventures*. Enjoy the book and remember us when you need equipment.

Sincerely,

Sonia Miller

Sonia Miller
Sales Manager
SM:mj

The salutation of a business letter includes the title and the last name of the person to whom you're writing. It's followed by a colon. Here are some examples:

Dear Mr. West:

Dear Ms. Johnson:

If the name of the person or persons to whom you're writing are unknown, you have several choices. Here are some examples:

Dear Sir:

Dear Madam:

Gentlemen:

Ladies:

Dear Sir or Madam:

To whom it may concern:

Another choice is to use the person's title as in this example:

Dear Sales Manager:

Notice that the salutation in a business letter is followed by a colon (:).

The signature in a business letter is usually typed four spaces below the closing. This method leaves room for a written signature directly under the closing. The signature should always be written by hand, even in a typed letter. Don't use a title (Mr., Ms., Mrs.) in a signature.

Here is an example:

Yours truly,

Barbara Bixley

Barbara Bixley

You will notice some added letters at the bottom of the sample business letter from Sonia Miller. The letters read SM:mj. Notations like these are used when the letter is typed by someone other than the writer. In this case Sonia Miller (SM) had her secretary, Mark Jones (mj), type the letter.

Activity 3

Use the second sample business letter (the block style sample on page 235) to answer these questions. The first one has been done for you as an example.

1. Who wrote the letter? Sonia Miller

2. What is the name of her company?

3. To whom was the letter written?

4. When was the letter written?

5. What was the inside address?

6. What closing was used?

7. What position does the letter writer have with the company?

8. Did the letter writer type her own letter?

Activity 4

Read the advertisement below. Then write a business letter ordering an item described in the ad.

Pro Baseball Caps
For a limited time only, you can order from our large selection of official professional baseball caps. We have colorful, high-quality caps at low, low prices.

The All-Wool Pro Model	**Available for**
Sizes 6 3/8, 7, 7 1/2, 7 3/4	Los Angeles Dodgers
$12.98	Oakland A's
or	Detroit Tigers
The Cotton Pro	San Francisco Giants
Sizes Small, Medium, Large	Cleveland Indians
$9.98	Boston Red Sox
	Chicago Cubs

Mail orders to
The Athlete's Closet
444 Westlake Drive
Mytown, PA 67221

Be sure to include all necessary information in your letter to get the product you want.

Addressing the Envelope

It's important that you correctly address the envelope for your letter. Notice the format of a properly addressed envelope:

```
┌─────────────────────────────────────────────┐
│  Mark Lee                          ┌ ─ ┐     │
│                                    │stamp│    │
│  2929 Lincoln Avenue               └ ─ ┘     │
│  Westmont, NY 10013                          │
│                                              │
│                                              │
│                        Mr. Bill West         │
│                                              │
│                        140 Maywood Road      │
│                                              │
│                        Boise, ID 60751       │
│                                              │
└─────────────────────────────────────────────┘
```

return address

main address

As your family receives mail this week, notice how the envelopes are addressed.

1. The *return address* (that's your address) goes in the upper left corner. This part is important in case the mail has to be returned to you.

2. The *main address* (the name and address of the person to whom you're writing) goes in the lower right quarter of the envelope.

Be sure to include the *zip code*. Otherwise, the letter will take a long time getting to its destination. If you don't know the zip code, call the post office and ask.

Also, use the post office's *abbreviations* for state names. A list of the abbreviations is on the next page. Notice that they're written in capital letters and don't need periods.

3. Put a *postage stamp* in the upper right corner of the envelope. Be sure you have the correct amount of postage.

Hint:
Be sure to use a waterproof ink on the outside of your envelopes.

State Postal Abbreviations

Alabama AL	Kentucky KY	Ohio OH
Alaska AK	Louisiana LA	Oklahoma OK
Arizona AZ	Maine ME	Oregon OR
Arkansas AR	Maryland MD	Pennsylvania PA
California CA	Massachusetts MA	Rhode Island RI
Colorado CO	Michigan MI	South Carolina SC
Connecticut CT	Minnesota MN	South Dakota SD
Delaware DE	Mississippi MS	Tennessee TN
District of Columbia DC	Missouri MO	Texas TX
Florida FL	Montana MT	Utah UT
Georgia GA	Nebraska NE	Vermont VT
Hawaii HI	Nevada NV	Virginia VA
Idaho ID	New Hampshire NH	Washington WA
Illinois IL	New Jersey NJ	West Virginia WV
Indiana IN	New York NY	Wisconsin WI
Iowa IA	North Carolina NC	Wyoming WY
Kansas KS	North Dakota ND	

What is the postal abbreviation for your state?

Activity 5

Place a sheet of paper width-wise on your desk. Draw a rectangle the size of a business envelope (about 4 inches high by 9 1/4 inches wide). In ink, address the envelope as if it contained a letter to Miss Wanda Webster, who lives at 444 Wexler Way, in Williams, Wyoming. The ZIP code there is 37210. Use your own name and address for a return address, and draw a picture of a postage stamp. (Use the chart above to find state abbreviations.)

Folding the business letter. Fold your letter in thirds, following these steps:

1. Lay the letter on a desk, face up.

2. Fold the bottom of the sheet up about one third of the way, and crease it.

3. Then fold the top down to within one-half inch of the bottom crease, and crease it again.

4. Holding the letter at the top crease, put it in a business envelope.

Folding the friendly letter. You may fold a friendly letter the same way as a business letter, or you may fold it this way:

1. Lay the letter on a desk, face up.

2. Fold the bottom of the sheet up to within one-half inch of the top, and crease it.

3. Then fold the letter in thirds, folding the sides in toward the middle.

4. Put the letter in a small envelope so that the receiver can start reading the letter as it unfolds.

Activity 6

Fold the business letter you wrote in Activity 4. Address a business envelope for the letter, and place the folded letter in the envelope.

Writing With Style

Which of the following letters would be most likely to encourage a prompt reply? Why? Point out specific problems with Letter A.

Letter A
Dear Pacific Comic Book Company,

I read that you were going to have a comic book show here. Do you know how I can get tickets? I have been collecting comic books since I was twelve. Will there be any old Superman comics at the show?

From Jack Turner

Letter B
1000 West Elm Street
Lansing, MI 10023
June 4, 1989

Pacific Comic Book Company
P.O. Box 771
Seattle, WA 65442

Dear Sir or Madam:

According to your advertisement in the May issue of *Collectors' World* magazine, you will be sponsoring a comic book show in Lansing this summer. I would appreciate more information on that show. Exactly when and where will it be held? How much will tickets cost?

Where might I purchase the tickets?

Please send me any information about your show. If possible, include a list of the comic books you will be showing.

Sincerely,

Jack Turner
Jack Turner

Vocabulary Builder

Words in the Real World: The World of Finance
The underlined words are commonly used when talking about business and finance.

Read each word as it's used in a sentence. Then on your own paper match each word with its definition. Use a dictionary if you need help.

example: 1. invoice = a.

1. The Markam Shoe Company sent me an invoice after I received the shoes.
2. We planned to rent a house at the beach for the weekend.
3. Before they moved into the apartment, they signed a lease.
4. The company sent out a catalog showing the spring line.
5. Harold sent a $10 money order to pay for a new pair of pants.
6. Hannah decided the speedboat was too expensive.

Definitions
a. a detailed bill giving the prices of goods sent
b. costly
c. payment made for use of something that belongs to another person
d. a written order that a certain sum of money be paid to a certain person; it can be purchased at a bank or post office as a safe way of sending money through the mail; it can be cashed at another bank or post office
e. a contract allowing someone to use property in return for rent
f. a book or paper listing items for sale

Chapter Review

Chapter Summary

- [ ] A friendly letter has five parts: heading, salutation, body, closing, and signature.

- [ ] The main address should be written or typed in the lower right quarter of an envelope. The return address should appear in the upper left corner. The stamp should be placed in the upper right corner.

- [ ] Use state postal abbreviations and include zip codes when addressing envelopes.

- [ ] A business letter has six parts: heading, inside address, salutation, body, closing, and signature.

- [ ] The salutation in a business letter is always followed by a colon (:).

- [ ] Fold a business letter in thirds and put it in a business envelope for mailing.

- [ ] A friendly letter may be folded in half, then in thirds, and put in a smaller envelope for mailing.

Writing Practice

Write a friendly letter. Is there someone who would like to hear from you? Perhaps you have a relative somewhere whom you haven't contacted in a long time. Maybe a friend moved away and would love to hear what you've been doing. Complete this assignment and get in touch with a relative or friend. Make sure you follow the guidelines for a friendly letter stated in Section 1 of this chapter.

Chapter Quiz

A. Identify the parts of the friendly letter.

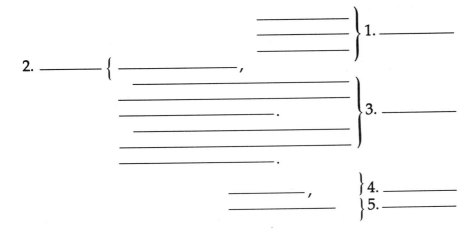

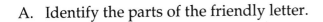

B. Identify the parts of a business letter.

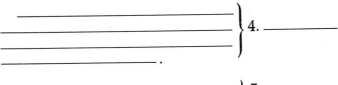

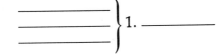

Chapter *17* Writing to Get a Job

Studs Terkel, a Chicago newspaperman, writes exciting and informative books based on his interviews with ordinary people. Hundreds of people told him their memories of the Great Depression for his book Hard Times. *In* Working, *he wrote about the everyday working lives of people from all walks of life.*

Good writers must learn how to gather and organize information.

Writers at Work: Studs Terkel (1912-   )

Chapter Learning Objectives

☐ Write a letter of application.

☐ Write a résumé.

☐ Fill out a job application.

Words to Know

inquire   to ask about something

qualify   to be suited; to have the necessary training

application   a form with questions you must answer when applying for a job

references   persons who can give information about someone else

interview   the meeting of a job-seeker and an employer when questions are asked and answered

résumé   an account of a person's education, experience, and qualifications

Writing a Letter of Application

Sooner or later almost everyone applies for a job. Most people look for new jobs many times in their lives. Job-hunting most often means a personal interview with the employer. Job-hunting also usually calls for some writing. Your goal in job-hunting is, of course, landing that job. Therefore, you'll want to put your best foot forward, not only in your interview, but in any written items as well.

In Chapter 16, you worked on writing letters. You wrote friendly letters and business letters. Sometimes applying for a job means writing a letter to an employer. Perhaps you see a job ad in the paper that asks interested workers to **inquire** by mail. Perhaps you know you'd like to work at a certain beach resort this summer. You'd probably write a letter asking if there will be any jobs available for which you **qualify**.

Of course, in writing a letter of **application**, you'll use the business letter format. Read the following sample letter of application. Notice the type of information that is included.

350 West Beach Drive
Juniper Beach, CA 97001
April 24, 1989

Kelly Long
Forest Glen Kennel
Juniper Beach, CA 97001

Dear Ms. Long:

Name the position that interests you.

I am interested in applying for a job as a dog groomer and kennel assistant.

Indicate your educational background and availability.

I will be graduating from Mission High School in June, and I will then be available for full-time work. Until then, I could work after school and on weekends.

Give a short summary of your experience and qualifications.

I have had a dog of my own since I was ten, and I have always taken full responsibility for his care. The dog is a long-coated husky, so I am experienced at brushing, bathing, and general grooming. In addition, I have taken care of other people's pets when the owners were away on vacation. I would be happy to provide you with references. I do love animals and enjoy caring for them.

Ask for an interview.

May I call you to arrange an interview?

Sincerely,

Diane Elliot

Diane Elliot

Notice the information provided and the questions asked in the letter.

☐ In the first paragraph, Diane asked about a specific job.

☐ In the second paragraph, she let the employer know what kind of work schedule she could handle.

☐ In the third paragraph, she sold herself just a little. (Don't be afraid to tell about your good points.) She described her experience and qualifications and offered **references**.

☐ In the fourth paragraph, she requested an **interview**.

The tone of the letter was friendly yet very businesslike. The letter gave a very brief explanation of Diane's qualifications. Letters of application should not be long. An interested employer will contact the writer for more information. If the letter is too long, a potential employer may not take time to read it.

Activity 1

Read the following job ads. Then write a letter expressing interest in one of the jobs. Be sure to give a brief explanation of your qualifications. You may make up information if you wish.

Playground Activities Director
Must be good with children of all ages. Should be creative and interested in games and sports. Job involves organizing summer activities. No experience necessary, but previous work with children preferred. Contact: Sue Hall, Elk Public Parks, P.O. Box 222, Elk, VT 77821.

Be sure your letter follows the proper business letter format. Take extra care with spelling, punctuation, and capitalization.

Clerk Video Store

Must be interested in films and be good at handling money and dealing with public. Should have some experience setting up video equipment and understand basic video recorders. Send letter of application to: William Palmeri, Star Video, 752 Roseway Blvd., Sherwood, NH 10988.

Cashier

Crestview Cinema needs box office cashier evenings and weekends. Must be good with numbers and at handling money. Prefer previous experience working with the public. Contact Mr. Welch, Crestview Cinema, 300 Main St., Crestview, WA 98771.

Note

Sometimes it's wise to follow up a job interview with a letter to the employer. Thank him or her for the interview and express a sincere interest in the job. This letter can also be a chance to include any information you may have forgotten to give during the interview.

Writing a Résumé

A **résumé** can be an important tool when you begin job hunting. A résumé is a short account of a person's education, experience, and skills. It gives an employer a look at a job applicant's qualifications.

Résumés follow a specific format. Look at the sample résumé on the facing page.

Kate Gilbert
4323 Old Orchard Road
Seattle, WA 80123
(303) 551-2213

Education

Pacific High School
Seattle, Washington
Graduated June 1989

Work Experience
5/88–9/88

Lifeguard, Bowman Park Pool, Seattle, WA 80123.
Supervised children and adults in park pool.
Operated cash register, collecting swim fees.
Managed locker room, towels, pool equipment.

6/87–9/88
11/86–1/87

Record Store Clerk, New Day Record Store,
14 River Mall, Seattle, WA 80123. General
salesperson. Operated cash register and
handled money.

6/86–9/87

Babysitter. Provided part time summer
child care for two toddlers for Mrs. Barbara
Moss, 302 Canyon Dr., Seattle, WA 80123.

Community Activities
1/88–present

Volunteer—Meals for the Homeless Program,
Seattle, Washington. Spend three to five hours
each week serving meals at community
center.

6/86–9/87

Volunteer guide at Seattle City Zoo. Led tour
groups and explained zoo exhibits.

Skills

Type 45 WPM
Hold Red Cross Lifesaving Certificate

References

Available upon request.

There are certain things you should notice about the résumé.

- [ ] The applicant's name, address, and phone number are provided at the top of the résumé.

- [ ] Categories are listed on the left, and information is given on the right.

- [ ] Most recent experiences are listed first.

Remember, you may be competing with others for the job. You want to make the best impression possible.

- [ ] All job experience and volunteer work is listed. Even jobs you weren't paid for can be impressive credits.

- [ ] References may or may not be listed on the résumé. If you decide to list references, give two or three and provide a name, a title, and an address for each one. For example, a reference listing might look like this:

  Mr. Seth Wade
  General Manager
  New Day Record Store
  14 River Mall
  Seattle, WA 80123

  Former employers, volunteer supervisors, fellow workers, coaches, and teachers all make good references. You should always ask if a person will provide you with a reference before you list his or her name.

Activity 2

Think of at least three people you know whom you could use for a reference. List their names, positions, and addresses.

Activity 3

Now write a résumé for yourself. As well as being an assignment in this book, this résumé can be a useful tool when you go looking for a job! Use the model résumé on page 251 as a guide. Because you're an individual, a different person than Kate Gilbert, your résumé will be similar in form but not the same in content.

Filling Out a Job Application

Have you ever filled out a job application? Were there any unusual questions on the form? Were there any questions you didn't understand? Discuss such questions with the class.

Job applications will vary. Some will ask for more information than others. Some will be quite long, and others very brief. It's important to read all the questions on a job application carefully. It's a good idea to look at all of them quickly before you even begin to answer. Fill out applications in ink. Make sure you understand the question before you begin writing so that your application will be neat. Take special care with spelling, punctuation, and capitalization. Remember, you're trying to make a good impression. You want the employer to notice your application. You want it to stand out not because it's messy or incomplete, but because it shows care and effort.

Fill in every item on the application. If the item doesn't apply to you, write NA. This means that this item is *not applicable* to you.

When you apply for a job, you'll probably have to fill out an application. Take a list of information with you. Then you won't have to look up addresses or try to remember dates.

Stop by a local store, restaurant, or other place of business, and ask for a job application form. Bring the form to class, and see if you understand how to complete it.

The amount of room to write on a job application is often limited. Write within the space given. Print information (except where signature is required) so that it's easy to read. There may not be room to list all your job experiences. List more recent experiences and those you think are relevant to the job you're seeking.

Answer honestly, but don't forget anything that might be in your favor. This isn't the time to be overly modest!

Read the sample job application on the facing page.

Activity 4

Write out all the information you would take with you if you were going job hunting. This list should include previous jobs (paid and volunteer) with dates, addresses, phone numbers, and supervisors' names. Don't forget postal zip codes and telephone area codes. Also include the address of the last school you attended. Some applications will ask for your social security number, so include that on your list. Write down the names and addresses of three people you can list as references. (You should have checked with them first.)

Activity 5

Think of a job you would really like to have. Write out the last part of the sample application by explaining in two or three sentences why you think you would be good at this job.

Job Application
Lake of the Woods Summer Camp

Position: **Camp Cook**

Date **4/24/89**

Name **Jean**   **M.**   **Perez**
First   Initial   Last

Address: **201 Webster St.**   **3A**
Number and Street   Apt. no.

San Pedro   **CA**   **90731**
City   State   Zip

Social Security #: **555-21-7810**

Date available for work: **6/14/89**

Previous jobs (paid and volunteer):

Employer	Position held	Dates of employment	Reason for leaving
Fred's Burgers	fry cook	6/88 - present	—
Long Hot Dogs	cook/clerk	6/87-9/87	school
Mrs. H. Wilson	babysitter	86-87	employer moved
Point Fermin Park	volunteer guide	6/86 - 9/86	school

Last year of education completed:

San Pedro High   1001 W. 15TH St., San Pedro, CA   1989
School   Address   Year completed

Write two or three sentences explaining why you think you would be good at this job.

I like the out-of-doors and would be an enthusiastic member of the camp staff. My experience at Fred's Burgers and at Long Hot Dogs taught me to cook for large groups. I have also taken some classes in diet and nutrition at Harbor College.

Writing With Style

If you were an employer which person would you most likely call in for an interview? Give specific reasons for your choice.

A.   Dear Mr. Chin,

I would like a job in your restaurant. I am trying to save enuf money to buy a car, and I think working in a restaurant would be fun. My friend Todd worked in your restaurant, and he likked the job a lot. I have never worked in a restaurant before, but I am sure I could do a good job. You can call me at 444-7562.

Thanks. Tim Tyler

B.   427 East Lincoln Drive
                                                             Denver, CO 87220
                                                             May 14, 1989

Oscar Chin
Snow Cap Cafe
602 Mountain Crest Road
Denver, CO 87220

Dear Mr. Chin:

Do you have any summer openings for a busboy at the Snow Cap Cafe? If you do, I would like to apply for the position.

 I have worked with the public before as a clerk at Martin's Minute Market. I have a 3.6 grade point average. I am very interested in the restaurant business and eager to learn all I can.

Please let me know if we might schedule an interview. I can be reached by phone at 779-6210.

Sincerely,

Matt Woods

Matt Woods

Vocabulary Builder

Words in the Real World: The Job Market

A. Number your paper from 1 to 5. After each number, write the letter of the definition that goes with the word.

1. application	a. a face-to-face meeting for questioning
2. career	b. a chosen occupation
3. employee	c. a person with a paid job
4. employer	d. a written request for a job
5. interview	e. a person who pays others to do a job

B. Now use the words listed above to fill in the blanks.

1. Sandy filled out an_____ for a job as a camp counselor.

2. Three days later, the camp director called Sandy in for an _____.

3. The director asked Sandy for the name of a former _____ as a reference.

4. Sandy hoped she would soon be an _____ of the Lake of the Woods Summer Camp.

5. Sandy is thinking about a future _____ working with children.

C. The words describing many careers end with the suffix *ist*. For example, a person can become a *scientist* or a *dentist*. Use the dictionary to find out what each of these people does for a career: (1) botanist, (2) cosmetologist, (3) zoologist, (4) journalist, and (5) pharmacist. Write your answers on a separate piece of paper.

Chapter Review

Chapter Summary

☐ A letter of application follows the form of a business letter. It should express your interest in a specific job, inquire about openings, and briefly describe your qualifications.

☐ A résumé is an outline giving a short account of a person's background. A résumé should include name, address, phone number, education, work experience, community activities, skills, and an offer of references.

☐ Most job interviews require you to fill out a job application. Applications will differ, but they should be filled out completely and neatly. Be prepared to fill out the application when you go job hunting.

Writing Practice

Imagine that you're Clyde or Claudette Clifford. You're interested in getting a job working as a clerk at a retail store. (You decide what the store sells. Make it something that interests you.) Your assignment is to apply for that job by writing a letter of application and a résumé. Clyde's or Claudette's background is briefly described below. Use your imagination to provide any other details.

- Graduating from George Washington High School this June
- Worked last summer as a fry cook at a fast foods restaurant
- Has sold advertisements for a neighborhood newspaper
- Has had babysitting experience
- Is a championship swimmer
- Can type 50 words per minute

Chapter Quiz

A. Decide if each of the following statements is true or false. On your paper, write true or false after each number.

1. A letter of application should be written in the form of a friendly letter.

2. A résumé is an outline of a person's background.

3. Employers are interested only in paid work experience, so you shouldn't include volunteer activities on a résumé.

4. You should not list your skills on a résumé, or it will sound like you are bragging.

5. It is a good idea to ask for a personal interview in a letter of application.

6. You should not worry about spelling on a job application unless good spelling is a requirement of the job.

7. On a résumé, you should list your most recent experience first.

8. You should always ask people if you may use them as references before you give their names on a job application or résumé.

9. All job application forms are exactly the same.

B. Which of the following would be listed on a résumé?

a. education
b. work experience
c. past residences
d. phone number
e. community activities
f. skills
g. favorite sports
h. names of family members
i. references
j. name
k. address
l. salary requirements

Chapter 18 Everyday Writing

Countee Cullen became well known during the Harlem Renaissance of the 1920s. His poetry explores such themes as the effects of racial prejudice and the black American's search for an African heritage. Unlike other poets of his day, he wrote in traditional English style.

Important social themes give writers something to write about.

Writers at Work: Countee Cullen (1903-1946)

Chapter Learning Objectives

☐ Write a thank-you note.

☐ Write get-well wishes and express sympathy in notes.

☐ Write an invitation.

☐ Write complete, clear messages.

☐ Write effective bulletin board ads and classified ads.

Words to Know

communication   sending and receiving messages

sympathy   the act of sharing another's feelings; feeling sorry for another's suffering

acceptance   answering "yes" to an invitation

regrets   polite refusal of an invitation

classified ads   short newspaper advertisements arranged in groups according to type

> example: homes for sale are offered in one section, pets for sale in another section

Writing Notes and Invitations

A note is a short **communication** from one person to another. A note is usually informal. However, it has the same purpose as any other writing: to communicate the writer's message as clearly as possible.

At certain times you will want to write a note. If someone gives you a present, it's appropriate to show your appreciation with a thank-you note. If someone invites you to an event, you may want to answer the invitation with a note. When friends are ill, notes can cheer them up. If someone you know has a death in the family, a sympathy note is appropriate.

Of course, stores sell greeting cards that provide messages. But a few words of your own will make each card more personal. You can add your own touch to a greeting card as Stan has done in this example:

Date	February 5, 1990
Greeting	Dear Bev,
Happy Birthday!	Happy Birthday!
Personal message	I wish I could spend your birthday with you, but I'll be thinking of you.
Closing	Your friend,
Signature	Stan

Thank-you Notes

A thank-you note is, of course, a way of saying "Thanks!" You should thank someone for a gift or for doing something especially kind and thoughtful. If you're a guest in someone's home, it's thoughtful to say "thank you."

When someone sends or gives you a gift, it's very important to respond right away with a thank-you note. If the present came in the mail, the note is one way of letting the sender know you received the gift. If you have been a guest in someone's home, you should respond with a thank-you note just a day or two after the visit.

When writing a note, remember your purpose. You want to say thank you and let the person know you appreciate his or her thoughtfulness. Aunt Rose sent Jill a sweater for her birthday. Read the sample thank-you note below. Notice its form is similar to a friendly letter's form.

Date	March 9, 1989
Greeting	Dear Aunt Rose,
What you're thankful for	Thank you for the beautiful, hand-knit sweater you sent me for my birthday. You chose my favorite colors. It is so bright and cheerful, just perfect for spring. I have lots of things to wear with it.
Why you liked the gift	I really appreciate all the time you spent making the sweater, and I will think of you when I wear it.
Closing	Your niece,
Signature	*Jill*

Jill wrote a nice thank-you note to Aunt Rose. She not only said thanks, but she also told her aunt how much she liked the present and what she liked about it.

A thank-you note after a visit would be similar. Always be specific. Pick out at least one thing you especially enjoyed about your visit, and mention that to your host or hostess.

Activity 1

List three specific things Jeff thanks Mrs. Wilson for in the following note.

December 28, 1988

Dear Mrs. Wilson,

Thank you so much for having me spend the holiday weekend with your family. It would have been rather lonely spending that time in my apartment alone.

I've told all my friends about the wonderful meal you cooked. That was the biggest turkey I have ever seen! I'm glad I got a chance to be a part of some of your family's holiday traditions. It was especially fun singing the traditional songs together.

You even arranged for snow to make my holiday visit complete. Thanks for everything. You know how to make a guest feel at home.

Sincerely yours,

Jeff Roth

Activity 2

Each of the following items describes a situation that calls for a thank-you note. Choose one, and write the note. Remember to be specific about why you're thankful. Use the sample thank-you notes as guides. Let your imagination supply any necessary names and details.

- You receive two tickets from your Uncle Harry. The tickets are for a professional baseball game. You take your friend with you to the game, and you're lucky enough to catch a foul ball.

- Your friend's family includes you on a trip to the beach. You spend the weekend in a cabin by the sea.

- For your birthday your friend, Jack, gave you a record album you had been wanting. It was a rare album, and it was hard to find.

- Perhaps you really do owe someone a thank-you note (for a gift or for a visit). You may write that person a note to complete this assignment.

Get-Well Notes and Sympathy Notes
People who are sick or injured usually have a lot of time on their hands. They probably miss seeing their friends. You can cheer people up with notes. Most of all, you can let them know you're thinking of them.

Date

Greeting

Express your feelings. Tell the person you hope for a quick recovery.

Send some news.

Closing

Signature

June 14, 1989

Dear Kim,

I was sorry to hear that you were hurt on your skiing trip. I hope you'll be on your feet and back at school again very soon.

We all miss you in science class. You would have laughed the loudest when the white mice escaped from their cages the other day. One mouse, in fact, is still missing. Maybe you'll find it when you come back.

Your friend,

Sally

Sometimes it's hard to know what to say when someone's friend or relative dies. However, it's important to let the person know that you care. A simple **sympathy** note can express your concern.

Heading	333 Lake Drive Chicago, IL 77211 April 4, 1989
Greeting	Dear Carl,
Express your feelings. *Say something specific* *about the person.*	I was sorry to hear about your mother's death. Your mother, Beth, was a warm, wonderful person. She was always so good to me when I visited your house. She treated me like one of the family, and I always felt at home.
Offer to help.	If I can be of any help to you and your family, please let me know. My current phone number is 553-7641.
Closing	With deepest sympathy,
Signature	*Mike Foster*

Mike hadn't seen Carl for quite a while, but he wanted to let him know he cared. Mike included his address and phone number in the note, so that Carl could contact him if he needed anything. There are three parts to the sympathy note: (1) Mike expressed his feelings, (2) Mike said something specific about why he liked the person who had died, and (3) he offered to help.

Activity 3

Choose one of the following situations and write a note expressing your feelings. Let your imagination supply any necessary details. Use the model get-well and sympathy notes as a guide.

- Your teacher, Mrs. Ward, is in the hospital after having her appendix taken out.

- Your friend's older brother was killed in an automobile accident. You have already talked to your friend and expressed your sympathy. Now you want to write a note to his parents.

- Do you know anyone who is sick and would be cheered by a get-well note? You can write that note for this assignment.

Invitations

Are you planning a party? You might call people on the phone and invite them to your get-together. You can also invite people to your party by sending invitations. It's important to include all the details of the event in your invitation.

What do you need to let people know?

When you receive an invitation, you should reply right away. Tell whether you will attend.

1. The kind of party it will be. (Sometimes it's a good idea to use the words *casual* or *formal* so people know how to dress.)

2. The time and date of the party

3. Where the party will take place

4. Whether the guests should bring anything

5. Write RSVP at the bottom of the invitation if you want people to let you know if they can come or not.

Those letters mean that people should respond with acceptance or regrets. Write your phone number after the RSVP. To cut down on responses, you can write "RSVP—regrets only." Then you can assume that anyone who doesn't call is coming to the party.

The letters RSVP are the first letters of the words in the French expression: *Repondez s'il vous plait.*

This translates to "Respond, if you please."

You can buy printed invitations in a store. These usually have spaces for time, date, and so on. Then all you have to do is fill in the blanks. Make sure to add any other necessary information at the bottom of the invitation.

If you write your own invitations, you will use the same form as you did for the other notes in this lesson.

Date invitation is sent	June 25, 1989
Greeting	Dear Linda and Ted,
Kind of party	Joe and I are having our Fourth of July celebration again this year. We hope you can come and join the group.
When, where *What to bring*	The party will be on Tuesday, July 4, from 4:00 P.M. until 10:00 P.M. at our house (4231 Mill Street). We will provide the meats to barbecue. Please bring a salad or dessert to share with others.
Other details	Dress casually and plan to stay late enough to see the fireworks display.
Closing *Signature* *Phone number for acceptance or regrets*	Your friend, Kate Oliver RSVP 773-1259

Activity 4

Use the model Fourth of July party invitation on the previous page to answer these questions.

1. Who is giving the party?

2. When will the party be held?

3. Where will the party be held?

4. What kind of party is it?

5. What should Linda and Ted bring?

6. Should Linda go out and buy a formal party dress? Why or why not?

7. What number should Ted or Linda call with **acceptance** or **regrets**?

Making Sure Others Get Your Message

Imagine you're babysitting for a Mrs. Betty Charles. At 7:00 P.M., her sister Anne calls with an important message. "Tell Betty," she says, "that I won't be able to pick her up tomorrow morning. Tell her that my car needs to go into the repair shop. I want her to pick me up at the Fourth Street Auto Garage at 10:00 A.M. If she has any questions, she can call me at 415-2291 before 8:00 tomorrow morning. If I don't hear from her, I will expect her at the garage."

You cannot depend on your memory to keep track of all that information. You'll have to give Mrs. Charles a written message.

While her sister Anne talks, you should take brief notes as in this example:

Can't pick you up, car in repair shop, pick her up—
Fourth St. Auto Garage—10:00 A.M.—any questions,
call 415-2291 before 8:00 A.M.

After you hang up, you should write out the
message to give to Mrs. Charles.

February 14

7:00 P.M.

Mrs. Charles,

Your sister Anne called. She can't pick you up
tomorrow morning as planned. Her car is in the
repair shop. She needs you to pick her up at the
Fourth Street Auto Garage at 10:00 A.M. If there
is a problem with that, call her at 415-2291
before 8:00 A.M.

Kim Edwards

Notice that the message includes the following
items:

• the time and date of the message

• the name of the person who called

• what the caller wanted

• a number to call back

• your name signed at the bottom to show who
took the message

Activity 5

What information is missing from each of the
messages on the next page?

1.

> January 5
> 7:00 A.M.
>
> Tom,
>
> Your friend called. He said he needed to talk to you. Call him back.
>
> Gina

2.

> Dad,
>
> Mr. Carlton said he would meet you at 8:00. He said it was important and that he needed to talk to you.
>
> Chris

3.

> March 5
>
> 4:00
>
> I won't be home for dinner.

You may need to give someone a message that includes directions. Have you ever tried to tell someone how to get to your house? Sometimes it's impossible to draw a map, and the directions must be given over the phone or in writing. It's important that the directions be clear and simple. Even more importantly, they must be accurate. Otherwise you could send someone wandering about the city.

Read these sample directions.

- Notice that they are short and simple.
- Notice that the directions for each turn are written on a new line.
- Notice that they are neat and easy to read.

> Directions from school to 215 Oak Street.
> Go north two blocks on Maple Street to Stevens Avenue.
> Turn left on Stevens and go half a block to Oak Street.
> Turn right on Oak and go three blocks to 215 Oak Street.

Now you try it.

Activity 6

Write directions telling someone how to get to your house from school or from some other place. Remember, keep the directions neat and simple, and write directions for each new turn on a separate line. (It might help to jot down some notes or draw a simple map before you begin to write the directions.)

Writing an Advertisement

There may be times when you'll have something to sell—perhaps something you no longer need or perhaps services for certain jobs. You can write ads to let people know you have something to sell.

Many stores, restaurants, schools, and other public places have bulletin boards where people place ads. Newspapers offer **classified ad** sections where people pay to place their ads.

Activity 7

Imagine that you have a twelve-speed bicycle to sell. List all the details you think you should include in an advertisement. (Use your imagination to come up with the details.)

example: red color, boy's bike

Now that you've finished making the list for Activity 7, check to see if you included all the details necessary to make a sale. Compare your list to this one:

- name the item (bike)
- give important facts that will attract buyers (type, brand name, color, condition, extras, price)
- tell how buyers can reach you (phone number)

Look at the two following ads. The first is a bulletin board ad for the bicycle. The second is a classified ad ready to be placed in a newspaper.

Headline catches attention and names item

Details
Condition
Price
Phone number

Bike for Sale

Boy's Smith 12-speed
Red frame, wide all-surface tires
Excellent condition
$125
Call Joe 771-6201

> Bike. Boy's Smith 12-speed, red, wide tires,
> excl cond, $125. 771-6201

People usually pay for classified ads by the line, so they make their ads as short as possible. They use abbreviations for some words. Notice the abbreviation *excl* is used for *excellent,* and *cond* is used for *condition.* That shortens the ad and saves money. These next two ads offer a service rather than an item for sale.

Bulletin board ad:

> **Yardwork**
> Experienced yard care offered by two high
> school seniors.
> Lawns mowed, shrubs trimmed, flowers
> planted and maintained
> References available
> $5.00 per hour
> Call Rick at 235-1387 or Dave at 222-9971

Classified ad:

> Yardwork. Lawns, shrubs, flowers.
> 3 yrs. experience, references. $5 per hr.
> Rick, 235-1387, or Dave, 222-9971.

What kind of work do Rick and Dave do? Have they ever done this kind of work before? How can people be sure they are good workers? How much do they charge? Where can they be reached? What abbreviations were used in the ad?

Now you try it.

Activity 8

Write your own ads. Write both a bulletin board ad and a classified ad. Sell either an item or your services for a certain job. Use the sample ads as a guide and remember to include all necessary information.

Some suggested items:

> record collection, motorcycle, speedboat, computer, puppies

Some suggested services:

> babysitting, house painting, dog walking

Writing With Style

Which of the following classified ads would probably get a better response? Why?

A.

> Canoe. 16', fiberglass, with 2 life jackets and paddles. Like new. $200. 255-8711

B.

> Canoe. 16', fiberglass, with 2 life jackets and paddles. A great buy.

Vocabulary Builder

Words in the Newspaper

Read the following paragraph. Then use the italicized "newspaper" words to fill in the blanks.

Our local newspaper just won an award for its fine *journalism*. The award came soon after the paper printed an exciting *feature* about crime on our city streets. "Local Crime Worst in 50 Years," the *headline* read. An *editorial* in the same *edition* of the paper blamed cuts in the police department for the rising crime.

1. An _____ is a piece of writing in a newspaper or magazine. It gives an opinion.

2. The work of gathering and reporting the news is called _____ .

3. A _____ is a special article in a newspaper or magazine.

4. An _____ includes all the copies of a newspaper or magazine printed at one time.

5. The title of an article printed in large, bold type is the _____ .

Chapter Review

Chapter Summary

☐ Send a thank-you note if someone gives you a gift or does something thoughtful.

☐ Be specific in your note. Tell what you liked or appreciated.

☐ The thank-you note should follow the same format as a friendly letter.

☐ Notes can also express get-well wishes or sympathy.

☐ Be sure your written invitations include all necessary information.

☐ Written messages should be clear and simple. They should always be dated with the day and the time.

☐ When directing someone to a place, write directions for each new turn on a new line.

☐ Written ads let people know you have something to sell. You can put ads on public bulletin boards or place them in the newspaper classified section.

Writing Practice

A. Pretend you're going to have a party. Write an invitation. What type of party do you want to have? (A swimming party? A dance? A beach party?) Use your imagination to supply the necessary details.

B. The party was a big success. You received some terrific presents. Now write a thank-you note to one of your guests thanking him or her for the great present. (Again, use your imagination to supply the details.)

Chapter Quiz

A. Match the occasion described in the column on the left with the proper written response from the column on the right.

1. Dr. Peters' office calls and says your father's appointment must be changed to 9:00 Wednesday.

2. The mother of your friend Harry dies.

3. You want to sell your ski equipment.

4. You're going to have a birthday party.

5. Your Aunt Helen sends you $10 for your birthday.

6. Your science teacher is in the hospital.

7. Jim will give you a ride to the football game. He'll pick you up at your house, but he has never been there before.

a. thank-you note

b. sympathy note

c. get-well note

d. invitation

e. phone message

f. written directions

g. classified ad

B. Write three sentences of your own. Use at least one of the following vocabulary words in each of your sentences: regrets, communication, sympathy.

Unit Review

A. Use a separate sheet of paper to answer each of the following questions.

1. Describe **two** differences between a friendly letter and a business letter.

2. What **three** items go on the envelope before a letter is mailed?

3. Name **five** items that will probably appear on a job application form.

4. What information appears at the top of a résumé?

5. Name **four** categories listed on a résumé.

6. Write **one** sentence explaining the purpose of a résumé.

B. Choose the correct item from each pair. Write the letter of the answer next to each number.

1. a. Dear Sirs: b. Dear Sirs,

2. a. Sincerely yours: b. Sincerely yours,

    Lynn   Lynn

3. a. Mr. Hal Collins   b. Mr. Hal Collins,

    4221 Lakeshore Drive   4221 Lakeshore Drive

    Sunnyvale, CA 94031   Sunnyvale, California

4. a. Sincerely,   b. Sincerely,

    Mr. Al White   Al White

5. a. My dear Aunt Mary: b. My dear Aunt Mary,

Unit Six

Writing in School

Chapter *19* Writing a Book Report

Gabriel Garcia Marquez, a Colombian, sets his short stories and novels in an imaginary new world, Macondo. His characters show what happens to people when their rural society collapses. Two of his best known novels are Love in the Time of Cholera *and* One Hundred Years of Solitude.

Good novels tell not only what **happens but** why **the characters behave as they do.**

Writers at Work: Gabriel Garcia Marquez (1928–   )

Chapter Learning Objectives

☐ Write a book report covering the major elements of a novel without telling the entire story.

☐ Describe the setting of a novel.

☐ Describe a main character's physical appearance and personality.

☐ Identify the conflict in a story, and explain how it's resolved.

Words to Know

report   an account of a particular subject

novel   a long work of fiction

elements   basic parts or features of the whole

setting   the time and place of an event, story, or play

character   a person in a story or play

plot   the main story of a novel or play

conflict   a problem caused by the clash of two opposing forces

incident   an event

resolution   a solution; an end to conflict

The Basic Book Report

After you have read a book you've enjoyed, are you eager to share it with others? Discussing a book can add to your enjoyment. Sometimes it's interesting to stop and think about why you liked a book so much.

Your teacher may ask you to write a **report** about a **novel** you've read. There are many ways to report on a book. This chapter will look closely at one common book report format.

As you begin, keep in mind this important fact about a book report: you can't tell everything that happened in a novel. It's not important to tell the story itself. It is important, however, that you show an understanding of the **elements** of that story.

What are the basic elements of a novel?

setting   when and where the story takes place

characters   the people in the story (at least one character will have a problem to be solved)

conflict   the main problem of the story

main incident   some important event that affects the conflict

resolution of the conflict   how the conflict is solved or decided

plot   the story line; what happens

A description of each of these elements makes a complete book report. You will probably conclude the report by giving your opinion of the book.

Look at the following sample book report carefully. The next sections in this chapter will take you through each part of the book report.

Sample Book Report

Title: <u>Dark Waters</u>

Author: Jack Summers

As you read, notice that this book report answers the who, what, when, where, why and how questions.

Setting: The story takes place aboard an ocean liner on the Atlantic Ocean. The time is during World War I, probably around 1915.

Main character: One of the main characters is a boy named David Starr. David is a handsome, red-haired, seventeen-year-old American traveling alone to England. At the beginning of the book, he's nervous about the trip. However, he overcomes his fears and turns out to be very brave. He shows his bravery by warning the ship's captain that a spy is on board and by finding a hidden bomb. David does this even though he knows the spy might catch him and kill him. David never gives up. "They just have

The conflict always involves a problem that must be solved.

to believe me," he tells his friend Anna. "Their lives depend on it. I must make them believe me." Although others on the ship say he's imagining things, David trusts his own feelings and keeps looking for the spy and the bomb.

Conflict: There is a spy and a bomb aboard a luxury liner. Will David Starr find them in time and save the ship?

Main incident: One exciting incident occurs when David and his friend Anna try to sneak into the spy's cabin. They want to find proof of the spy's evil plans and take that proof to the captain. They have to pick the lock of the cabin with Anna's hairpin. While they are inside the cabin, they find what they need—a book of secret codes and some letters from the Germans. But the spy, Arnold Stone, returns while they're in the cabin. They hide in a closet, hoping they won't be discovered. Luckily, they escape and take the book and letters to the captain.

Resolution of conflict: Only minutes before the bomb is to go off, David convinces the captain to search the ship. Because David and Anna would not give up, the bomb is discovered, disarmed, and the ship and all its passengers are saved.

Opinion: This book was very exciting. I worried that no one would believe David and Anna and that the ship would blow up, killing everyone on board. I liked the main characters, David and Anna, because they never gave up. I hated the evil Arnold Stone because he didn't care about anyone but himself. The book also taught me some interesting facts about World War I. I hadn't known that German submarines attacked nonmilitary boats. In all, <u>Dark Waters</u> was easy to read and packed with suspense.

Activity 1

Use the sample report on the book *Dark Waters* to answer these questions.

When you use the title of a book in your writing, make sure you underline it.

1. Who wrote *Dark Waters*?
2. When did the story take place?
3. Where did the story take place?
4. Name a main character in the story.
5. Write two adjectives that describe David Starr.
6. What problem did David have to solve?
7. What two items did David and Anna find in the spy's cabin?
8. If David and Anna were the good guys in the novel, who was the bad guy?
9. Were David and Anna able to save the ship?
10. Did the person who wrote the book report like the novel or not?

Setting

When you report on the setting of a novel, you must describe *where the story takes place* and *when the story takes place*. These elements are important because they affect how the story is told. For example, imagine a story about a bank robbery set in a cowboy town of the Old West. Now imagine a bank robbery story set in modern New York City. They would be very different stories, wouldn't they?

Sometimes an author will come right out and tell the *when* and *where* of the story. Somewhere in the early pages, he or she might mention, for example, the city of Tombstone, Arizona, and the date 1890. Then it's easy to describe the setting in your report. However, sometimes the author doesn't tell exactly when and where the story is set. Then you must look for clues, and they are usually easy to find. How do the people dress? Do they ride horses or drive automobiles? How do they talk? Does it seem as if they are in a big city or a small town? Sometimes you may not be able to give the place a specific name. However, you should be able to say something to identify the place: a small American town, a big city in the East, a tropical island, and so on. Likewise, you should be able to identify the time even if you can't give a specific date: modern times, long ago, the days of cowboys and Indians, colonial days, the future, and so on.

Activity 2

The following paragraphs don't tell the setting in specific words. However, you can use clues to decide when and where the action takes place. What is the setting (the when and where) of each paragraph? On your own paper, list clues you used to arrive at your answer.

A. Big Jim pushed his ten-gallon hat back and wiped the sweat off his forehead. He took a long drink of water from his canteen. Then he patted his horse and whispered under his breath, "We'll catch those train robbers yet! If I have to ride fifty miles across this desert, I'll have them in my jail by sundown."

B. Sharon held the briefcase full of money tightly against her body. She knew the two men were still after her. She waited nervously for the subway train to arrive.

The subway station was crowded, and people pushed against her. She was glad. She could hide in the crowd. At last the train arrived. "Hey, move it!" someone yelled to her. She hurried aboard the subway train. She took a seat next to a frowning young man with a black leather jacket and pink hair standing up in tall spikes.

Characters

It's better to give a good description of one main character in the book than to merely list all of the characters. Choose a main character that really interests you—someone you especially like or dislike. Then write a paragraph or two describing that character.

Sometimes the villain is as interesting a character as the hero or heroine. Don't forget about the bad guy when you're choosing a character to describe.

Here are some topics you might discuss:

- Describe the character's physical appearance.
- Describe the character's personality.
- Tell about one thing the character did that made you like or dislike him or her.
- Tell about any difficulties or hardships the main character overcomes.
- Tell about any changes in the main character. What caused the change?
- What problem did the main character face?

When you write about the character, follow these guidelines:

- Use specific examples.

When you say that a character is, for instance, brave, give an example of something brave that he or she did. If you say you liked a character, tell why. Then give an example of something he or she did that earned your admiration.

Notice how specific examples are used in the character section of the sample book report (pages 284–285). The statement that David is brave is supported by an example of something brave that he did.

- Use direct quotations from the book to support your points.

If you say that your character is, for example, cruel, copy a quotation from the book to prove your point. Find something cruel that the character says. Copy the words directly from the book, putting them in quotation marks.

Notice the direct quotation in the character section of the sample book report on pages 284–285. The quotation supports the idea that David is determined and never gives up.

Activity 3

Choose a main character from a novel you have recently read. Write a one-paragraph character description. Use the following headings and topic sentence for your paper.

Book:

Character's name:

Character description:

The character _____ in _____ was a very interesting person.

Plot

*Remember, it's **not** your job in a book report to retell the whole story.*

Think about a story you have read recently. In what other ways might the conflict have been resolved? Imagine the story with a totally different ending.

When students start describing the plot of a book, they often run into trouble. They find themselves telling every little detail and soon discover they can't include everything. Their discussion ends up going nowhere and becoming very confusing indeed. It's best to look at the separate elements that make up the plot. Then you can briefly describe how they were handled in the book.

Every story must have a **conflict**. The conflict makes a story. It's what makes people want to read to the end. They want to find out how the conflict is solved. The conflict is simply a problem. Will the lost boys find their way out of the woods? Will the police detective find the person who murdered her partner? Will the family be able to explain the creature from another planet living in their house? A story could be written around each of those conflicts.

Notice how the sample book report on page 284–285 describes the conflict of the book *Dark Waters*.

___

Activity 4

Think about the plot of a television show or movie you saw recently. Write one or two sentences describing the conflict in that show.

Stories are made up of many **incidents** that all work toward a **resolution** of the conflict. Some of the incidents lead to the solution of the problem. Some incidents make matters worse, increase the problem and heighten the suspense.

The incident described in the sample book report takes the conflict one step closer to a resolution. By finding the code book and the letters, David and Anna can convince the captain there is a spy on board and save the ship.

It's very difficult to describe everything that happens in a book. It's better to describe one important event very clearly.

Activity 5

Write one paragraph describing an interesting incident in a book you recently read, in a television show, or in a movie. Tell how that incident affected the conflict in the story. (Did it make matters worse, or did it lead to a resolution of the problem?)

For every conflict, there is a **resolution**. The events of the story take the reader toward that resolution. The plot is built around that conflict and its resolution. Your book report should answer the question, "How is the conflict (the problem) resolved?"

What is your favorite novel? Why did you like it so well? What makes it stand out from all the other books you have read?

The last part of your report involves giving your opinion of the book. Again, the key is to **be specific**. Don't merely say you liked the book. Tell **why** you liked it. Give reasons for your opinion. Don't merely say you liked it because it was exciting. Give a **specific example** of something exciting that happened. Reread the opinion section of the *Dark Waters* book report. Notice how the person who wrote the report used specific detail to back up the statement that the novel was exciting.

Use the paragraphing skills you learned in earlier pages of this book (especially Chapter 10) to write a well-developed opinion paragraph.

Writing With Style

The following paragraphs give two readers' opinions of Jack London's novel *The Call of the Wild*. Which paragraph do you think is better? Why?

A. I liked Jack London's <u>The Call of the Wild</u> very much. I thought that it was a very good book. It was exciting and interesting, and I could hardly put it down. It was very well written. In fact, <u>The Call of the Wild</u> was one of the best books I have ever read. I think that people would really enjoy reading <u>The Call of the Wild</u>.

B. I thought Jack London's <u>The Call of the Wild</u> was an excellent book. London made me understand the feelings of the main character, a big dog named Buck. I wanted Buck to survive. I worried about him when he fought other dogs and fell into the hands of cruel masters. London also described the setting, the frozen Arctic, so clearly that I could see it in my mind. <u>The Call of the Wild</u> was an exciting adventure I would recommend to most readers.

Vocabulary Builder

Finding Hard Words

Read the following paragraph. Find at least three words that you think are hard to understand. Perhaps you don't know the meanings. Perhaps you think other people might not know the meanings. Look up each hard word in the dictionary. Write a definition for the word and use the word in a sentence.

For example, if you found the word *rave* and didn't know its meaning, you would first write a definition:

rave—to talk wildly

Then you would use it in a sentence:

The man <u>raved</u> about the new car he had bought.

Now, find at least three hard words in this paragraph:

The prisoners were planning their escape. Dangerous Dan and California Slim had been in jail for ten long years. Now they were digging a tunnel to freedom. The only implement they had was a rusty old spoon. The men took turns digging with that spoon. Every night for six months, Dan and Slim burrowed through the hard, dry earth. At last one night, just around midnight, Dan called to Slim. His voice was hoarse with anticipation. He whispered that he saw a light at the end of their tunnel. Dan believed that light meant freedom.

Chapter Review

Chapter Summary

- ☐ Don't try to tell the whole story in a book report. Instead, choose several elements of the novel and discuss those in some detail.

- ☐ Describe the setting. If the book doesn't give the exact setting, use clues to decide when and where the story takes place.

- ☐ Describe the physical appearance and personality of a main character.

- ☐ Don't try to tell the whole plot. Instead, point out conflict, describe one specific incident, and tell how the conflict is resolved.

- ☐ Give your opinion of the book. Use specific examples to support your opinion.

Writing Practice

Choose a book that you have read recently, and write a book report like the one discussed in this chapter. Use the following guide:

Title:

Author:

Setting:

A main character:

Conflict:

A main incident:

Resolution of conflict:

Opinion of novel:

Chapter Quiz

A. On a separate sheet of paper, match each number to a letter.

1. title
2. setting
3. character
4. conflict
5. resolution
6. opinion

a. Sam Swanson, a clever detective who uses every trick to catch a criminal

b. Will Sam Swanson discover who murdered the wealthy movie star?

c. Hollywood, California, during the 1950s

d. Murder in the Mansion

e. The book was exciting. Until the very end, it was impossible to guess who committed the murder.

f. Detective Sam Swanson proves that the movie star's boyfriend, Carter Cutler, was the murderer.

B. Pretend you are a character in a novel you have read. Use the six items listed above to write a book report about an adventure you would like to have. Write your book report on a separate sheet of paper.

Chapter 20 Writing Answers on Tests

Richard Wright was the first to use the phrase "black power." Raised in poverty in the South, he worked his way to Chicago by age 19, and began to write. He is best known for his novel Native Son *and his autobiography* Black Boy.

Memories of childhood provide the richest story material for many writers.

Writers at Work: Richard Wright (1908–1960)

Chapter Learning Objectives

- ☐ Write answers to questions in complete sentences.
- ☐ Begin answers by restating the subject of the question.
- ☐ Write essay answers in well-developed paragraphs.
- ☐ Read essay questions carefully and answer the specific question that is asked.

Words to Know

restate to say something again or in a different way

identify to show to be a particular person, place, or thing

Short-Answer Questions

Some tests ask questions that call for short, written answers. When you're asked this type of question, it's time to remember your writing skills.

Here is a question that calls for a short answer:

Question: Why is Paul Revere famous?

Answer: Paul Revere is most famous for his midnight ride to Concord. He warned the American patriots that the British soldiers were coming.

Note
The answer is written in complete sentences.

Each sentence has a subject, a predicate, and it expresses a complete thought.

Can you recall taking a test that had questions calling for short answers?

The first sentence of the answer **restates** the question.

Why is Paul Revere famous?

Paul Revere is most famous for . . .

It is very important to restate the question. This starts you off on the right track and helps you stick to the point.

Here is an example of a science question and its answer:

Question: *What is a barometer?*

You can see that writing skills are not only important in English class.

Answer: A *barometer* is an instrument that measures the pressure in the atmosphere.

Notice again that the answer restates the subject of the question.

___

Activity 1

On a separate sheet of paper, answer each of the following questions with one or two sentences. Make sure that you answer in complete sentences. The first two items have been started for you. Use them as a model.

1. Who is George Bush?
   George Bush is . . .

2. What is your favorite food?
   My favorite food is . . .

3. What is a tricycle?

4. Why do we celebrate the Fourth of July?

5. What makes a group of words a complete sentence?

You first read about characteristics in Chapter 12. Turn back if you need help remembering.

You're often asked to **identify** some person, place, or object in test questions. You might be asked to identify people, places, or things. To identify something means to name its characteristics. What makes a thing what it is? What features are different from others of its type? These are characteristics.

For example:

> **Question:** *Identify* Jackie Robinson.

> **Answer:** Jackie Robinson was the first black baseball player to play in the major leagues.

Notice that the answer tells why Robinson is famous. It tells what makes him different from other people.

Notice that the answer is written in a complete sentence. And it restates the subject of the question.

Activity 2

A. Read each of the following questions and its answers. Write **CS** if the answer is a complete sentence. Write **NS** if it is not a complete sentence.

1. Q: What is the smallest state in the United States?

   A: Rhode Island

2. Q: What happened at the Boston Tea Party?

   A: At the Boston Tea Party, a band of American patriots disguised themselves as Native Americans. Then they dumped tea into Boston harbor. They were protesting against a British company that sold tea at a price American tea merchants could not match.

3. Q: Identify Wyatt Earp.

   A: a gunfighter and law officer of the Old West

4. Q: Identify Thomas Jefferson.

   A: Thomas Jefferson wrote the Declaration of Independence. He was also the third president of the United States.

5. Q: What is Jupiter?

   A: the largest planet

B. You should have found three answers that were not complete sentences. Now rewrite those answers as complete sentences.

Note
Always restate the subject of the question in the first sentence of your answer. Do not use a pronoun to replace the subject.

Here is an example:

> **Question:** Identify Abraham Lincoln.
>
> **Poor answer:** He was the sixteenth president of the United States.
>
> **Better answer:** *Abraham Lincoln* was the sixteenth president of the United States.

Notice that the first answer used the pronoun *he* instead of stating the subject. The better answer named the subject of the question.

Activity 3

Choose the best answer for the following question. Be ready to explain your choice.

Question: Identify Topeka.

Answer 1: It is the capital of Kansas.

Answer 2: capital of Kansas

Answer 3: Topeka is the capital of Kansas.

Challenge

If you need help, use a reference book (encyclopedia or almanac) to identify each of the following people. Answer in complete sentences.

1. Identify Sally Ride.

2. Identify Michael Jackson.

3. Identify Davy Crockett.

4. Identify John Adams.

5. Identify Harriet Tubman.

Answering Essay Questions

An essay question calls for a longer answer. It asks you to discuss a topic in detail. Your answer will be a little essay of one or more paragraphs. Some essay questions can be answered quite briefly. Others require more detail. You must decide how much detail to include. Be thorough but don't go overboard!

Here is an example of an essay question and its answer:

Question: Describe the Hawaiian island of Kauai.

Answer: The island of Kauai is often described as the most beautiful of the Hawaiian islands. Kauai's Waimea Canyon is very colorful. Some people compare it to the Grand Canyon. The smooth rocks of Waipahee Falls make a natural slide for swimmers. Most of the island is sunny. Kauai's Mount Waialeale however, is the rainiest spot in the world. Because of its lush

Can you recall taking a test that included essay questions?

What essay questions might a science teacher ask? What essay questions might a social studies teacher ask?

plant life, beautiful Kauai is sometimes called the "Garden Island."

Note

The answer is written as a paragraph.

Remember, a well-developed paragraph has a topic sentence. *(The island of Kauai is often described as the most beautiful of the Hawaiian islands.)*

A well-developed paragraph has at least three sentences of supporting details. *(Waimea Canyon sentences, Waipahee Falls sentence, Mount Waialeale sentence)*

A well-developed paragraph has a concluding sentence. *(Because of its lush plant life, beautiful Kauai is sometimes called the "Garden Island.")*

The topic sentence restates the subject of the question.

As in the short-answer questions, you should not refer to the subject with a pronoun. The writer did not say, *"It* is often described as the most beautiful of the Hawaiian islands." Rather, the subject, *Kauai,* was restated.

Activity 4

On your own paper, write a topic sentence that could begin a one-paragraph essay answer for each of the following questions. You will not be presenting any details in this exercise. Just write a topic sentence.

example:

Question: Describe Alaska's natural resources.

Topic sentence: The state of Alaska is rich in natural resources.

Notice the sample topic sentence merely restates the question as a statement, but adds the descriptive word <u>rich.</u> A good topic sentence points the way in which a paragraph will develop.

1. Q: Explain how the woodpecker is a helpful bird.
   topic sentence:

2. Q: Describe how Americans celebrate the Fourth of July.
   topic sentence:

3. Q: Discuss how television can be educational.
   topic sentence:

Note

Always read essay questions carefully. Read the question two or three times to be sure you understand it. Then begin your essay. Make sure the information you are writing down really answers the question.

What is wrong with the answer to this essay question?

Question: Describe three uses of the helicopter.

Answer: Helicopters are very useful. Helicopters are often used as ambulances. They carry injured people from an accident to the hospital. They can get people to the hospital much faster than regular ambulances. Helicopters do not have to depend on roads, as cars do, or on landing strips, as regular airplanes do. Helicopters save lives.

The answer above contains useful information. But, it does not answer the question. The question asked for three uses of the helicopter. Read the following answer. Is it a better answer? Why?

Helicopters are very useful. For example, helicopters are used as ambulances to carry injured people from an accident to the hospital. Forest-fire fighters use helicopters to search for fires in the mountains. The army uses helicopters, too. Helicopters carry troops directly into battle and move wounded soldiers from battlefields to hospitals. Helicopters do jobs no other vehicles can do.

Note

The answer about helicopters could also have been written in three paragraphs. One paragraph might have discussed helicopters used as ambulances. A second paragraph might have discussed how forest-fire fighters use helicopters. A third paragraph could say how helicopters are used in battle. With three paragraphs, the writer could have given many more details. You must determine how long and detailed an answer your teacher expects.

Watch for key words in essay questions. Here are a few examples:

Describe = tell about; make a picture with words

Explain = make clear; give the details

Discuss = tell about; give good and bad points; share your opinion

Watch for numbers. Does the question ask you to give *three* reasons, to discuss *two* points, and so on?

Activity 5

Choose one of the numbered questions and write a one-paragraph answer. It is often a good idea to make some notes before you begin writing your answer. For example, if you choose the first question below, your notes might look like this:

great-grandfather

came from Poland

traveled to America alone at thirteen

was very tall, very brave, very clever

couldn't speak English until he was nineteen

saved enough money to open a small fruit stand

eventually owned a large supermarket

1. Describe your great-grandfather or great-grandmother.
2. Describe two major industries in your state.
3. Explain how the holiday of Thanksgiving began.
4. Discuss three ways a person can stay healthy.
5. Discuss cats as pets.
6. Explain this quotation by Thomas Jefferson: "All men are created equal."
7. Explain this proverb: "You can catch more flies with honey than with vinegar."
8. Identify a famous person from your state.
9. Describe two ways bees help people.
10. Explain how tennis is played.

Writing With Style

Students in a science class were given the following essay question. Which answer, A or B, do you think deserves the better grade? Why?

Question: Describe three ways frogs are valuable.

Answer A:
They eat insects. They are also a good source of food for people. In France, they are a popular food. In the United States, some people eat their legs. In Germany, people often cook and eat the entire frog.

Answer B:
Frogs are valuable creatures. First, they eat many harmful insects. Second, they are a source of food for some people. Frogs are a delicacy in France and Germany. Third, frogs serve as food for other animals. Snakes and birds living near water eat frogs. Even some fish eat frogs. Frogs, indeed, have some important uses.

Vocabulary Builder

Checking Your Dictionary Skills

Words in the dictionary are arranged in alphabetical order. If the first letter of two words is the same, you decide their order by looking at the second letter. If the second letter is also the same, you look at the third letter.

A. Alphabetize the following words.

coffee   fire   control   arrow

eye   freeze   fan   art

B. Look at the following dictionary entry for the word *snake*. Use the entry to answer the questions below.

The entry word shows the number of syllables in the word.

The pronunciation shows how to say the entry word.

Some definitions use examples to make meanings clear.

snake (snāk) n. 1. a crawling reptile with a long, thin body covered with scales and with no legs. 2. a person who cannot be trusted: *The snake cheated me out of my money.* 3. a long, flexible rod used to clear blocked pipes. v. to move, twist, wind, or curve like a snake.— snaked, snaking

Some words have more than one meaning. Each meaning is numbered.

The dictionary may show other forms of the word.

The part of speech is often abbreviated.

n = noun
v = verb
adj = adjective
adv = adverb
prep = preposition
pron = pronoun

1. Can *snake* be used as a noun?

2. Can *snake* be used as a verb?

3. Can *snake* be used as an adverb?

4. How many definitions are given for *snake* as a noun?

5. What does *snake* mean when it is used as a verb?

6. Write your own sentences using *snake* as a noun and a verb.

Chapter Review

Chapter Summary

- ☐ Some test questions call for short written answers. Always write such answers in complete sentences.

- ☐ Always restate the subject of the question.

- ☐ Answer essay questions by writing one or more well-developed paragraphs.

- ☐ The topic sentence should restate the subject of the question.

- ☐ Read essay questions carefully. Make sure that the paragraph you write does, indeed, answer the question.

Writing Practice

Choose one of the topics listed below and write a one paragraph essay answer.

1. Identify _____ (any famous person you choose).
2. Describe _____ (a well-known tourist attraction).
3. Explain why we celebrate _____ (any holiday).
4. Discuss the good and bad points of having a _____ (any animal) as a pet.
5. Explain why _____ (some fact of science: for example, why things fall down, why the sun sets in the West, why it rains, what causes tides . . .)

Remember to begin with a topic sentence that clearly states the subject and the point.

Chapter Quiz

Number your paper from 1 to 5. Beside each number write **Good** (good answer) or **Poor** (poor answer). If you decide an answer is poor, rewrite it, making it better.

example: Q: Identify Neil Armstrong.

A: first person to walk on moon

Poor.   Neil Armstrong was the first person to walk on the moon.

1. Q: Who was Harriet Beecher Stowe?

   A: a famous writer

2. Q: Who is Pelé?

   A. Pelé is a Brazilian soccer star who scored 1,280 goals during his twenty-two-year career.

3. Q: Why did France give the United States the Statue of Liberty?

   A: because they wanted to show friendship toward the U.S.

4. Q: What did the Nineteenth Amendment to the U.S. Constitution do?

   A: It gave women the right to vote.

5. Q: Who was Neptune?

   A: Neptune was the god of the sea in Roman mythology.

Chapter *21* Writing a Report

Ray Bradbury is a popular American writer of science fiction. His highly imaginative, suspenseful tales have appeared in both novel and short story form. Two of his best known works are The Martian Chronicles *and* Dandelion Wine. *Many of his stories are set in fantastic, "other worlds."*

A lively imagination is the science fiction writer's most important tool.

Writers at Work: Ray Bradbury (1920–   )

Chapter Learning Objectives

☐ Identify good report topics.

☐ Identify the card catalog, reference books, and the *Readers' Guide to Periodical Literature.*

☐ Use index cards for selective note taking.

☐ Organize notes and write an outline for a report.

☐ Identify the introduction, the body, and the conclusion of a report.

☐ Write a bibliography.

Words to Know

research the gathering of facts and other information

source any book, place, person, or material from which you gather information

example: That scientist is the *source* of my information.

periodicals publications such as newspapers or magazines that are published at regular intervals

card catalog a file in the library that contains information cards for every book

cross-reference a reference to another part of a book or to another source of information on the same subject

Dewey Decimal Number the specific number assigned in a library to each book, pamphlet, and so on that classifies the item according to subject

reference book a source of information

bibliography a list of books or sources for a particular topic

quote to repeat or copy exactly the writing or speech of another

Choosing the Topic of a Report

When a teacher first assigns a report, it can seem like a big task. However, if you approach the job step by step, the task is much simpler.

Here are the steps you will take when you do a research report:

1. Choose a topic.
2. Do the **research**. Find information and take notes.
3. Write an outline.
4. Write the report. (Write a rough draft. Then proofread, revise, and write a final copy.)
5. Write a bibliography.

Each section in this chapter will help you through one of the steps. This section begins, of course, with the first step, choosing a topic.

What are some topics that interest you?

If possible, choose a topic you like.
Sometimes a teacher will assign your report topic. At other times you will be free to choose your own topic. A report usually takes quite a bit of time and effort. It is certainly best if you choose a topic that interests you. A report assignment is often a chance to learn new things and to meet new people.

Make sure your topic is narrow enough.
Many students have trouble with reports because they try to research a topic that is too broad. For example, what would happen if you tried to write a three-page report on the country of Peru? Where would you begin? You could not possibly cover the entire subject or sort through all the available material. You would be much better off limiting your topic. Perhaps you might write about the people of Peru or discuss Peru's history or how it is governed.

Writing a report can be hard and confusing if your topic is too broad. Make it easy on yourself; narrow your topic to a size you can manage.

Activity 1

In each pair listed below, choose the topic that would be narrow enough for a three-page report. Write your answers on a separate sheet of paper.

1. a. Automobiles
   b. Henry Ford and the Model T

2. a. Native Americans
   b. Educational opportunities for Native Americans

3. a. The story of the Frankenstein monster
   b. Monsters

4. a. Fighter planes of World War I
   b. Airplanes

5. a. Fashion
   b. How people will dress in the 1990's

Now you try it.

Activity 2

For each of the broad topics listed below, write three different, narrower topics. Choose topics you feel would be appropriate for a three- to five-page report.

1. rock music	2. the Olympics	3. outer space
a.	a.	a.
b.	b.	b.
c.	c.	c.

Warning!
Always make sure you can find enough information on your topic.

Once you have chosen a topic, make sure you have enough **sources** for a good report. Suppose you saw one magazine article on your subject. That doesn't mean you will find more information. And one source is usually not enough.

For example, perhaps you heard about a woman named Holly Hanson who was a big game hunter in Africa. You decide she would be an interesting topic for a research paper. However, when you go to the library, you find only one half-page magazine article on Hanson. Don't be stubborn. Give up on Hanson and find a new topic.

Before you actually begin gathering information and taking notes, check to see if information is, indeed, available. Be willing to change your topic if you cannot find enough information.

Finding Information and Taking Notes

Your school library or the public library is the place to begin your research. Books and **periodicals** can usually provide the information you need. And sometimes you might consult a person for information about your topic. For example, if you are writing about a scientific topic, you might want to use your science teacher as one source.

The Card Catalog

The library's **card catalog** is the place to begin looking for books with information on your topic. The card catalog contains cards for every book in the library.

In the card catalog, there are three cards for every book. There is a subject card, an author card, and a title card. The same information appears on each card, but it is arranged differently. The cards are in alphabetical order and are **cross-referenced**. Author cards are alphabetized by the author's last name.

For example, if you want information on the midnight ride of Paul Revere, you could look under *Revere, Paul* or *American Revolution*. (These would be subject cards.)

If you knew you wanted a specific book on Paul Revere called *Brave Silversmith*, you could look in the "B" drawer of the card catalog under *Brave Silversmith*. (This would be a title card.)

If you knew that Walter Smith wrote the book *Brave Silversmith*, you could also look in the "S" drawer under Smith, Walter. (This would be an author card.)

For a nonfiction book the cards will give you the **Dewey Decimal Number** of the book. That number will tell you where to find the book on the shelf. Once you have that number, a librarian can also help you. For a work of fiction, the book will be listed on the shelf alphabetically by the author's last name.

Activity 3

Does your school have a library? Where is the nearest public library? Do you have a library card?

If you were using the card catalog . . .

1. Under which letter would you look to find a book called *Scary Stories to Read in the Dark?* Would you be looking for a title card, an author card, or a subject card?

2. Under which letter would you look to find a book about Greek mythology? Would you be looking for a title card, an author card, or a subject card?

3. Pretend you really enjoy reading novels by an author named Alice Wald. Under which letter would you look to see if her books are available in your library? Would you be looking for a title card, an author card, or a subject card?

Challenge

Go to a library and see if it has the following books. If it has the book, write down the author's name. If it does not have the book, write "No."

1. *The Pigman*
2. *Jane Eyre*
3. *The Fox Steals Home*
4. *Where the Red Fern Grows*
5. *Mystery on White Pine Lane*

Use the card catalog to answer these questions.

1. Did the author of *The Fox Steals Home* write any other books besides that one? If so, list three.

2. Did the author of *Jane Eyre* write any other books besides that one? If so, name one.

3. Pretend you are writing a report about Martin Luther King, Jr. Write the title and author of one book that might contain information you need.

Reference Books

You can also find information in the library by looking in reference books. You do not need to read an entire **reference book**. You can look up the topic you need either in the index or table of contents. Usually you cannot check reference books out of the library. You must use them at the library.

Most libraries have a reference shelf. You can find these books and others like them on the reference shelf:

Encyclopedia   This tool is divided into volumes and contains alphabetized entries on almost any subject.

Almanac   This book contains facts, statistics, records, and information for current and past years. It is a good place to look for quick information.

Atlas   This book contains maps and facts about places.

Who's Who in America, Current Biography   These books contain alphabetized entries with information about famous people. *Current Biography* is divided into volumes.

Periodicals

Do you read any periodicals regularly? Do you or any member of your family subscribe to any periodicals?

Very up-to-date information can often be found in magazine articles and newspapers. These materials are called periodicals. But how do you ever find an article about your topic? You certainly cannot look through every magazine in the library!

A publication called the *Readers' Guide to Periodical Literature* can help you find your article. The *Readers' Guide* lists articles from major magazines.

Suppose you were writing a report on the rock music group, the Rolling Stones. Suppose you looked under Rock 'n' roll groups in *Readers' Guide.* You might find this entry there.

Rolling Along: Rolling Stones. J. Cook. Newsday 81:120 N 17 '70

title of article   **author**   **magazine**   **volume**   **page**   **date**

Activity 4

Use the sample entry below to answer the questions.

The Rolling Stones on the Road. B. Taylor. *Music Digest* 78:24-26 Ja 6 '69.

1. What is the name of the magazine article?
2. Who wrote the article?
3. In what magazine will the article be found?
4. On what pages can the article be found?
5. What is the date of the magazine issue?

Taking Notes

Once you have found your sources, you will need to read them and to take notes. Use the table of contents and index in books to help locate the information you need.

Take your notes on index cards not on regular paper. Then when the time comes to organize your material, you can move the cards around and arrange them according to subtopics.

Each note card will have two headings. One heading will indicate the subtopic the information

covers. Imagine that your paper is on World War I airplanes and you are taking notes on the British Sopwith. You would write "Types of planes—British Sopwith" at the top of your card.

The second heading will indicate your source. Perhaps you found the information in the *American Encyclopedia*. Note <u>American Encyclopedia</u> at the top of the card. Also note the volume and page number in case you need to look the material up again. Always keep a complete listing of all sources you use on separate cards. Write down the title of the book, author or editor, volume number, publisher, place of publication, and copyright date. You will need this information later for your **bibliography**.

Study this sample note card:

Types of planes—British Sopwith

<u>American Encyclopedia</u>,
vol. A, pg. 122

British Sopwith Triplane—nicknamed Tripe—1st used in battle in 1916

British Sopwith Camel—two machine guns—one above wing, one behind propeller

"The British Sopwith engaged in dogfights, or battles in the air with enemy planes."

In the sample note card above, observe that notes are not written in complete sentences. If a source contains information you want to use word for word, copy that information exactly and put quotation marks around the **quote**. Do not copy any other information word for word from the source. Summarize main points found in the source. Be brief, but accurate.

Activity 5

Assume that you are writing a report on the dodo bird. Read the following selection. Take notes on information you think you could use in the report. Remember, the notes should be brief and to the point. They should not be in complete sentences unless you are copying a direct quotation.

The Dodo Bird

The dodo bird was a rather strange creature. The last dodo bird was seen around 1681. It was about the size of a turkey, but it had very short legs, a gigantic beak, and stubby wings. A short tail of curly feathers added to the dodo's odd appearance. The dodo was quite a large bird, often almost three feet high. Because it was so heavy and because its wings were so small, the dodo could not fly.

Organizing Notes and Writing an Outline

When you have finished taking notes, you will have many note cards. Separate them according to their headings. Put all the notes on one subtopic together.

Then look at your piles of note cards. You can see how much you have to say on each subtopic. If one pile is very small, you might want to omit that subtopic. If a pile is very large, you might want to divide that one subtopic into two or more parts.

Think about the person who was writing a report on World War I fighter planes. This person might have ended up with four piles of notes: one on different types of planes, one on special features of the World

War I plane, one on famous air squadrons of World War I, and one on famous pilots of World War I. Each of the piles of notes would represent a section of the report. As the writer organizes the note cards, the report begins to take shape.

Activity 6

A student was writing a report on the famous magician, Harry Houdini. Some of the facts are listed below. Organize those facts into subtopic groups by matching each numbered fact with a lettered subtopic. Write your answers on a separate sheet of paper.

facts	subtopics

facts

1. Houdini could free himself after being handcuffed, nailed in a box, and thrown into deep water.

2. His real name was Ehrich Weiss.

3. He once was a trapeze performer in a circus.

4. He considered magic a skill that could be learned.

5. He did not believe in the supernatural.

6. He could escape from prison cells.

subtopics

A. A description of Houdini's early life

B. Houdini's magic tricks

C. Houdini's attitude toward magic and the supernatural

Once your note cards are divided into groups, it is time to write an outline. You may remember working with essay outlines in Chapter 14. Your report outline should be done in very much the same way. Look at the following sample outline for a report on World War I airplanes. The writer should have a pile of note cards for each main section of the outline.

World War I Airplanes

I. Introduction

II. Different types of World War I planes
    A. British planes
        1. Sopwith
        2. Vickers
        3. Handley-Page twin-engine
    B. German Fokker
    C. French Spad

III. Special features of World War I planes
    A. Attack features
        1. First use of machine guns on planes
        2. Bombing devices
            a. First threw bombs by hand
            b. Later developed electrical bombing device
    B. Safety features
        1. Telephones in oxygen masks
        2. Armored pilot seat
    C. Engines

IV. Famous air squadrons of World War I
    A. French squadrons
    B. British squadrons
    C. American squadrons

V. Famous pilots of World War I
    A. Roland Garros
        1. French pilot who carried pistols and rifles
        2. First fighter pilot
    B. Quentin Roosevelt
        1. Youngest son of President Theodore Roosevelt
        2. Shot down behind enemy lines
    C. Eddie Rickenbacker
        1. American race car driver
        2. Leading American "ace"

VI. Conclusion

Writing the Report

Do you remember how to write a good paragraph (Unit Two) and how to organize an essay (Unit Four)? You will use the same skills to write your report. Like an essay, the report has an *introduction*, a *body* of supporting paragraphs, and a *conclusion*. Just be sure to follow your outline and write a clear topic sentence for each paragraph.

Read on for a few hints:

Your Introduction (the first paragraph)
Your introduction does not need to be long. Keep it simple and direct. The introduction should define your topic and explain the purpose of your research.

Read this example:

> In recent wars, the skies have been a battlefield. However, World War I was the first war in which soldiers took to the air. Today, computers fire missiles. Those earliest pilots shot pistols at each other from their open cockpits. I think it is amazing how much military planes have advanced. For this reason, I decided to research and discuss those early war planes, the fighter planes of World War I.

Direct Quotations in the Body
Most of your report will be written in your own words. However, you may want to quote a source directly once or twice. When you use a direct quotation, you must put the words in quotation marks and identify the source.

Read this example:

> Many American World War I pilots were after adventure. According to the *American Encyclopedia*, "Many of the daring pilots in the slow-flying planes of World War I looked upon war as a game." American race car driver Eddie Rickenbacker became one such pilot.

Your Conclusion (the last paragraph)

At the end of your report, you will need a conclusion. Like the introduction, it should be short and simple. It should refer back to the introduction. Look at this sample conclusion. Then reread the sample introduction above. Notice how they are alike.

> During my research, I read fascinating stories of the earliest fighter planes and the men who flew them. I was amazed to find that such a short time ago planes were so very different. The warplanes of World War I may have been slow and primitive compared to today's aircraft, but they were exciting. They were the first fighters in the sky.

Of course, you will proofread and edit the rough draft of your report before writing the final copy. The final copy should be written in ink or typed.

Activity 7

Number your paper from 1 to 5. Write <u>true</u> if the statement is true. Write <u>false</u> if the statement is false.

1. A report has an introduction, a body, and a conclusion.

2. The introduction tells what the report is about.

3. The body is only one paragraph long.

4. The conclusion is very much like the introduction.

5. Anything copied word for word from a source must be put in quotation marks, and the source must be identified.

Writing the Bibliography

A bibliography is a list of the sources you used in your research. Your sources will include any books, reference books, or periodicals that you used.

You should list the items in your bibliography in *alphabetical order*. Bibliographies must be written in a special way. Look at the sample bibliography that follows. Notice how each entry is written.

Bibliography

Arnold, William T. <u>The History of American Aircraft.</u> New York: Smith Publishing Co., 1985.

"Airplanes." <u>The American Encyclopedia,</u> Vol. 1. Chicago: Ace Education Inc., 1982, pp. 34-52.

Hart, C. L. "Flying Aces." <u>Newsday,</u> May 1987, Vol. 21, p. 22.

Write down bibliographical information as you use each source. You do not want to make an extra trip to the library just to find bibliographical information.

Activity 8

Write a bibliography with at least four entries. Use the sample bibliography as a guide. Be sure to alphabetize the entries.

Writing With Style

A research report takes a lot of work and time. You will want to present it in a way that reflects all your effort. Staple your papers together in the top left corner. Your report should include a *title page*, the *report* itself, and a *bibliography*.

The *title page* is the first thing your readers will see. Follow the sample title page below, and present your paper with style.

Airplanes

of World War I

by

Ann Roth

May 4, 1989

Vocabulary Builder

Words in the Library

The paragraph below contains words common to the world of books and learning. Read the paragraph and then write down each of the italicized words. Next to each word, write the number of its definition (definitions follow the sample paragraph). Use context clues (the way the word is used in the paragraph) to help you.

example: *librarian—4*

> My teacher assigned a report on a famous person, so I went to the library to look for information. The *librarian* suggested that I read a *biography*. At last, I decided to write my report on Emmett Kelly, the famous clown. I found a book on circus clowns right away. I looked in the *table of contents* and saw that the book had a whole chapter on Kelly. The *index* of the book told me he was mentioned on other pages, too. The *publisher* had included a large *illustration* showing Emmett Kelly in a colorful clown suit. The book on clowns was rather old. The *copyright date* was 1950. However, the information was still very interesting.

Definitions

1. a book about a person

2. a list of chapters in a book that is found in the front of the book

3. a list at the end of the book telling subjects the book covers

4. a person who works in a library

5. a person or company who organizes the printing of a book, magazine, newspaper, and so on for distribution to the public

6. the year a book was published

7. a picture

Chapter Review

Chapter Summary

☐ Narrow your report topic so you can discuss it fully.

☐ Make sure there is enough information available on your topic. If not, be willing to change your topic.

☐ Use the card catalog to locate books in the library.

☐ Use the *Readers' Guide* to find magazine articles on your topic.

☐ Take notes on index cards. Label the cards with subtopic and source headings.

☐ Do not copy information word for word. Summarize main points; be brief.

☐ Organize note cards according to subtopics.

☐ Write an outline showing the parts of your report (introduction; body of supporting, detailed paragraphs; conclusion).

☐ Write a rough draft, using your outline as a guide.

☐ Write a bibliography listing your sources.

Writing Practice

Imagine that you are writing a report about haunted houses. Write an introduction that clearly states your topic and that would interest your readers. Review the sample introduction on page 323 of this chapter before you write.

Chapter Quiz

A. Answer the following questions in complete sentences.
   Remember what you learned in the last chapter about
   answering questions with complete sentences.

   1. Would *American history* be a good topic for a report? Why
      or why not?

   2. What are the three kinds of catalog cards for every
      nonfiction book in the library?

   3. Why would a person take notes on index cards rather
      than on notebook paper?

   4. What is the purpose of an outline?

   5. What are the three main parts of a research paper?

   6. What is a bibliography?

B. Match the type of information with the most likely source.

   1. atlas

   2. *Readers' Guide to
      Periodical Literature*

   3. *Who's Who in America*

   4. card catalog

   a. a magazine article on the
      Boston Celtics basketball team

   b. information on the life of
      Ronald Reagan

   c. a map of Brazil

   d. a book about Eskimos

Unit Review

A. Write an answer to one of the following short essay questions. Remember to write in complete sentences and to state the subject of the question in your first sentence.

1. Describe the conflict in a book you read recently and explain how that conflict was resolved.

2. Describe one of your favorite fictional characters.

3. Describe in detail the five steps involved in writing a report.

4. If you could write a report on anything you wanted, what topic would you choose? Explain why you would choose that topic.

B. Choose the item that best completes each sentence.

1. A character description should (a) just describe the way a character looks. (b) just describe a character's personality. (c) describe a character's looks and personality.

2. A card catalog will contain (a) one card for every book. (b) two cards for every book. (c) three cards for every book.

3. Research notes (a) should be taken on index cards. (b) should be taken on paper. (c) are not necessary.

4. The bibliography should be found (a) right after the title page. (b) at the end of the report. (c) at the bottom of the first page.

Unit Seven

Imaginative Writing

Chapter 22 Creating Characters

Agatha Christie, a British mystery novelist, produced 66 detective novels in 56 years of writing. Two of her best known stories are The Murder of Roger Ackroyd *and* Murder on the Orient Express. *Her plots are clever, often humorous, and they always keep the reader in suspense.*

Constructing a good plot takes careful thought and organization.

Writers at Work: Agatha Christie (1890–1976)

Chapter Learning Objectives

☐ Write character descriptions based on real people.

☐ Write character descriptions that appeal to all the senses.

☐ Write about characters who are interesting.

☐ Write effective dialogue.

☐ Write correctly punctuated dialogue.

Words to Know

traits   special qualities

unique   being the only one of its kind

habit   a thing a person does regularly without thinking about it

imaginary   not real; existing only in one's mind

villain   an evil or wicked character in a story

hero   the most important male character in a story; usually he is good

heroine   the most important female character in a story; usually she is good

dialogue   a conversation between two or more people

indirect quotation   repeating what a character says, but not in exact words

example: *Tom said that he was hungry.* = an indirect quotation.

Tom said, "I am hungry." = a direct quotation

Drawing on Real Life

Have you ever read a book and felt as if you really knew a character? Are there some characters that you just can't forget? Authors who create such characters have done their job well. A good writer can make characters come alive.

The world is full of characters—people with interesting faces, shapes, and personalities. When writers create fictional characters, they often draw on some of the **traits** of real people they have known.

Think about some "real people," beginning with yourself.

It can be hard to describe yourself. It's often easier to see unusual traits in other people. This first activity will give you a chance to look closely at yourself.

Activity 1

A. On a separate sheet of paper, copy any adjectives from the list below that describe you. Then write five more adjectives of your own that describe you.

friendly	shy	serious	energetic
quiet	funny	kind	lazy
happy	tough	clumsy	sad
lonely	attractive	slim	artistic
plump	athletic	intelligent	nervous

B. On your own paper, complete each of the following sentences.

My favorite food is _____ .

My favorite season is _____ .

If I could be doing anything I wanted, I would be _____ .

I hated the time that _____ .

Other people say that I am _____ .

The one possession I treasure most is _____ .

I admire people who _____ .

The strangest thing about me is _____ .

Now write two more sentences about yourself.

C. On your own paper, draw a picture of yourself. You don't have to be a great artist. Any little sketch will do.

Now complete these sentences:

My best physical feature is my _____ .

My worst physical feature is my _____ .

My best personality feature is my _____ .

D. Use the information above. Write one paragraph describing yourself physically. Then write a second paragraph describing your personality. Be sure to tell what makes you special, or different from other people.

Have you ever heard the expression, "What a character!"?

A person who is called a character is usually someone who is unusual. A "character" is special. A "character" stands out in a group. These **unique** traits make people interesting. Consider the people you know, perhaps the people in your classroom. Try to identify their special **habits** or traits.

Activity 2

Complete each sentence with the name of someone you know.

1. _____ has a most unusual way of laughing.

2. _____ wears the strangest clothes.

3. _____ has the most interesting hairdo.

4. _____ has a sad smile.

5. _____ is the funniest person I know.

6. _____ is the most serious person I know.

7. _____ takes a lot of risks.

8. _____ has an unusual face.

9. _____ is the friendliest person I know.

10. _____ is the meanest person I know.

Now write a paragraph of description based on one of the sentences above. Describe the unusual trait of the person you have named. For example, describe how and why Sally Wilson takes a lot of risks or why Joe Brown's smile seems so sad.

Can you write a whole paragraph on just one trait? Yes, if you really pay attention to detail. Try to make your reader see what you describe. Use examples. You might write about one of Sally's recent exploits—how she wanted to join the track team. Use comparisons. Joe's smile is like a rainy day.

Use all your senses. You might describe how Sally's face looks when she's made up her mind to do something risky—how her mouth snaps shut and she bites her lips. Stretch your imagination and creativity. Then you will find you can write a whole paragraph about that one trait.

The person you just described was a real person. Often authors draw on real people to create **imaginary** characters.

You have all kinds of freedom when you're creating an imaginary character. You can combine the unusual traits of many people to make an interesting character. You might use one person's walk and another's hairdo. The real people you draw upon for ideas can be people you know.

On the other hand, they can be people you only saw once but remember well. Perhaps an old man waiting for the bus caught your eye because he looked so angry. Perhaps you remember a couple's interesting comments that you overheard in a restaurant. That conversation may inspire you to write dialogue.

You first read about exaggeration in Chapter 11. Turn back if you need help remembering.

Writers have the freedom to exaggerate characteristics to make a character unforgettable. Use what you know from real life and real people. Then add your imagination to create a unique fictional character.

Activity 3

Create a fictional character. Use characteristics from people you really know or have seen. Again, try to write two paragraphs. The first paragraph should describe the character's physical appearance. The second paragraph should describe his or her personality. Give your character a name and bring him or her to life.

Begin your description by completing the following sentence:

_____ is a most unusual person.

Challenge

Draw a picture of your character, or find a picture in a magazine or newspaper that shows how you picture your character.

Appealing to All of the Reader's Senses

Look at the description you wrote for Activity 3. What senses did you call upon to describe your character? Did you describe the way the character looked? Did you describe how the character sounded or smelled?

Read the following character description. To what senses does the writer appeal?

Sometimes the sound of a person's voice is as interesting and unique as the way that person looks.

The girl entered the room with a jangle of bracelets and a strange tinkling of bells. I watched her. She was different from anyone I had ever seen. Other people were looking at her, too. She wanted to be noticed. She had dyed her hair a bright pink color and wore matching pink eye shadow bold and shiny on her eyelids. The tinkling sound, I saw, came from her shoes. She had tied tiny silver bells on each yellow shoelace. She was in the room only a moment. Then she was gone, leaving the sweet smell of perfume hanging heavy in the air.

Did you notice that the writer described the way the girl looked, sounded, and smelled? All those senses were used to create a character. Did you also notice the writer's reaction to the girl? Do you feel you know something about this girl? Do you know anything about the writer? When you write, you create character but you also reveal or disguise *yourself* as well. Writing can be a powerful act.

Challenge

Use the character just described for this activity. Picture the girl in your mind. You know a little about her now. Create even more character by describing what you think she would be wearing. Describe her outfit in detail. Can you write more about why she wants to be noticed? Does she say anything? Creating character begins in saying how someone looks, but beyond that, it tells us about personality and emotion as well.

Activity 4

Choose one of the following, and write your description on a separate sheet of paper.

A. Rewrite your paragraph from Activity 3, adding description that appeals to a sense other than sight.

or

B. Pretend that you're blind. You're sitting in a room alone, and a stranger walks in. Write a one-paragraph description of that stranger.

Winning Sympathy for Your Character

You have finished the book. You wipe tears from your eyes and realize that you feel as if you actually lived the story you just read. "That was a good book!" you exclaim.

Can you name a fictional character you will never forget?

One of the reasons you feel that way is that the author won your sympathy for the characters. You really cared about what happened to the characters. Whenever you create a character, one of your goals should be making the reader care about that person.

How do you make your reader sympathize with your character? One way is to use a lot of detail. Let the reader know the character. Show the character doing things and saying things that the reader will believe are real. The reader will usually sympathize with the character that he or she knows best.

Become the Character

As a writer, you can create a believable character by putting yourself in that character's place. Become the character as you write. You may not be a fifteen-year-old country boy who has suddenly moved to New York City. But, if that boy is your character, try to think as he would. Try to picture things through his eyes. How would he react to a crowded subway train? How would he see the holiday lights on Fifth Avenue?

Activity 5

Practice putting yourself in the place of a character who is very different from yourself. Choose an object that is not alive. Maybe you will pick a doorknob, a roller skate, a football, a flag, or a computer. Bring that object to life as a character. Be that character! Write one or two paragraphs from the first-person point of view (using "I"). Describe yourself as the object, and describe your feelings.

Point of View

A story is usually told with the focus on one character's point of view. It is that character who usually wins the reader's sympathy.

For example, imagine a war between two countries, Lumboland and the Kingdom of Woo. Suppose the story is written about a fellow from Woo who leaves his beloved wife and fourteen children to fight for his country, the reader will probably see Lumbolanders as enemies. The reader will sympathize with the soldier from Woo.

However, the same tale of war could focus on the people of Lumboland. A writer can easily win sympathy for a young, Lumboland warrior who is kind and gentle and does good deeds.

You can win sympathy for your character by presenting events from his or her point of view.

Refer back to Chapter 15 if you need to review point of view.

A story told by "I" is said to be written from the first-person point of view. When a story is told in terms of the pronouns *she, he,* or *they,* it is one told from a third-person point of view.

Activity 6

Practice looking at things from different points of view. Choose one of the writing assignments below. Write your paragraph on a separate sheet of paper.

A. Describe a mud puddle. First, write one paragraph describing a mud puddle from a five-year-old's point of view. Then write a paragraph describing the same mud puddle from the child's father's point of view.

B. Someone tied Billy O'Connor's shoelaces to his desk legs. When the bell rang, Billy got up to leave the classroom. He tripped, fell, and pulled the desk down on top of him. Write a paragraph describing the incident from Billy's point of view. Then write a paragraph describing the incident from the point of view of the person who played the joke on Billy.

C. Describe an automobile accident. First write a paragraph describing the accident from the point of view of the driver of one car. Then write a paragraph describing the accident from the point of view of the driver of the second car.

The Bad Guy

Just as you win your reader's sympathy for the good characters, you can make your reader dislike the bad characters. Create an evil **villain** just as you would create a **hero** or **heroine.** However, in characterizing a villain, you will point out the bad things the character has done instead of the good. You will probably emphasize unattractive physical characteristics. You might make the villain *whine* and *snarl* and *growl* instead of *speak*. Your reader should hope that the villain loses out in the end!

Make Your Characters Speak—Writing Dialogue

Dialogue is conversation between characters speaking to each other. Read these two examples of dialogue:

A. "Excuse me, sir," the woman said, "but I believe you are standing on my toe."

B. "Hey, buddy," the woman said, "get your fat foot off my toe."

As you see, dialogue can say a lot about a character. By writing dialogue, you can build a character's personality. How is the woman in sentence A different from the woman in sentence B? You could say the woman in sentence A is too polite. You could say the woman in sentence B is probably angry.

Activity 7

On your own paper, write an adjective or a phrase that describes the speaker in each of the following groups of sentences:

1. "What a beautiful day!" Sarah exclaimed. "The sun is shining, the flowers are blooming, and the air is warm."

2. "It's too hot!" George complained. "That sun is beating down on me, and those stupid flowers are making me sneeze."

3. "I can hardly wait until the tryouts for the spring play," said Amy. "I'm going to try out for the leading role."

4. "Are the tryouts for the spring play really tomorrow?" asked Seth. "I don't know my lines very well. Maybe I'm catching a cold and should stay home."

The Reference Guide *in the back of this book will tell you more about punctuating quotations. See Punctuation 14, 15, and 16.*

When you use dialogue, you must write it correctly. Follow these rules when you write dialogue.

1. Put quotation marks around a direct quotation (a speaker's exact words).

example: ***"Stop teasing that kitten,"*** *shouted Jean.*

2. Only the exact words are put inside the quotation marks. Explaining words are outside the quotation marks.

> example: *"I didn't mean to hurt the cat,"* **said Wilma.**

3. Separate the direct quotation from the explaining words with a comma, a question mark, or an exclamation point. The punctuation mark at the end of a quotation goes within the quotation marks.

> examples: *"I will cook a fine dinner," said the chef.*
>
> *"What's in the stew?" asked Molly.*
>
> *"Help me!" screamed the man on the raft.*

4. Capitalize the first word of a quotation.

> example: *The waiter said, "***The** *cook is very sorry about the fly in your soup."*

5. A direct quotation may be placed at the beginning or at the end of a sentence. It may also be divided by the explaining words.

> examples: *"Uncle Paul's car is here. My favorite uncle has finally arrived," cried Julie.*
>
> *Julie cried, "Uncle Paul's car is here. My favorite uncle has finally arrived."*
>
> *"Uncle Paul's car is here," Julie cried. "My favorite uncle has finally arrived."*

Note

If the divided quotation is all one sentence, do not capitalize the word that begins the second part of the quotation

> example: *"Uncle Paul," Julie cried, "has finally arrived."*

6. Begin a new paragraph each time a different character speaks.

> example: *Mrs. Marcus said, "Today's lesson deals with writing quotations and punctuating them properly."*
>
> *"Ugh!" exclaimed Rose. "I would rather be sailing."*

7. If you do not use the speaker's exact words, but some other form of them, do not use quotation marks. This method is called an **indirect quotation.**

> example: *Rose said that she would rather be sailing.*

Activity 8

On a separate sheet of paper, copy each of these direct quotations and punctuate them correctly.

1. Wendy whispered I think this will be an exciting adventure.
2. This spaceship will leave in one hour the captain announced.
3. Where can I buy a ticket I asked.
4. The ticket booth, a woman answered, is at the end of the hall.
5. All aboard for Mars the captain shouted.

Read the following selection. Dialogue has been used to tell a story. Notice how each character reveals his personality through conversation.

"What is the matter?" Alfred asked Jerry. "You don't really believe in haunted houses, do you?"

"Of course not," Jerry lied. He looked around at the spider webs in the empty room. "Maybe we should get out of this old house. We don't really belong here."

"Don't be silly," Alfred said. "Those guys dared us to spend the night here, and I have never turned down a dare."

"What's that?" Jerry cried. He looked up at the top of the wooden staircase and pointed. "What . . . what . . .what . . ." Jerry could no longer speak. His words froze in his throat.

"Don't be afraid," Alfred said. "It's only someone dressed in a bed sheet playing tricks on us." But Alfred turned pale when the strange figure in white began to float down the stairs.

What kind of person is Alfred?

What kind of person is Jerry?

Now you try it.

Activity 9

Write a conversation between two people. Let what the characters say reflect their personalities. Choose one of the following situations below.

Write a conversation between:

- a clerk in a store and a customer trying to return an item

- an umpire and an angry baseball fan

- two space creatures who have just landed on Earth

- a traffic police officer and a person getting a speeding ticket

- two children who have run away from home

Activity 10

The names you choose for your characters can be important. Different kinds of names give the reader different mental pictures of what a character looks like. Think about the names in the following list. Then write a short description of that character's physical appearance. Use your imagination.

Spike Boznowski	Matilda Marblehead
Reverend Van Cleef	Mrs. Grundy
Jane Doe	Coach Mills
R. Wentworth Biddle	Bert Duff

Now write four short conversations that these characters might have with one another. For example, what might R. Wentworth Biddle have to say to Mrs. Grundy? What might Matilda Marblehead and Jane Doe have to talk about? Make each dialogue at least four sentences long.

Writing With Style

Which of the selections below makes you care more about what happens to the main character?

What do you know about Christine in paragraph A? What do you know about Christine in paragraph B? How does one selection win more sympathy for Christine than the other?

A. When Christine woke up, she found herself at the bottom of a deep canyon. She realized that she had fallen from a cliff. She had been knocked out when her head hit the rocks. She moved carefully, checking to see if any bones were broken.

Luckily, she was all right. She looked up the smooth sides of the steep cliff. Then she realized the truth. There was no way out of the canyon. She was trapped.

B. When Christine woke up, she found herself at the bottom of a deep canyon. She realized that she had fallen from a cliff while walking with her dog. She moved carefully, checking to see if any bones were broken. Her blue jeans were torn and her knee was cut, but otherwise she was all right. Then Christine thought about her family. Her husband Gary would be worried. She should have returned long ago. And what about Jake, her little boy? He would be crying for his mother. Christine looked up the smooth sides of the steep cliff. She could hear her dog Snowball barking wildly from somewhere far away. Christine's gentle, blue eyes filled with determination as she realized the truth. There seemed to be no way out of the canyon. But nothing was going to keep her from getting out of there and back to her family.

Vocabulary Builder

Let Your Imagination Go
Make up a totally new word. Then use it in a paragraph. Let the context (the way you use the word in sentences) reveal the word's meaning.

example: *made up word—quimble*

I went to Miller's Pet Shop to buy a quimble. I had been saving my money for months because a quimble is very expensive. The clerk at Miller's said that they kept the quimbles in the back of the shop because most people weren't interested in them. The back of the shop was dark and cool. Quimbles like it that way. I heard the quimbles making a tiny chirping sound. The first quimble I saw was the one I wanted. It was soft and brown and furry. I paid my money, and the clerk put my new quimble in a little cage. I hurried out of the store, anxious to take my new quimble home.

Now you try it.

Make up your own new word and use it in an original paragraph.

Chapter Review

Chapter Summary

☐ Draw upon interesting traits of real people to create fictional characters.

☐ Appeal to other senses in addition to the sense of sight when you describe people.

☐ A good writer creates characters that readers care about.

☐ Try to put yourself in the place of your character. Try to see things from that character's point of view.

☐ A character's dialogue can show a lot about his or her personality.

Writing Practice

Find a picture of someone in a magazine. Look carefully at the person in the picture. Give this person a name. Spend some time imagining what kind of life this character leads. Describe an imaginary incident involving the character. The incident you describe should give clues to the character's personality.

Chapter Quiz

A. Copy the following conversation, adding quotation marks wherever necessary.

I have a riddle for you, Mark said to Gina.

Your jokes are always so silly, Gina said. Go ahead and tell it to me anyway.

Mark grinned and said, Knock, knock.

Who's there? Gina asked with a sigh.

Darryl, said Mark.

Gina knew what she was supposed to say. Darryl who? she answered.

Darryl never be a joke stupider than this one! laughed Mark.

B. The things characters say show a lot about their personalities. Match each comment with an adjective that would describe the speaker.

1. "All right, let's all get in line now. I want to see this done the right way. Follow my instructions and everything will turn out fine!"

   a. bossy

   b. generous

2. "I'm not sure if I want to meet her today. I haven't worked out, and I know I won't be able to think of a thing to say."

   c. insecure

3. "Don't you think that old man could use some help? He looks so frail and tired. I hate to see him carrying those heavy groceries all by himself. I think I will take a few minutes to help him."

Chapter 23 Writing a Story

Zane Grey, after a trip west in 1908, gave up his career as a dentist and began to write western stories. At first he had a hard time finding a publisher. Then, in 1912, his first book came out; Riders of the Purple Sage *went on to sell one million copies. His novels are realistic, colorful tales of frontier life.*

Believable characters are created by using many details from real life.

Writers at Work: Zane Grey (1875–1939)

Chapter Learning Objectives

☐ Identify character as a story element.
☐ Identify setting as a story element.
☐ Identify plot as a story element.
☐ Identify mood as a story element.
☐ Explain the term *resolution of conflict.*

Words to Know

distinct   different or separate

mood   a state of mind or feeling

background   the events that came before

What Is a Story?

Storytellers have power. They can transport others into a different world. For a little while, they can turn dreams into reality.

The cave people drew pictures on the walls of their caves, and those pictures told stories. The pictures told stories of struggles with wild animals. They told stories of hard times when food was scarce and the weather was bad. People continued telling stories through the years. In all lands, they told tales of troubles, of triumphs, and of heroes and heroines. We are still telling stories today.

Your teacher says, "Today we will write stories. Everyone loves a good story. This should be fun."

Writing a story can, indeed, be fun, but not unless you understand what a story is. What does the teacher mean by a "story"?

A story tells what happened.

The tale of "what happened" can be true, or it can be made up. It can be short (just a paragraph) or long (hundreds of pages).

A story has a conflict.

You can read more about conflict in Chapter 19, Writing a Book Report.

You may call a conflict a problem, or a struggle. But remember that a story has to have one in order to be a story. The conflict is the heart of the story. Everything else revolves around it.

The conflict can be between two people, as in the following example:

> Tim comes to live at his cousin Dick's house. Dick thinks that Tim is a boring pest. Dick teases Tim all the time. The two boys fight and argue. Tim, who is really a very lonely boy, must not only live in Dick's house but must share his room.

The conflict can be between a person and some outside force, as in the following example:

> Connie takes the little girl she is babysitting on a rowboat ride on the lake. When a storm comes up she has to save not only her own life, but the child's life too.

The conflict can be within one character's mind. It can involve a decision that he or she must make, as in the following example:

> Diane knew that the other girls in school thought that Becky was a stranger. She knew that they would laugh at her if she invited Becky to her party. But she also knew that Becky needed a friend. A party invitation would mean more to Becky than anything in the world. Diane could make Becky happy, but it could mean losing other friends. What would Diane do?

Activity 1

To write a story of your own, you need to recognize what a conflict is. Read about each of the following situations. Decide if each contains a conflict.

Unless there is a problem, there is no conflict.

Number your paper from 1 to 5. Then write *conflict* or *no conflict* by each number.

1. Pete has skipped school and is spending the day in the park. While he is at the park, he sees a robbery. He is the only one who sees the attack on the old man, and he can clearly identify the robber. However, if Pete tells the police what he saw, his parents will find out he skipped school. He will be punished.

2. Pete has skipped school and is spending the day in the park. It is a beautiful day. The sun is shining, and the park is not crowded as it is on the weekends. Pete buys some popcorn and feeds the ducks in the duck pond. He has a great day.

3. Sarah and Kim have always been good friends. They both try out for the same swim team. They both make the team. They both want to swim in the butterfly event.

4. Sarah and Kim have always been good friends. They both try out for the same swim team. They both make the team. The team is great, and they have a winning season.

5. Lisa discovers that her father's factory is dumping dangerous waste material in the town river. She wants to be loyal to her family, but she knows that the river could be destroyed.

Activity 2

Think of three situations that contain conflict. They can be real experiences you have had or have heard about. Perhaps you were once lost, faced danger, or competed with someone. The situations can also be imaginary. On your own paper, write a brief description (like those in Activity 1) for each of the situations.

The People in the Story

A story must have characters, a setting, and a plot. The characters are the people in the story. In a good story, the characters seem real. In a good story, the reader cares what happens to the characters. Remember the discussion of character in the last chapter. Review it if you need to.

Characters are also discussed in Chapter 19, *Writing a Book Report*, and in Chapter 22, *Creating Characters*.

When you write a short story, you should limit the number of characters. If you have too many characters, your reader may not be able to keep them all straight. Have you ever read a story where you were confused by too many characters?

It is better to concentrate on getting your reader to know two or three characters well than to introduce lots of people. Remember your goal. You want your reader to care about your characters.

Give your characters names that are very different from each other. Give them different sizes and shapes, different hair colors, and different personalities. Make them wear different types of clothing. Make sure the characters are **distinct** from each other.

Activity 3

On a separate sheet of paper, copy and complete the lists below. Make the characters very distinct from each other. You might base your characters on two real people you know who are quite different from each other.

Character 1

name:
age:
hair color:
size:
clothing style:
personality:
interests:

Character 2

name:
age:
hair color:
size:
clothing style:
personality:
interests:

Challenge

Rewrite the following paragraphs. Change the characters' names so that they are not so alike. Give each character some distinguishing characteristics.

You might consider these qualities as you rewrite: hair colors, personalities, and interests.

You might try making the reader like one of the characters and dislike the other one. Or you might decide their conflict is not very important or is a cliché (a cliché is an overused expression or situation). Create a different conflict for them if you like.

Annie and Amy were on their own at last. It was their first year of college, and they were roommates. They had been friends since grade school. They had been at the university only for one week, and already both had fallen in love. Annie described her new boyfriend as tall, handsome, and athletic. Amy said her boyfriend was all those things, too. He was also, she said, smart, sweet, and gentle.

Then Annie saw Amy and a young man walking hand in hand in front of the library. Annie was shocked and angry. Amy was holding hands with Annie's boyfriend! They were both in love with the same man.

The Setting Can Create a Mood

The setting is where and when the story takes place. The writer must make the setting clear early in the story. The setting can create a **mood** for a story.

You can read more about setting in Chapter 19, Writing a Book Report.

What kind of a mood is created by the following description of setting?

> Dark clouds moved in over the lake. The outline of the shore looked far away. Although the sky was dark, the late afternoon was very calm. There was not a breath of wind. It was strange, indeed, for the air to be so still. The water was as dark as the sky. Not a ripple disturbed its black surface. Then I saw a strange shape pass by my little rowboat. It was a long, white shape that seemed to be just a few feet under the water. It passed again, going against the current now. This large object was no fish!

Could you say the above setting creates an air of mystery and of danger? If so, how does it manage to do this? Using the right details are important, aren't they?

Activity 4

On a separate sheet of paper, rewrite the following paragraph so that it sets up a mood of danger, evil, and mystery.

> It was night. I walked up the steps of the house. I opened the door and stepped inside. The clock on the mantel was just striking. I looked around the room. At first, I thought the room was empty. Then I saw a woman standing in the corner with her back to me. She turned around.

You are responsible for letting your reader know the setting early in your story. You are also responsible for giving your reader a little **background** material. Let your reader know the situation as the story opens. Tell a bit about what has already happened in the characters' lives.

Notice how this paragraph fills the reader in on background details.

> Jenny decided to enter a pie-baking contest. Now, this may not seem very unusual or very exciting, but for Jenny, it was an amazing event. She had grown up in a penthouse in New York City. When her family ate at home, their meals were prepared by cooks and served by maids and butlers. Most often, they dined in restaurants. Then, just last September, Jenny got married and moved to a farm in Ohio. Jenny had never cooked a meal or shopped in a grocery store. However, once she got into her own kitchen, she found she liked it there. When the Ohio State Fair opened that summer, Jenny decided she would not only enter the pie-baking contest. She decided she would win it!

The conflict is set up: Will Jenny bake a prize-winning pie?

Enough background is provided so that the reader will know why pie-baking is such a big deal for Jenny. The reader also has been introduced to the main character and already knows quite a bit about her.

Notice that all details provided have something to do with the story. We are not told, for example, that Jenny was an orchestra member in high school. We are not told that her parents are divorced, or that her new husband is a champion chess player. These things would not affect this story, and so they are not mentioned.

Activity 5

Here is a story idea:

Conflict: The Websters' house is on fire. Eight-year-old Will Webster is inside. Can anyone save him?

On your paper, write the numbers of the details that are important to the story. Don't write the numbers of details that seem unnecessary.

1. The Websters live way out in the country. The only fire station is fifty miles away.

2. Will Webster has a broken leg.

3. Mr. Webster is a clerk in a clothing store.

4. The Websters' house is old and made of wood.

5. The Websters grow vegetables in a garden behind their house.

6. Will Webster has been known to play with matches.

7. Will Webster goes to Junction City Grade School.

8. A next-door neighbor, Stan Swift, is home when the fire breaks out.

9. Stan Swift, is an excellent athlete. He is strong and brave and likes Will very much.

10. Stan's mother is a teacher.

The Plot—Solving the Conflict

The plot is the series of events that leads to the resolution of the conflict. The plot includes the events that happen to make the problem better or worse, and that in the end cause the problem to be solved. These events make up the body of the story.

You can read more about plot in Chapter 19, Writing a Book Report.

You should be able to list the events in a plot, as in the following example:

Linda Gray is frightened when she can't find her two-year-old daughter, Tammy.

She looks all around the back yard where she last saw Tammy playing. She calls the neighbors, but no one has seen Tammy.

She sees an unfamiliar black van pull away from the curb and speed off down the street.

Linda, sure that her daughter has been kidnapped, calls the police.

The police arrive and question Linda. They ask her if she has searched the house. Linda realizes she has not.

It is usually best to present the events in a story in chronological order (in the order they happened).

The police search the house and find Tammy asleep on her bedroom floor.

When you write a story, you must decide who the narrator of your story will be. Do you want to tell the story from the first-person or the third-person point of view? To review point of view, see Chapter 15, Writing Better Essays.

Why do you think the detail about the black van was included in the story? It really has nothing to do with the final outcome. The detail about the black van adds suspense. It plants the idea that Tammy may have been kidnapped.

Before you write a story do the following things:

1. Write a sentence describing the conflict.
2. List your characters.
3. Write a brief outline of the events.
4. Write a sentence telling how the conflict will be resolved.

If you follow the four steps listed above, you should write a good story. You will not become confused. You will know where you are heading the moment you begin writing. Your story will not go on and on. You will not find yourself well into the story and suddenly wonder, "How am I going to end this?"

Too often, teachers get stories from students that end: "I woke up to find that it was all a dream."

That ending shows that the writer did not plan ahead. The writer had no idea how the story was going to end when he or she began writing. With no way to solve the character's problem, the writer took an easy (and uninteresting) way out. Your ending should be as strong as your beginning. Plan ahead, and it will be.

The title of your story will probably be the last thing you will write. It will, however, be the first thing your reader will see. The title should catch the reader's attention. It should also suggest the main idea of your story.

Challenge

Working Backwards

Choose one of the following story endings. Write a beginning (setting, background) and middle (events of a plot) so that you have a complete story.

- Then I saw the window, and I knew I could escape. When I was free, I hurried down the road without looking back. I left the big, dark house behind me. I knew I would never forget that place. I knew, too, that I would never talk to strangers again.

- I watched as the father and his child hugged each other. I had been through a lot to make this moment happen, but it had been worth it. They were together again.

- When I opened my eyes, the people around my bed were crying. "Welcome home," they said.

- In spite of everything, we won that game. No one had been able to stop us. We were the champs.

Activity 6

Number your paper from 1 to 4. Use complete sentences to answer the questions below.

1. A story is built around a conflict. Explain the meaning of *conflict.*

2. A story must have characters. What are *characters?*

3. A story needs a setting. What is a *setting?*

4. Every story has a plot. What makes up the *plot?*

Writing With Style

Which beginning, A or B, makes you more interested in reading the story? Why?

A. Janie Nichols met the old man in the park one Saturday. He seemed lonely and sad. Janie decided that he needed a friend. Janie, in fact, also needed a friend. She had just moved to the city and knew very few people. She hadn't found a job yet, and she lived all alone in a little apartment. The old man wanted to talk, and Janie wanted to listen.

He told Janie stories. He told her about all the strange places he had visited when he was young. Then one day he gave Janie a gift.

"This box," he said, "contains a precious treasure. Do not open it until you are alone." He smiled a crooked smile from behind his thick, gray beard.

In her apartment that evening, Janie began to unwrap the box. She had just pulled off the dirty old string when the box moved. The movement made Janie jump. She stared at the box, not sure what to do next. Then, from within the box, came the whisper of a human voice.

B. Janie Nichols met the old man in the park one Saturday. He seemed very nice. The man and Janie became good friends. They would sit and talk for hours every time they met. Some days they would feed the pigeons. The park was filled with pigeons. There were gray ones and white ones, and there were some with brightly colored feathers.

One day the old man said, "I have a present for you, Janie." He gave her a box. She was very grateful for the gift. She did not get many presents. When she opened it, she found it was a blue sweater. It was beautiful and soft and had come from the finest department store in town.

Vocabulary Builder

Everybody Says "Said"

Sometimes you will use dialogue in a story. Your conversations will be more interesting if you don't always use the word *said* in conversations. Improve your writing by sometimes using more interesting, descriptive verbs to replace *said*.

This lesson presents some words you might use to replace *said*. Complete each sentence by giving the speaker something to say. Use the meaning of the verb (in italics) to decide just what the speaker would say. If you don't know what the verb means, look it up in the dictionary before you complete the sentence.

example: 1. "Save me! I'm drowning!" *exclaimed* Jill.

1. "_____!" *exclaimed* Jill.

2. "_____," *bawled* Dora.

3. "_____," *bellowed* the boss.

4. "_____," Doug *mumbled*.

5. "_____?" Luke *queried*.

Chapter Review

Chapter Summary

- ☐ A story tells what happened.

- ☐ Every story has a conflict.

- ☐ A story must have characters, a setting, and a plot.

- ☐ Make sure characters are distinct from each other.

- ☐ You can use setting to create a mood.

- ☐ You should know how the conflict will be resolved before you begin writing a story.

- ☐ Before you write a story do the following things: (1) write a sentence describing the conflict, (2) list your characters, (3) write an outline of the events, and (4) write a sentence telling how the conflict will be resolved.

Writing Practice

Now it's time to write a two- to three-page story. Plan ahead. Follow these four steps before you begin: (1) write a sentence describing the conflict, (2) list your characters, (3) write a brief outline of events, and (4) write a sentence describing how the conflict will be resolved.

Once you have done those things, write your story.

If you can't think of a story idea you like, perhaps this idea will get you started:

The time had come. I had to stand up to that bully.

Chapter Quiz

Read the following story. Then answer these questions:

1. What is the conflict of the story? 2. Who is the main character? 3. What is the setting of the story? 4. Is this story told from the first- or third-person point of view? 5. How is the conflict resolved?

Carla felt as if she were going to scream. She was stuck in a crowded elevator. The chubby man beside her was beginning to sweat. The baby in the stroller was beginning to cry. Carla was getting dizzy.

Carla didn't like close places. In fact, they upset her very much. It was getting hot. There just wasn't enough air for all eight people on the elevator. Carla was beginning to panic.

Then Carla heard a moan from behind her. She turned her head in time to see an elderly woman sink to the floor of the elevator. The woman was clutching her chest.

"She's having a heart attack!" the plump man cried. "Somebody do something."

Suddenly Carla's dizziness disappeared. Her voice was calm when she spoke. She ordered everyone to move to the edges of the elevator and make some room. Carla forgot her own fears. She forgot she was trapped in that little box. She loosened the stranger's blouse and talked to her softly.

"My pills," the woman gasped, pointing to her purse. Carla found the pills and placed one under the woman's tongue. Carla held her hand and kept her calm while a janitor began to work on the elevator from somewhere above them.

"You saved my life," the woman whispered to Carla when they were finally rescued.

"And you changed mine," Carla replied. She knew she would never be afraid of close places again. She would not panic in a crisis. She had found a new confidence in herself.

Chapter 24 Writing Poetry

Robert Frost was almost forty before he published any of his work. He is admired for his ability to turn plain speech and everyday language into poetry. Some of his most popular poems are "Birches," "Death of the Hired Man," and "Mending Wall."

The art of the poet is to make ordinary words deliver extraordinary messages.

Writers at Work: Robert Frost (1874–1963)

Chapter Learning Objectives

☐ Identify the poetic devices of alliteration and onomatopoeia.

☐ Write a cinquain.

☐ Write a haiku.

Words to Know

verse   a short poem or a section of a poem

alliteration   the repetition of the same first sound in a group of words or line of poetry

example: *Sixty silver salmon swam swiftly up the stream.*

onomatopoeia   a word whose sound suggests its meaning

example: *hiss, buzz*

rhyme   the repetition of similar sounds

example: *park, mark, lark*

rhythm   any regular, recurring pattern

cinquain   a five-line poem that follows a particular pattern

haiku   a Japanese verse form in three lines of five, seven, and five syllables

Listening to Words

Does the idea of writing poetry frighten you? Actually, writing poetry lets you relax, play with words, and dream a little. So far in this book, you have learned to follow a lot of writing rules. You have had to write some fairly long papers. However, there are very few rules for writing poetry. And poems are often short! Sometimes they're only a few words. Sometimes they're several **verses** long.

In many ways, writing poetry is more fun than writing anything else.

Poetry lets people take a close look at their world and at their feelings. It lets people express those feelings in just a few, carefully chosen words.

Listen to the words of poems. Each word plays a part in creating a mood and expressing an idea. Each word in a poem has more than one job. The word expresses an idea through its meaning. And it also creates a kind of music. The very sounds of the words often add to a poem's effect on us.

You can review figures of speech in Chapter 11, Writing to Describe.

One way poets can use sound in their writing is to use a figure of speech called **alliteration**. Alliteration means that the same first letter or letters is repeated in several words. This method can create an interesting effect. The repeated letter not only makes a sound but can add meaning.

Look at the following example of alliteration:

> The strong, smooth snake slithered across the sun-baked sand.

Did you notice how all the *s* sounds created a snaky feeling?

Here is another example:

> Forceful winds fanned the fierce, flashing flames.

Here is one more example:

> Donna definitely disliked doughnuts.

Now you try it.

Activity 1

Write a sentence of description for two of the following subjects. Use alliteration in your description. Begin two, three, or four words with the same letter.

> example: *summer—Sweet summer sounds filled the air like singing.*

> example: *autumn leaves—The crisp, crunchy autumn leaves crackled underfoot.*

Look for examples of alliteration in advertisements.

1. a train
2. summer
3. rain
4. a bee
5. a fire engine
6. snow
7. autumn leaves
8. flowers
9. bugs
10. any subject you choose

Some words actually copy sounds. For example, the word *buzz* imitates the sound a bee makes. This type of word is another figure of speech. It is called **onomatopoeia** (onna-mata-PEE-a). Think about these "sound words" as you do the next activity.

Activity 2

Write a sound word for each of the following:

> example: pig = oink

1. a water pipe
2. an alarm clock
3. a train
4. a horn
5. rain
6. a cow
7. a donkey
8. a rooster
9. bacon frying
10. a person who has been hit in the stomach
11. a laugh
12. a strong wind
13. a home run

Painting a Picture with Poetry

Do you remember the goal of writing that has been repeated so often in this book? You want to let your reader experience what you are experiencing. Poems can do that job in very few words. Before you write any poems for the following activities, take time to picture what you will write about. Go slow. See it. Hear it. Smell it. Taste it. Feel it. And think about how your topic makes you feel.

Now, it's time to write a poem.

Activity 3

Think of this activity as making a picture poem. You will be describing something. Your poem doesn't have to **rhyme**. It does not have to have any special **rhythm**. There is only one rule: Each line should paint a picture.

Highway

The highway stretches out ahead of me,
Hard, black asphalt as far as I can see.
A yellow line runs down the middle.
That line is faded now but once was bright.
The highway goes on and on, flat and straight,
right toward the sun.
I cannot see the end.

Can you picture the highway? Notice that each line is like a brush stroke on canvas, adding to the picture of the highway.

You may choose your topic for a picture poem from the list below. Or you may come up with a topic of your own.

clouds	waterfall	a car
headlights	ski slope	an insect
the swimming pool	snow	night
last day of school	hurricane	sunrise
the desert	police officer	a rock star

The next activities will give you a chance to write some different types of poems. Don't be surprised if you find that writing poems can be easy, and fun.

A Reminder:
Before you write, take time to picture your subject. Use all your senses. Think about how your subject makes you feel. Suppose for example, you are going to write about an old woman you know. You picture her. You see her thin, frail body. You see her hair done up tightly in a bun. You smell the sweet odor of the peppermint candy she always eats. You feel her cold, dry hand on yours. Finally, you think about how sad you feel because you know that she is lonely.

Activity 4

In French, "Cinq" means five.

By taking just five steps, you can write a poem. These five-line poems are called **cinquains** (SAN kanez).

Carefully read the five steps, take a look at some of the examples, and you are on your way.

Step 1: Write a noun (a person, place, or thing).	**icicles**
Step 2: On the next line, write two adjectives (words that describe the noun in line 1). Separate the two adjectives with a comma.	**long, silver**
Step 3: On the third line, write three verbs. These verbs should be things that the noun on the first line does.	**glitter, sparkle, drip**
Step 4: On the fourth line, tell how you feel about your noun, or compare it to something else (a simile).	**they look like silver daggers.**
Step 5: On the fifth line, repeat the word you wrote on the first line, or write a synonym for that word.	**icicles**

Read a few more examples of cinquains before you write your own.

Actress	*Midnight*
Beautiful, glamorous	*Dark, lonely*
Smiling, bowing, gesturing	*Covering, hiding, concealing*
Who is she, really?	*A scary time of night*
Star	*The witching hour*
Frogs	*Stream*
Green, bug-eyed	*Shallow, icy*
Croaking, hopping, climbing	*Bubbling, gurgling, flowing*
Some people eat them!	*A friend that cools my toes*
Toads	*Tiny river*

Now you try writing a cinquain. Just follow the five steps.

You may write about one of the topics listed below or choose a topic of your own.

trees	eagles
babies	the moon
teachers	ocean
baseball	love
fire engines	television

Activity 5

The Japanese often write haiku to describe the beauty and wonders of nature.

The Japanese invented a form of verse called **haiku** (HI koo). Students often enjoy writing a haiku because it's short and follows a simple pattern. Think of a haiku as an expression of one brief moment in time.

The haiku pattern is based on the number of syllables in a line. The entire poem has only seventeen syllables. The first line has five syllables. The second line has seven syllables. The third line has five syllables.

Read the following examples of haiku before you try writing your own.

Fog blankets the bay
Fishing boats are like white ghosts
Ropes moan against docks.

Race cars on the track
Tires shrieking, round and round
Going nowhere fast.

The flag flaps wildly
Declaring a nation's pride
Bright, brave colors wave.

A fiery wind blows
Across the empty desert
Nothing can live here.

Now write your own haiku. Remember that the point is to capture a moment and share it with your reader. Write about one of the topics listed below, or choose your own topic.

flowers	jazz	sunset
turtles	frozen pond	junkyard
sun	spider web	cemetery
caterpillars	candy	rooftop
quilts	football	slums

Express Yourself

So far in this chapter, you have used your "picturing" and "describing" skills to write some poems. You have been looking at things in the world. Now look inside your own mind.

Activity 6

A. Complete each of the following sentences in a different way.

1. I wish . . .

2. I wish . . .

3. I wish . . .

4. I wish . . .

5. I am happy when . . .

6. I am happy when . . .

7. I am happy when . . .

8. I am sad when . . .

9. I am sad when . . .

10. I am sad when . . .

B. Now choose the one sentence from Part A that you like the best. Expand that sentence into a poem. Build on the idea expressed in the sentence. The poem should reveal the way you feel. Look at some of the following examples before you write your own poem.

I wish . . .
That people didn't call me a shrimp
And laugh at me because I'm small.
Sometimes it makes me feel as if
I don't exist at all.

I wish . . .
I had a million bucks,
And I could buy all my friends
The most amazing toys.
I'd watch them smile bigger
And bigger until their faces
Almost burst.

I am happy when . . .
It is late at night, and the house is quiet.
Then darkness wraps around me like a blanket.
My brothers and sisters are safe in bed.
We are together.
No one can get in or out.
I am sad when . . .
Halloween is past,
And I pack my mask away.
I have to be myself again.
No more daring, dashing pirate—
Time to get back to real life.

Concrete Words and Poems

Think of the word *concrete.* Your first thought may be about the hard substance that is used to make sidewalks. But concrete has another meaning. It means real, or having a physical existence. Something concrete is something you can actually see. Objects you can touch are concrete; ideas are not.

You can have some fun with words by thinking in a concrete manner.

Look at these examples of concrete words.

Activity 7

Now try writing some concrete words of your own.
You can use any words you want. Here are some
suggestions.

flower	rain	huge
flag	waterfall	repeat
parallel	war	dizzy
downhill	sad	absent
mountain	snake	crowded

You can write concrete poems, too. Again, the
physical shape will reflect meaning. Read the
following example of a concrete poem.

The King

From the top of
the park slide, I
  could

   see

    the

     whole

     world

    then

     ZOOM I was back to earth again.

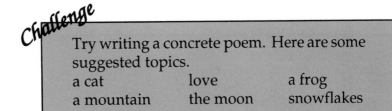

Challenge

Try writing a concrete poem. Here are some
suggested topics.

a cat	love	a frog
a mountain	the moon	snowflakes

Writing With Style

What makes a collection of words a poem? Look at the following two descriptions. Which one would you define as a poem? What qualities does it have that make it a poem?

A. The Moon

The moon is a natural satellite of the earth. It is sometimes seen in a full, rounded shape. At other times, it can be seen as a crescent shape. Some people say the moon has strange powers. One superstition says people can become insane from looking at the moon. Such people are said to be "moonstruck."

B. The Moon

Great, white orb of the night

You are a mystery.

Some evenings just a pale sliver of light,

Your surface hidden by the dark.

Sometimes full and round and glorious

You invite all to come stand and stare

At your brilliance.

Vocabulary Builder

Clichés

Clichés are overused expressions. People often use them so that they don't have to say things in their own words. Everyone uses clichés once in a while when speaking. However, it's wise to avoid using clichés in your writing. It's better to be original than to rely on overused expressions. Use your own voice. Express yourself.

You will often hear clichés, and it is interesting to think about what they mean. Clichés usually do not actually mean what they seem to say. For example, "turn over a new leaf" is a cliché. It means "make a new start." A person who uses this cliché is not talking about trees.

A. The italicized words below are clichés. Read the sentences. Then, in your own words, tell what each cliché means. Use context clues to help you figure out meanings.

1. Hank worked so hard at the factory that he would sleep *like a log* every night.

2. Susan always uses the same excuse. She sounds like a *broken record*.

3. I bet a dollar that the Cleveland Indians would win the game, even though it was *a long shot*.

4. Steven always looks angry. He has a real *chip on his shoulder*.

5. I have heard that joke before. It is *as old as the hills*.

6. Don't say the wrong thing to Cindy. She has a *short fuse*.

B. Think of three more clichés. List them on a separate sheet of paper.

Chapter Review

Chapter Summary

- ☐ Each word in a poem should be carefully chosen to create an image or express an idea.

- ☐ Poets sometimes use alliteration and onomatopoeia to emphasize meaning through sound.

- ☐ A poem may or may not rhyme or have a specific rhythm.

- ☐ Cinquains and haiku are short poems that follow definite patterns.

- ☐ You can show meaning with an actual picture by writing concrete words and poems.

Writing Practice

Write a poem by thinking about the words you associate with something. First, take a word or phrase. Next, just think about the word and the things you associate with it. Just let your thoughts go.

When you are finished with your list, read it over. Choose your favorite words and phrases. Arrange them in an order that seems appropriate. You have written a poem.

Here is an example of a "free association" poem:

First Day of School

Dressed right?

Who's in my class?

Check out the new kid!

Where's room 205?

Forgot my lunch!

Homework already?

Can I switch teachers?

Where did summer go?

Chapter Quiz

Choose the best answers. Write them on a separate sheet of paper.

1. Do not touch the pot.

   It must be very hot.

   This is an example of:
   (a) alliteration   (b) rhyme   (c) onomatopoeia

2. The babbling brook bubbled cheerfully through the beautiful meadow.

   This is an example of:
   (a) alliteration   (b) rhyme   (c) haiku

3. The duck quacked angrily. "Get away, get away," it seemed to say.

   This is an example of:
   (a) a cinquain   (b) alliteration   (c) onomatopoeia

4. s   ep   arat   e

   This is an example of:
   (a) a concrete word   (b) haiku   (c) a cinquain

5. April

   Sunny, windy

   Flowering, showering, changing

   Can't you make up your mind?

   Springtime

   This is an example of:
   (a) haiku   (b) a cinquain   (c) alliteration

Unit Review

A. Choose words from the box below to fill in the blanks in the following sentences. Write your answers on a separate sheet of paper.

setting	character	plot
dialogue	senses	

1. A person in a story is called a _____ .

2. A conversation between people is called a _____ .

3. Seeing, hearing, tasting, smelling, and feeling are the five _____ .

4. When and where a story takes place is called the _____ .

5. The events of a story make up the _____ .

B. Practice your poetry by following these directions. Use a separate piece of paper.

1. Use alliteration by adding two adjectives that begin with a *t*: The _____ , _____ tiger tramped through the jungle.

2. Use onomatopoeia to describe the sound made by a sleeping person.

3. A cinquain has _____ lines.

4. "5, 7, 5" describes the number of syllables in the lines of a _____ .

5. Turn *backwards, giraffe,* and *rattlesnake* into concrete words.

Appendix

Glossary

Reference
Guide

Index

Glossary

abbreviation a shortened form of a word

acceptance answering "yes" to an invitation

adjective a word that adds meaning to a noun or pronoun

adverb a word that adds meaning to a verb, an adjective, or another adverb

alliteration the repetition of the same first sound in a group of words or line of poetry

anecdote a short, interesting story about an event or a person

antecedent the noun a pronoun replaces

application a form with questions you must answer when applying for a job

background the events that came before

bibliography a list of books or sources for a particular topic

body main part

card catalog a file in the library that contains information cards for every book

character a person in a story or play

characteristics distinguishing features; features that make something or someone special and individual

chronological order events arranged in the order they happened

cinquain a five-line poem that follows a particular pattern

classified ads short newspaper advertisements arranged in groups according to type

command a sentence that gives an order

communication sending and receiving messages

comparison the act of noting the likenesses and differences of things

complex sentence a sentence with a subordinate clause and an independent clause

composition an essay

compound predicate two or more predicates with the same subject

compound sentence two simple sentences joined by a comma and a coordinating conjunction (and, but, or)

compound subject two or more subjects with the same predicate

conclude to bring to an end

conflict a problem caused by the clash of two opposing forces

conjunction words used to join or link words, phrases, ideas, and sentences; common conjunctions are *and, but,* and *or*

connotation idea or ideas associated with a word in addition to its actual meaning

content the ideas in a piece of writing

cross-reference a reference to another part of a book or to another source of information on the same subject

description a picture in words; the details that create a picture of something

details all the small parts of something that make up the whole

Dewey Decimal Number the specific number assigned in a library to each book, pamphlet, and so on that classifies the item according to subject

dialogue a conversation between two or more people

differences points that are not alike

distinct different or separate

edit to prepare a piece of writing for the final copy by finding and correcting any mistakes in facts, point of view, and style

elements basic parts or features of the whole

essay a short piece of writing about a particular subject

exaggeration something stretched beyond the truth; something made larger or greater than it really is

explanatory paragraph a paragraph that explains, clarifies, and gives details

fact something known to be true

fiction imaginative writing; something made up or invented

figure a number

figure of speech an expression in which words suggest an image that is different from the literal meaning of words

first person the personal point of view; uses the pronoun *I*

format the plan, style, or layout of something

fragment   a group of words that is not a complete sentence but is punctuated as if it were

gender   classification given to nouns and pronouns according to the sex of the person or thing described

habit   a thing a person does regularly without thinking about it

haiku   a Japanese verse form in three lines of five, seven, and five syllables

hero   the most important male character in a story; usually he is good

heroine   the most important female character in a story; usually she is good

identify   to show to be a particular person, place, or thing

imaginary   not real; existing only in one's mind

implies   suggests in an indirect way

incident   an event

indented   set in from the margin

independent clause   a clause that can stand alone as a complete sentence

indirect quotation   repeating what a character says, but not in exact words

informative paragraph   a paragraph that gives information and shares knowledge

inquire   to ask about something

interview   a meeting of a job-seeker and an employer when questions are asked and answered

literal   actual, real, exactly as things are

logical   something that is reasonable, or makes sense

mechanics   the spelling and punctuation of a piece of writing

metaphor   a figure of speech in which one thing is compared with another by suggesting a likeness between the two

moderation   the opposite of exaggeration; neither too much nor too little

mood   a state of mind or feeling

narrative paragraph   a paragraph that tells of events and experiences

narrator   the one telling the details

nonfiction   writing based on real people and events

noun   a word that names a person, a place, or a thing

novel   a long work of fiction

object of the preposition   the noun or pronoun that follows the preposition in the prepositional phrase

onomatopoeia   a word whose sound suggests its meaning

opinion   a belief, attitude, or a viewpoint

outline   a plan that lays out the main part, but not all the details

paragraph   a group of sentences placed together because they all relate to the same idea

periodicals   publications such as newspapers or magazines that are published at regular intervals

personal   of one's own; for example, a *personal* experience is a person's own experience

persuade   to get someone to do something or believe something; to convince

plot   the main story of a novel or play

plural   expressing more than one

point of view   the eyes through which something is written; the way in which something is viewed

precision   saying exactly what a thing is; every detail accurately described

predicate   the part of the sentence that tells something about the subject

preposition   a word that shows the relationship of a noun or pronoun to some other word in the sentence

prepositional phrase   the preposition and its object taken together

pronoun   a word used in place of a noun

proofread   to read over a piece of writing in order to find and mark any mistakes in mechanics

qualify   (1) to limit, make less strong; (2) to be suited, to have the necessary training

quote   to repeat or copy exactly the writing or speech of another

reference book   a source of information

references   persons who can give information about someone else

regrets   polite refusal of an invitation

report   an account of a particular subject

research   the gathering of facts and other information

resolution   a solution; an end to conflict

restate   to say something again or in a different way

résumé   an account of a person's education, experience, and qualifications

rhyme   the repetition of similar sounds

rhythm   any regular, recurring pattern

rough draft   the first, unpolished copy of a piece of writing

run-on sentence   two or more sentences that have not been properly separated or properly joined

second person   the point of view of a narrator who speaks to the reader; uses the pronoun *you*

senses   the faculties of sight, hearing, smell, taste, and touch

sentence   a group of words that expresses a complete thought; a sentence has a subject and a predicate. It begins with a capital letter and ends with a punctuation mark.

setting   the time and place of an event, story, or play

similarities   points of likeness: the state of being close to the same

simile   a figure of speech in which two things are compared by using the word *like* or *as*

simple predicate   the verb or verb phrase in the sentence

simple sentence   a group of words that expresses a complete thought and has one subject-predicate combination

simple subject   the most important noun or pronoun in the sentence; what the sentence is about

singular   expressing only one

sources   any book, place, person, or material from which you gather information

subject   the part of the sentence that tells who or what the sentence is about

subordinate clause   a clause that adds to the meaning of another clause but makes no sense by itself

subordinate conjunction   a conjunction that introduces a subordinate clause

summary   a short statement that brings the important points or details together

support   to add strength to

sympathy   the act of sharing another's feelings; feeling sorry for another's suffering

synonym   a word with the same or nearly the same meaning as another word

thesis statement   a sentence that presents the idea that the essay will support

third person   the point of view of a narrator who stays outside the writing and tells about the subject; uses the pronouns *he, she,* and *they*

topic sentence   the sentence that states the main idea of the paragraph

traits   special qualities

transition   the act of moving from one thing to another

transitional words   words that help a reader move from one idea to another. They show how one idea relates to and connects with another idea.

unique   being the only one of its kind

variety   many different forms or kinds of things

verb   a word that expresses action or being

verse   a short poem or a section of a poem

villain   an evil or wicked character in a story

vivid   clear, distinct, colorful

zip code   a postal code designed to speed up mail service by assigning special numbers to each area of the country

Reference Guide

Sentences

Grammar 1. Definition of a sentence

A sentence is a group of words that expresses a complete thought. Every sentence must have a subject and a predicate. (See Grammar 3-6) Every sentence begins with a capital letter and ends with a punctuation mark.

> That leopard has already killed 400 people.

> Is it still hungry?

> Be careful!

Sometimes a sentence may have only one word. (See Grammar 5.)

> Listen. Hurry!

Grammar 2. Kinds of sentences

There are four different kinds of sentences.

A *declarative sentence* makes a statement. A declarative sentence ends with a period.

> A volcano in the Canary Islands is for sale.

An *interrogative sentence* asks a question. An interrogative sentence ends with a question mark.

> Who would want to buy a volcano?

An *imperative sentence* gives a command. An imperative sentence ends with a period.

Show me the list of buyers.

An *exclamatory sentence* expresses excitement. An exclamatory sentence ends with an exclamation point.

They must be crazy!

Grammar 3. Subjects and predicates in declarative sentences

Every sentence has two main parts, the subject and the predicate. The subject names what the sentence is about. The predicate tells something about the subject.

In most declarative sentences, the subject is the first part. The predicate is the second part.

A famous sea captain   was often sick.

He   suffered from seasickness.

In some declarative sentences, the predicate is the first part. The subject is the second part.

Back and forth rolled the captain's ship.

Grammar 4. Subjects and predicates in interrogative sentences

Every interrogative sentence has a subject and a predicate. In some interrogative sentences, the subject is the first part. The predicate is the second part.

Who   solved the mystery?

Which clue   was most important?

In most interrogative sentences, part of the predicate comes before the subject. To find the subject and predicate, rearrange the words of the interrogative sentence. Use those words to make a declarative sentence. (The declarative sentence will not always sound natural, but it will help you.) The subject and predicate of the two sentences are the same.

| Why did | the butler | lie about it? |

| The butler | did lie about it why? |

Grammar 5. Subjects and predicates in imperative sentences

Only the predicate of an imperative sentence is spoken or written. The subject of the sentence is understood. That subject is always you.

(You) Try an underhand serve.

(You) Please show me how to do it.

Grammar 6. Subjects and predicates in exclamatory sentences

Every exclamatory sentence has a subject and a predicate. In most exclamatory sentences, the subject is the first part. The predicate is the second part.

Kotzebue Sound, Alaska, is frozen over nearly all of the time!

In some exclamatory sentences, part of the predicate comes before the subject.

What terrible weather that city has!

(That city has terrible weather!)

Grammar 7. Compound subjects in sentences

A sentence with a compound subject has two or more subjects with the same predicate.

> **Jesse James and his brother Frank** were famous outlaws in the Old West.

> **Cole Younger, James Younger, and Robert Younger** were all members of the James gang.

Grammar 8. Compound predicates in sentences

A sentence with a compound predicate has two or more predicates with the same subject.

> The postal workers **took in the tailless cat and named him Kojak**.

> Kojak **lives in the post office, catches mice, and earns a salary**.

Grammar 9. Compound sentences

A compound sentence is made up of two shorter sentences joined by a coordinating conjunction. (See Grammar 45.) A compound sentence has a subject and a predicate followed by another subject and another predicate.

> G. David Howard set a record in 1978, and it remains unbroken.

> Howard told jokes for more than 13 hours, but not all of them were funny.

Nouns

Grammar 10. Definition of a noun

A noun is a word that names a person, a place, or a thing.

> That brave **man** crossed the **ocean** in a **rowboat**.

Grammar 11. Singular and plural forms of nouns

Almost every noun has two forms. The singular form names one person, place, or thing.

> Only one **worker** in that **factory** can name the secret **ingredient**.

The plural form names more than one person, place, or thing.

> Several **workers** in those two **factories** can name the secret **ingredients**.

Grammar 12. Spelling plural forms of nouns

For most nouns, add s to the singular form to make the plural form.

> joke—jokes   character—characters
>
> cartoon—cartoons

If the singular form ends in **s**, **ss**, **sh**, **ch**, or **x**, add **es**.

> bus—buses   witch—witches
>
> kiss—kisses   fox—foxes
>
> wish—wishes

If the singular form ends in a consonant and **y**, change the **y** to **i** and add **es**.

spy—spies   discovery—discoveries

mystery—mysteries

If the singular form ends in **f**, usually change the **f** to **v** and add **es**. If the singular form ends in **fe**, usually change the **f** to **v** and add **s**. There are some important exceptions to these rules. Look in a dictionary if you are not sure of the correct plural form.

half—halves   wife—wives

loaf—loaves   knife—knives

Some exceptions

roof—roofs   chief—chiefs safe—safes

If the singular form ends in **o**, add **s** to some words and **es** to others. Look in a dictionary if you are not sure of the correct plural form.

studio—studios   tomato—tomatoes

piano—pianos   zero—zeros

Some nouns change in other ways to make the plural form.

child—children   mouse—mice

woman—women   goose—geese

A few nouns have the same singular form and plural form.

sheep—sheep   deer—deer

moose—moose

Grammar 13. Proper nouns and common nouns

A proper noun is the special name of a particular person, place, or thing. Each word in a proper noun begins with a capital letter.

> Then **Max** stopped in **Junctionville** and ate a **Big Mac**.

A common noun is the name of any person, place, or thing.

> Then the **man** stopped in a small **town** and ate a **hamburger**.

Grammar 14. Possessive nouns

The possessive form of a noun shows ownership. Usually the possessive form of a noun is made by adding an apostrophe and s. (See Punctuation 20.)

> A **piranha's** teeth are as sharp as razors.

The possessive form of a plural noun that ends in s is made by adding only an apostrophe. (See Punctuation 20.)

> Nobody believed the **explorers'** story.

Grammar 15. Nouns of address

A noun of address names the person being spoken to. One or two commas separate a noun of address from the rest of a sentence. (See Punctuation 9.)

> Where are you going, **Ricky?**

> I told you, **Lucy,** that I have a rehearsal tonight.

Grammar 16. Appositive nouns

An appositive noun renames or identifies the noun that comes before it in a sentence. An appositive noun is usually part of a group of words. The whole group of words is called an appositive. One or two commas separate an appositive from the rest of a sentence. (See Punctuation 10.)

> A Ford was the preferred car of John Dillinger, **the famous gangster.**

> Even his sister, **the president of her own company,** would not hire him.

Verbs

Grammar 17. Definition of a verb

A verb is a word that expresses action or being.

> The volcano **erupted** suddenly.

> It **was** a terrific surprise.

Almost all verbs have different forms to show differences in time.

> Sometimes puffs of smoke **rise** from the volcano.

> A huge cloud of heavy gray smoke **rose** from it last week.

Grammar 18. Action verbs

Most verbs are action verbs. An action verb expresses physical action or mental action.

> The committee members **banned** Donald Duck comic books.

> They **disliked** the duck's behavior.

Grammar 19. Linking Verbs

Some verbs are linking verbs. A linking verb tells what the sentence subject is or is like. The most common linking verb is be. (See Grammar 23.)

> A black and white dog **became** a mail carrier in California.

> The dog's name **was** Dorsey.

Grammar 20. Verb phrases

A verb phrase is made up of two or more verbs that function together in a sentence. The final verb in a verb phrase is the main verb.

> The 13,000-pound bell **had disappeared**.

> Somebody **must have stolen** it.

The verbs before the main verb in a verb phrase are helping verbs. The most common helping verbs are forms of be (is, are, am, was, were), forms of have (has, have, had), and forms of do (does, do, did). (See Grammar 23.)

> That radio station **is sponsoring** a contest.

> The station **has** already **received** 45,217 postcards.

Grammar 21. Agreement of verbs with nouns

Verbs that express continuing action or existence and verbs that express current action or existence are in the present tense. Almost all present-tense verbs have two different forms. These two different forms go with different sentence subjects. The verb in a sentence, or the first helping verb in a sentence, must agree with the most important word in the subject of that sentence.

One present-tense form of a verb agrees with singular nouns. This verb form ends with s.

> A tick **sucks** blood from larger animals.

The other present-tense form of a verb agrees with plural nouns.

> Ticks **suck** blood from larger animals.

Grammar 22. Agreement of verbs with compound subjects

The present-tense verb form that agrees with plural nouns also agrees with compound subjects. (See Grammar 7.)

> Beth Obermeyer and her daughter Kristen **hold** a record for long-distance tap dancing.

Grammar 23. Forms of the verb be

The verb be has more forms than other verbs. Be has three present-tense forms: is, are, and am. Is agrees with singular nouns. Are agrees with plural nouns. Am agrees with the pronoun I.

> Mary Lou Retton **is** a famous gymnast.
>
> Many people **are** her fans.
>
> I **am** a pretty good gymnast, too.

Most verbs have one past-tense form that tells about action or existence in the past. Be has two past-tense forms: was and were. Was agrees with singular noun subjects. Were agrees with plural noun subjects.

> The argument **was** noisy.
>
> Several neighbors **were** very angry about it.

Grammar 24. Irregular verbs

Usually the past-tense form of a verb ends in d or ed.

> William Baxter **invented** an important part of the Morse code.

Some verbs change in other ways to form the past tense. These are called irregular verbs. Look in a dictionary if you are not sure of the correct past-tense form of a verb.

> Samuel Morse **took** all the credit.

Pronouns

Grammar 25. Personal pronouns

A personal pronoun is a word that takes the place of one or more nouns.

> Superman tried to enlist in the Army during World War II, but **he** was found unfit to serve.

Grammar 26. Subject forms and object forms of personal pronouns

Each personal pronoun has a subject form and an object form. These different forms are used in different ways in sentences. (The pronouns it and you are the same in the subject form and the object form.) These are the subject forms of personal pronouns: **I, you, he, she, it, we, they.** These are the object forms of personal pronouns: **me, you, him, her, it, us, them.**

> **He** saw through a wall and read the wrong eye chart.

> The army did not accept **him**.

Grammar 27. Antecedents of pronouns

A personal pronoun refers to the noun it replaces. That noun is the antecedent of the pronoun.

> **Roy Rogers** became famous in movies. **He** was usually accompanied by his horse, Trigger, and his dog, Bullet.

If a personal pronoun takes the place of two or more nouns, those nouns together are the antecedent of the pronoun.

> **Roy Rogers and Dale Evans** often worked together. **They** made dozens of movies.

Grammar 28. Subject-verb agreement with personal pronouns

The present-tense verb form that agrees with singular nouns also agrees with the pronoun subjects **he, she, and it.**

> She **tests** new planes.

The present-tense verb form that agrees with plural nouns also agrees with the pronoun subjects **I, you, we, and they.**

> **They** test new planes.

Grammar 29. Indefinite pronouns

A word that refers to a general group but does not have a specific antecedent is an indefinite pronoun.

> **Nobody** can be right about **everything.**

One common indefinite pronoun, **no one**, is written as two words.

Grammar 30. Subject-verb agreement with indefinite pronouns

The present-tense verb form that agrees with singular nouns also agrees with most indefinite pronouns.

> Almost everyone **remembers** the Alamo.

> No one **knows** exactly what happened there.

> Of the accounts written of the battle, several **claim** to be factual.

Grammar 31. Possessive pronouns

A personal pronoun that shows ownership is a possessive pronoun.

These possessive pronouns pronouns are used before nouns in sentences: **my, your, his, her, its, our, their.**

> Why are **my** gym shoes in **your** locker?

These possessive pronouns stand alone in sentences: **mine, yours, his, hers, its, ours, theirs.**

> Are these gym shoes **mine,** or are they **yours?**

Unlike possessive nouns, possessive pronouns are not written with apostrophes.

Grammar 32. Reflexive pronouns

A pronoun that refers back to a noun or pronoun in the same sentence is a reflexive pronoun. These words are reflexive pronouns: **myself, yourself, himself, herself, itself, ourselves, yourselves, themselves.**

> The witness had been talking to **himself.**

> You should have bought **yourself** a ticket.

Grammar 33. Demonstrative pronouns

A word that points out one or more people or things is a demonstrative pronoun. These four words can be demonstrative pronouns: **this, that, these,** and **those.**

> **These** are the funniest cartoons.

> Nobody laughed at **those.**

If the word **this, that, these,** or **those** is followed by a noun, the word is not a demonstrative pronoun. (See Grammar 34.)

Adjectives

Grammar 34. Definition of an adjective

A word that adds to the meaning of a noun or pronoun is an adjective. Adjectives usually tell what kind, which one, or how many.

> **Those exhausted** men have been playing tennis for **nine** hours.

Adjectives that tell what kind can sometimes stand alone.

> They were **exhausted.**

Adjectives that tell which one or how many always come before nouns.

> **Both** players have used **several** rackets.

Grammar 35. The adjectives a and an

The adjectives **a** and **an** are usually called *indefinite articles.* (The adjective **the** is usually called a *definite article.*) **A** is used before words that begin with consonants or with a "yew" sound.

> **A** penguin cannot fly.

> Cooking is **a** useful activity.

An is used before words that begin with vowels or with an unsounded **h**.

> **An** ostrich cannot fly.

> Brutus is **an** honorable man.

Grammar 36. Predicate adjectives

An adjective that comes after a linking verb and adds to the meaning of the subject noun or pronoun is a predicate adjective.

> Maria Spelterina must have been **brave.**

> Her tightrope walks across the Niagara Falls were **dangerous.**

Grammar 37. Proper adjectives

An adjective that is formed from a proper noun is a proper adjective. Each word in a proper adjective begins with a capital letter.

> The **American** dollar is worth less than the British pound.

> The new **Spielberg** film is great!

Grammar 38. Comparative and superlative forms of adjectives

Adjectives can be used to compare two or more people or things. When only two people or things are compared, use the comparative form of an adjective. To make the comparative form, add **er** to adjectives with one syllable. Use **more** (or **less**) before some adjectives with two syllables. Look in a dictionary if you are not sure of the correct comparative form of an adjective.

> Buster Keaton was **funnier** than Charlie Chaplin.

> Buster Keaton was **more amusing** than Charlie Chaplin.

When more than two people or things are compared, use the superlative form of an adjective. To make the superlative form, add **est** to adjectives with one syllable and many adjectives with two syllables. Use **most** (or **least**) before some adjectives with two syllables and all adjectives with more than two syllables. Look in a dictionary if you are not sure of the correct superlative form of an adjective.

> Buster Keaton was the **funniest** movie actor who ever lived.

> Buster Keaton was the **most amusing** movie actor who ever lived.

The comparative and superlative forms of the adjective **good** are **better** and **best.**

> Buster Keaton was a **better** actor than Charlie Chaplin.

> Buster Keaton was the **best** movie actor who ever lived.

The comparative and superlative forms of the adjective **bad** are **worse** and **worst.**

> The Revenge of the Killer Tomatoes was a **worse** movie than The Fly.

> The Revenge of the Killer Tomatoes was probably the **worst** movie ever made.

Adverbs

Grammar 39. Definition of an adverb

A word that adds to the meaning of a verb or verb phrase is an adverb. Adverbs usually tell where, when, how, or how often.

> The rodeo rider **bravely** mounted the mustang **again.**

Grammar 40. Comparative and superlative forms of adverbs

Adverbs can be used to compare the actions of two or more people or things. When only two people or things are compared, use the comparative form of an adverb. To make the comparative form, usually use **more** (or **less**) before the adverb. Add **er** to a few short adverbs.

Polly speaks **more clearly** than that other parrot.

Polly can fly **higher** than that other parrot.

When more than two people or things are compared, use the superlative form, usually use **most** (or **least**) before the adverb. Add **est** to a few short adverbs.

Of all those parrots, Polly speaks **most clearly.**

Of all those parrots, Polly can fly **highest.**

The comparative and superlative forms of the adverb **well** are **better** and **best.**

That parrot behaved **better** than your pet cat.

Of all the unusual pets in the show, the parrot behaved **best.**

The comparative and superlative forms of the adverb **badly** are **worse** and **worst.**

Your pet monkey behaved **worse** than that parrot.

Of all the unusual pets in the show, your cat behaved **worst.**

Grammar 41. Using adjectives and adverbs

Use an adjective to add to the meaning of a noun or a pronoun.

> The **proud** actor accepted the prize.

Use an adverb to add to the meaning of a verb or a verb phrase. *Many (but not all) adverbs end in* **ly**.

> The actor accepted the prize **proudly.**

Grammar 42. The adverb *not*

The adverb **not** changes the meaning of the verb or verb phrase in a sentence.

> The soldiers in the fort would **not** surrender.

> Help did **not** arrive in time.

Grammar 43. Avoiding double negatives

The adverb **not** is a negative word. Other common negative words are **no, never, no one, nobody, nothing, nowhere, hardly, barely,** and **scarcely.** Use only one negative word to make a sentence mean **no** or **not.**

> **No one** ever understands how I feel.

> My friends **never** understand how I feel.

> **Hardly** anyone understands how I feel.

Grammar 44. Adverbs used as intensifiers

Certain adverbs add to the meaning of adjectives or other adverbs. These special adverbs are sometimes called intensifiers.

> One **terribly** nosy neighbor heard the whole conversation.

> **Very** nervously, she told the police all about it.

Conjunctions

Grammar 45. Coordinating conjunctions

A word used to join two equal parts of a sentence is a coordinating conjunction. The most common coordinating conjunctions are **and, but,** and **or.**

> Many people have driven across the country, **but** these two men did it the hard way.

> Charles Creighton **and** James Hargis drove across the country **and** back again.

> They never stopped the engine **or** took the car out of reverse gear.

Grammar 46. Subordinating conjunctions and complex sentences

A word used to begin an adverb clause is a subordinating conjunction. The most common subordinating conjunctions are listed below.

after	before	though	when
although	if	unless	whenever
because	since	until	while

An adverb clause is a group of words that has a subject and a predicate but that cannot stand alone as a sentence. An adverb clause functions like an adverb. It tells when, where, how, or why. An adverb clause usually comes at the end or at the beginning of a sentence. (See Punctuation 8.) A sentence formed from an adverb clause (which cannot stand alone) and a main clause (which can stand alone) is called a *complex sentence*.

Otto E Funk played his violin **while he walked from New York City to San Francisco**.

When he finished his musical journey, both his feet and his hands were tired.

Whenever it is threatened, an opossum plays dead.

It can be poked, picked up, and even rolled over **while it remains completely rigid**.

Interjections

Grammar 47. Definition of an interjection

A word that simply expresses emotion is an interjection. A comma or an exclamation point separates an interjection from the rest of a sentence. (See Punctuation 11.)

Oh, now it makes sense.

Wow! That's terrific news!

Prepositions

Grammar 48. Definition of a preposition

A word that shows the relationship of a noun or pronoun to some other word in a sentence is a preposition. The most common prepositions are listed below.

about	before	during	over
above	behind	for	since
across	below	from	through
after	beneath	in	to
against	beside	into	under
along	between	like	until
among	beyond	of	up
around	by	off	upon
at	down	on	with

Grammar 49. Prepositional phrases

A preposition must be followed by a noun or a pronoun. The preposition and the noun or pronoun that follows it form a prepositional phrase.

> A new record **for sit-ups** was set **by Dr. David G. Jones**.

> His family and friends were very proud **of him**.

Often, other words come between the preposition and the noun or pronoun. Those words are also part of the prepositional phrase.

> He set a new record **for consecutive straight legged sit-ups**.

Grammar 50. Objects of prepositions

A preposition must be followed by a noun or a pronoun. That noun or pronoun is the object of the preposition.

> One of the main **characters** of Star Trek didn't appear until the second **season**.

Grammar 51. Personal pronouns in prepositional phrases

A personal pronoun that is the object of a preposition should be in the object form. These are object-form pronouns: **me, you, him, her, it, us, them.**

> The other presents for **her** are still on the table.

> The most interesting present is from **me**.

Grammar 52. Prepositional phrases used as adjectives

Some prepositional phrases are used as adjectives. They add to the meaning of a noun or pronoun in a sentence.

> The Caribbean island **of Martinique** is a department **of the French government**.

Grammar 53. Prepositional phrases used as adverbs.

Some prepositional phrases are used as adverbs. They add to the meaning of the verb or verb phrase in a sentence.

> **In 1763**, Napoleon Bonaparte's wife, Josephine, was born **on Martinique**.

Sentence Parts

Grammar 54. Simple subjects

The most important noun or pronoun in the subject of a sentence is the simple subject of that sentence. The object of a preposition cannot be the simple subject of a sentence.

> A 27-year-old **man** from Oklahoma swam the entire length of the Mississippi River.

> **He** spent a total of 742 hours in the river.

Grammar 55. Simple predicates

The verb or verb phrase of a sentence is the simple predicate of that sentence.

> Actor W. C. Fields **may have had** 700 separate savings accounts.

> Fields **used** a different name for each account.

Grammar 56. Direct objects

A word that tells who or what receives the action of a verb is the direct object of the verb. A direct object must be a noun or a pronoun. A personal pronoun that is a direct object should be in the object form. These are object-form pronouns: **me, you, him, her, it, us, them.**

> The first aspirin tablets contained **heroin.**

> A German company sold **them** for 12 years.

Grammar 57. Indirect objects

A word that tells to whom (or what) or for whom (or what) something is done is the indirect object of the verb expressing the action. An indirect object comes before a direct object and is not part of a prepositional phrase. An indirect object must be a noun or pronoun. A personal pronoun that is a direct object should be in the object form. These are object-form pronouns: **me, you, him, her, it, us, them.**

> Professor Sommers gave his **students** the same lecture every year.

> He told **them** a familiar story.

Grammar 58. Predicate nominatives

A word that follows a linking verb and renames the sentence subject is the predicate nominative of a sentence. A predicate nominative must be a noun or a pronoun. A personal pronoun that is a predicate nominative should be in the subject form. These are subject-form pronouns: **I, you, he, she, it, we, they.**

The best candidate was **Andrea**.

In my opinion, the winner should have been **she**.

Capitalization Rules

Capitalization 1. First word in a sentence

Begin the first word in every sentence with a capital letter.

Who won the eating contest?

That man ate 17 bananas in two minutes.

Capitalization 2. Personal pronoun I

Write the pronoun **I** with a capital letter.

At the last possible minute, **I** changed my mind.

Capitalization 3. Names and initials of people

Almost always, begin each part of a person's name with a capital letter.

Toby Ohara   Rosie Delancy

Sue Ellen Macmillan

Some names have more than one capital letter. Other names have parts that are not capitalized. Check the correct way to write each person's name. (Look in a reference book, or ask the person.)

Tim O'Hara   Tony de la Cruz

Jeannie McIntyre

Use a capital letter to write an initial that is part of a person's name.

B. J. Gallardo   J. Kelly Hunt

John F. Kennedy

Capitalization 4. Titles of people

Begin the title before a person's name with a capital letter.

Mr. Sam Yee   **Captain** Cook

Dr. Watson   **Governor** Maxine Stewart

Do not use a capital letter if this kind of word is not used before a person's name.

Did you call the **doctor**?

Who will be our state's next **governor**?

Capitalization 5. Names of relatives

A word like grandma or uncle may be used as a person's name or as part of a person's name. Begin this kind of word with a capital letter.

Only **Dad** and **Aunt Ellie** understand it.

Usually, if a possessive pronoun comes before a word like grandma or uncle, do not begin that word with a capital letter.

Only **my dad** and **my aunt** understand it.

Capitalization 6. Names of days

Begin the name of a day with a capital letter.

Most people don't have to work on **Saturday** or **Sunday**.

Capitalization 7. Names of months

Begin the name of a month with a capital letter.

At the equator, the hottest months are **March** and **September**.

Capitalization 8. Names of holidays

Begin each important word in the name of a holiday with a capital letter. Words like **the** and **of** do not begin with capital letters.

They usually have a picnic on the **Fourth of July** and a fancy dinner party on **Thanksgiving**.

Capitalization 9. Names of streets and highways

Begin each word in the name of a street or highway with a capital letter.

> Why is **Lombard Street** known as the most crooked road in the world?

Capitalization 10. Names of cities and towns

Begin each word in the name of a city or town with a capital letter.

> In 1957, the Dodgers moved from **Brooklyn** to **Los Angeles**.

Capitalization 11. Names of states, countries, and continents

Begin each word in the name of a state, country, or continent with a capital letter.

> The story was set in **Nevada**, but they shot the film in **Mexico**.

> There are very high mountain peaks in **Antarctica**.

Capitalization 12. Names of mountains and bodies of water

Begin each word in the name of a mountain, river, lake, or ocean with a capital letter.

> Amelia Earhart's plane was lost somewhere over the **Pacific Ocean**.

Capitalization 13. Abbreviations

If the word would begin with a capital letter, begin the abbreviation with a capital letter.

> On the scrap of paper, the victim had written, "**Wed.—Dr.** Lau."

Capitalization 14. Titles of works

Use a capital letter to begin the first word, the last word, and every main word in the title of a work. The words **the, a,** and **an** do not begin with capital letters except at the beginning of a title. Coordinating conjunctions and prepositions also do not begin with capital letters. (See Grammar 45 and Grammar 48.)

> Archie and Edith were the main characters in the television series **All in the Family**.

Capitalization 15. Other proper nouns

Begin each major word in a proper noun with a capital letter. A proper noun is the special name of a particular person, place, or thing. (See Grammar 13.) Usually, the words **the, a,** and **an,** coordinating conjunctions, and prepositions do not begin with capital letters. (See Grammar 45 and Grammar 48.)

> Jerry rushed to the **Burger King** and ordered three **Whoppers**.

Capitalization 16. Proper adjectives

Begin each word in a proper adjective with a capital letter. A proper adjective is an adjective that is formed from a proper noun. (See Grammar 37.)

> That **American** author writes about **English** detectives.

> She loves **Alfred Hitchcock** movies.

Capitalization 17. Direct quotations

Begin the first word in a direct quotation with a capital letter. (See Punctuation 14-16.)

> Dr. Pavlik said, "**There** are simply no teeth in the denture law."

If the words that tell who is speaking come in the middle of a quoted sentence, do not begin the second part of a quotation with a capital letter.

> "**There** are simply no teeth," said Dr. Pavlik, "**in** the denture law."

Capitalization 18. Greetings and closings in letters

Begin the first or only word in the greeting of a letter in a capital letter.

> **Dear** Mr. Lincoln: **Dear** Uncle Abe,

Begin the first or only word in the closing of a letter with a capital letter.

> **Sincerely** yours,   **Very** truly yours,

> **Love,**

Capitalization 19. Outlines

In an outline, begin the first word of each heading with a capital letter.

    II. **Houses** by mail order

        A. **First** sold by Sears, Roebuck in 1903

            1. **Build**-it-yourself kits

            2. **Included** all materials and instructions

        B. **Other** companies now in business

In an outline, use capital Roman numerals to label main ideas. Use capital letters to label supporting ideas. For ideas under supporting ideas, use Arabic numerals. For details, use small letters. Use a period after each Roman numeral, capital letter, Arabic numeral, or small letter.

    I. **Miner** George Warren

        A. **Risked** his share of Copper Queen mine in bet

            1. **Bet** on race against George Atkins

                a. Warren on foot

                b. Atkins on horseback

            2. Lost property worth $20 million

Punctuation Rules

Punctuation 1. Periods, question marks, and exclamation points at the ends of sentences

Use a period, a question mark, or an exclamation point at the end of every sentence. Do not use more than one of these marks at the end of a sentence. For example, do not use both a question mark and an exclamation point, or do not use two exclamation points.

Use a period at the end of a declarative sentence (a sentence that makes a statement).

> A hockey player must be able to skate backward at top speed.

Also use a period at the end of an imperative sentence (a sentence that gives a command).

> Keep your eye on the puck.

Use a question mark at the end of an interrogative sentence (a sentence that asks a question).

> Who is the goalie for their team?

Use an exclamation point at the end of an exclamatory sentence (a sentence that expresses excitement).

> That was a terrific block!

Punctuation 2. Periods with abbreviations

Use a period at the end of each part of an abbreviation.

Most titles used before people's names are abbreviations. These abbreviations may be used in formal writing. (**Miss** is not an abbreviation and does not end with a period.)

Dr. Blackwell   **Mr.** Bill Tilden

Ms. Maureen Connolly

Most other abbreviations may be used in addresses, notes, and informal writing. They should not be used in formal writing.

Lake View **Blvd.**   **Mon.** and **Thurs.**

Fifth **Ave.**   **Dec.** 24

Do not use periods in the abbreviations of names of government agencies, labor unions, and certain other organizations.

Tomorrow night **CBS** will broadcast a special program about the **FBI**.

Do not use periods after two-letter state abbreviations in addresses. This special kind of abbreviation has two capital letters and no period. Use these abbreviations only in addresses.

Their new address is 1887 West Third Street, Los Angeles, **CA** 90048.

Punctuation 3. Periods after initials

Use a period after an initial that is part of a person's name.

Chester **A.** Arthur   **C.C.** Pyle

Susan **B.** Anthony

Punctuation 4. Commas in dates

Use a comma between the number of the day and the number of the year in a date.

Hank Aaron hit his record-breaking home run on **April 8, 1974.**

If the date does not come at the end of a sentence, use another comma after the number of the year.

April 8, 1974, was an exciting day for Hank Aaron's fans.

Do not use a comma in a date that has only the name of a month and the number of a year.

Aaron hit his final home run in **July 1976.**

Do not use a comma in a date that has only the name of a month and the number of a day.

April 8 is the anniversary of Aaron's record-breaking home run.

Punctuation 5. Commas in place names

Use a comma between the name of a city or town and the name of a state or country.

> The world's largest chocolate factory is in **Hershey, Pennsylvania.**

If the two names do not come at the end of a sentence, use another comma after the name of the state or country.

> **Hershey, Pennsylvania,** is the home of the world's largest chocolate factory.

Punctuation 6. Commas in compound sentences

Use a comma before the conjunction—**and, but,** or **or**—in a compound sentence. (See Grammar 9 and Grammar 45.)

> Eighteen people tried**, but** no one succeeded.

Punctuation 7. Commas in series

Three or more words or groups of words used the same way in a sentence form a series. Use commas to separate the words or word groups in a series.

> **Jamie, Mitch, Kim, Lou, and Pablo** entered the contest.

> Each contestant **swam one mile, bicycled two miles, and ran five miles.**

Punctuation 8. Commas after introductory phrases and clauses

Use a comma after a phrase that comes before the subject of a sentence. A phrase is a group of words that usually functions as an adjective or an adverb. One kind of phrase is a prepositional phrase. (See Grammar 49.)

In the old dresser, Penny found the diamonds.

If the entire predicate comes before the subject of the sentence, do not use a comma. (See Grammar 3.)

In the old dresser lay the diamonds.

Use a comma after an adverb clause at the beginning of a sentence. (See Grammar 46.)

When he was first named hockey's most valuable player, Wayne Gretzky was only 18 years old.

Punctuation 9. Commas with nouns of address

Use a comma after a noun of address at the beginning of a sentence. (See Grammar 15.)

Fernando, that was a teriffic pitch!

Use a comma before a noun of address at the end of a sentence.

That was a teriffic pitch, **Fernando!**

If the noun of address comes in the middle of a sentence, use one comma before the noun and another comma after it.

That, **Fernando,** was a teriffic pitch!

Punctuation 10. Commas with appositives

Use a comma before an appositive at the end of a sentence. (See Grammar 16.)

> This costume was worn by George Reeves, **Hollywood's first Superman.**

If an appositive comes in the middle of a sentence, use one comma before the appositive and another comma after it.

> George Reeves, **Hollywood's first Superman,** wore this costume.

Punctuation 11. Commas or exclamation points with interjections

Usually, use a comma after an interjection. (See Grammar 47.)

> **Well,** we should probably think about it.

Use an exclamation point after an interjection that expresses excitement.

> **Wow!** That's a terrific idea!

Punctuation 12. Commas after greetings in friendly letters

Use a comma after the greeting in a friendly letter.

> Dear John,   Dear Uncle Theodore,

Punctuation 13. Commas after closings in friendly letters and business letters

Use a comma after the closing in a letter.

Love,   Yours sincerely,

Punctuation 14. Quotation marks with direct quotations

A direct quotation tells the exact words a person said. Use quotation marks at the beginning and at the end of each part of a direct quotation.

"Look!" cried Tina. "That cat is smiling!"

"Of course," said Tom. "It's a Cheshire cat."

Punctuation 15. Commas with direct quotations

Usually, use a comma to separate the words of a direct quotation from the words that tell who is speaking. (See Punctuation 16.)

Jay asked, "Who won the game last night?"

"The Cubs won it," said Linda, "in 14 innings."

Punctuation 16. End punctuation with direct quotations

At the end of a direct quotation, use a period, a comma, a question mark, or an exclamation point before the closing quotation marks.

If the direct quotation makes a statement or gives a command at the end of a sentence, use a period.

> Linda said, "The Cubs won last night's game."

> Jay said, "Tell us about the game."

If the direct quotation makes a statement or gives a command before the end of a sentence, use a comma.

> "The Cubs won last night's game," said Linda.

> "Tell us about the game," Jay said.

If the direct quotation asks a question, use a question mark.

> "Was it an exciting game?" asked Jay.

If the direct quotation expresses excitement, use an exclamation point.

> Linda yelled, "It was great!"

Punctuation 17. Quotation marks with titles of works

Use quotation marks around the title of a story, poem, song, essay, or chapter.

> **"Happy Birthday to You"** is the most popular song in the world.

If a period or a comma comes after the title, put the period or comma inside the closing quotation mark.

> The most popular song in the world is **"Happy Birthday to You."**

Punctuation 18. Underlines with titles of works

Underline the title of a book, play, magazine, movie, television series, or newspaper.

> One of the best movies about baseball was **<u>The Natural.</u>**

Punctuation 19. Apostrophes in contractions

Use an apostrophe in place of the missing letter or letters in a contraction.

> is not—isn't   Mel is—Mel's   I will—I'll

Punctuation 20. Apostrophes in possessive nouns

Use an apostrophe and **s** to write the possessive form of a singular noun. (See Grammar 14.)

> This cage belongs to one bird. It is the **bird's** cage.

> This cage belongs to Tweeter. It is **Tweeter's** cage.

Use only an apostrophe to write the possessive form of a plural noun that ends in **s**.

> This is a club for boys. It is a **boys'** club.

Use an apostrophe and **s** to write the possessive form of a plural noun that does not end in s.

> This is a club for men. It is a **men's** club.

Punctuation 21. Colons after greetings in business letters

Use a colon after the greeting in a business letter.

> Dear Mrs. Huan: Dear Sir or Madam:
>
> Dear Senator Rayburn:

Punctuation 22. Colons in expressions of time

When you use numerals to write time, use a colon between the hour and the minutes.

> 5:45 P.M.   9:00 A.M.   12:17 P.M.

Punctuation 23. Hyphens in numbers and fractions

Use a hyphen in a compound number from twenty-one to ninety-nine.

> thirty-seven   fifty-eight   seventy-three

Use a hyphen in a fraction.

> one-quarter   two-thirds   seven-eighths

Index